SOCIAL IMPACT OF MILITANCY IN KASHMIR

SOCIAL IMPACT OF MILITANCY IN KASHMIR

BASHIR AHMAD DABLA

GYAN

Social Impact of Militancy in Kashmir

ISBN: 978-81-212-1099-7

Published in 2012 in India by
Gyan Publishing House
23, Main Ansari Road, Daryaganj,
New Delhi-110002
Phone : 23282060, 23261060
Fax : (011) 23285914
E-mail : books@gyanbooks.com
Website : gyanbooks.com
Lasser type setting : Lucky Graphic, Delhi
Printed at : G. Print Process.Delhi

CONTENTS

LIST OF ABBREVIATIONS

AAI	Action Aid International
AISC	All India Sociological Conference
A	Anantnag
ADP	Association of Disappeared Persons
B-1	Baramulla
BPL	Below Poverty Line
BJP	Bhartiya Janata Party
BML	Bihari Migrant Labour
BSF	Border Security Force
B-2	Budgam
CRPF	Central Reserve Police Force
CSSCD	Centre for the Study of Social Change and Development
CL	Child Labour
DD	Delhi Darbar
DVAW	Domestic Violence Against Women
DOSSW	Department of Sociology and Social Work
DK	Drvida Kazzagam
DM	*Dukhtarane Millat*
E	Employer
Govt.	Government
GMC	Government Medical College
GO	Government Official
GOI	Government of India
HC	Handicraft Centre

HC [G]	Hurriat [Geelani]
HC [M]	Hurriat [Mirwaiz]
ITBP	Indo-Tibetian Border Police
IAK	Indian Administered Kashmir
ICSSR	Indian Council of Social Science Research
IK	Indian Kashmir
IM	Indian Muslim
IMPA	Institute of Management and Public Administration
INC	Indian National Congress
IPC	Indian Penal Code
IT	Information Technology
ICDS	Integrated Child Development Scheme
ICWS	Integrated Child Welfare Scheme
JI	Jamaat-e-Islami
JK/J&K	Jammu and Kashmir State
JKAP	Jammu and Kashmir Armed Police
JKNC	Jammu and Kashmir National Conference
JKPDP	Jammu and Kashmir People's Democratic Party
JP	Janata Party
JS	Jan Sangh
JC	Juvenile Court
JD	Juenile Delinquincy
JH	Juvenile Home
JJS	Juvenile Justice System
KC	Kashmir Christians
KI	Kashmir Identity
KM	Kashmiri Muslim
KMS	Kashmiri Muslim Society
KN	Kashmiri Nationalists
KP	Kashmiri Pandit

KS	Kashmiri Sikh
KU	Kashmir University
KY	Kashmiri Youth
K	Kupwara
LA	Legislative Assembly
LOC	Line of Control
MC	Muslim Conference
ML	Muslim League
MP	Member of Parliament
MUF	Muslim United Front
DWB	Doctors Without Borders
NCPCR	National Commission for Protection of Child Rights
NHPC	National Hydro-power Corporation
NKP	Naya Kashmir Programme
NGO	Non-governmental Organization
NWISA	North-West Indian Sociological Association
PK	Pakistani Kashmir / Panun Kashmir
PAK	Pakistan Administered Kashmir
P	Parents
PUCL	People's Union for Civil Liberties
PUDR	People's Union for Democratic Rights
PF	Plebiscite Front
PTSD	Post-traumatic Stress Disorder
PSA	Public Safety Act
RSS	Rashtriya Sarvesevek Sangh
RSD	Right to Self Determination
RRC	Region, Religion and Culture
SAC	State Accountability Commission
SC	Save the Children
SHRC	State Human Rights Commission

SEATO	South East Asian Treaty Organization
SKEYWSY	Sheri Kashmir Employment and Youth Welfare Scheme
SMA	Sheikh Mohammad Abdullah
STF	State Task Force
SCI	Supreme Court of India
SVO	State Vigilance Organization
UN	United Nations
UNICEF	United Nations International Children's Emergency Fund
USA	United States of America
VAW	Violence Against Women
VOK	Voice of Kashmir

PREFACE

1. The Kashmiri society experienced most difficult challenge which stands unparalleled in its modern history due to two-decade long armed conflict and its larger-deeper social implications. In actuality, it proved a devastating experience for the survival of this society. It brought catastrophic impact in totality in the entire Kashmiri society, especially in the fields related to large scale economic destruction, widespread social disorder; social disorganization and social chaos; educational backwardness and dropout; mass psychological depression; physical and mental health deterioration; mass humiliation and people's helplessness; forceful cultural aggression; political suppression, oppression and domination; demographic manipulation; and social crisis and anarchy and pathological social situation characterized by deviance, crime, delinquency, drug addiction, suicides and social apathy. This socially degenerated situation was faced by all members living in Kashmir throughout this period.

2. This qualitative and quantitative impact was felt in all sectors and sections of Kashmiri society. Economically, all sectors of economy and all classes and groups in society faced extreme economic downfall, especially people related to handicraft, tourism, hotel and horticulture sectors. The *Hanji* community which is totally dependent on tourism faced near-starvation situation. Educationally, people in general in rural as well as in urban areas faced backwardness in terms of increasing drop outs, decreasing admissions and destruction of educational of educational infrastructure. Culturally, the composite and plural character of Kashmir got non-composite and singular character. The tolerant and non-violent ethos was replaced by intolerant and violent ethos. Linguistically, the Kashmiri language lost its relevance to all communities, especially the Kashmiri Pandits. Politically, while Kashmiri masses were denied their basic rights, they were suppressed and oppressed. The local youth was denied the ideological liberty and

hundreds of them were thrown in to prisons under draconian laws. Socially, Kashmiris faced extreme social crisis in the emergence of structural and functional undesirable changes at micro and macro level and pain and agony of suffering groups, and cruel and pathetic conditions of the prime victims of violence. Psychologically, there emerged miserable condition of thousands mental and physical health patients. In this way, all fields of life collapsed and a decent and civilized life became difficult. This was crisis and anarchy of the highest order which a human can think about.

3. The preceding situation gave birth to radical changes in the existing social order whose Ideological and functional basis were eroded. A new situation was created in which new social groups, new ideologies, new ethics, new values and norms, new standards and new criteria for social desireabilities were born, which all were opposed to traditional Kashmiri culture and civilization. The birth of new social groups of militants, government militants, widows, orphans, half widows, disappeared from custody and their social role and social interaction with broader society was a shocking experience. Never in the written history of Kashmir, the Kashmiris had faced such a human catastrophe and had never faced such a wrath.

4. The dynamics created by armed conflict had also given birth to new social trends which Debade, rather destroyed, the moral, ethical and social basis of Kashmiri society. These trends were identified as late marriage, no marriage, disability, deviance and delinquency, violation of patriarchal authority, petty conflict and antagonism between various old and new classes-groups led to a situation characterized by ideological-religious-moral confusion and crisis of confidence.

5. The social dynamics of militancy and militarization had corrupted the entire social mileau and cultural ethos of traditional society. This was totally different social unit in comparison to its comparison with pre-militancy social unit. Now, the present social unit has developed the prominent features of crime, drug abuse, moral degeneration, mass corruption, prostitution and sexual promiscuity, social anarchy, and so on. These social problems has contributed to delegitimization of social justification of social solidarity, social harmony and social continuity. All major social processes and social institutions have become defunct, unproductive and under siege. Thus the

fundamental societal dynamics has led to its misdirection and degeneration.

6. All these negative social developments have contributed to moral-cum-social tragedy in the Kashmiri society. In this social environment evolved over a period of two decades, every member of a family has been abused, injured, mal-treated and dishonoured; all elders were abused and mal-treated, all youth were suppressed, threatened, tortured and brutally treated; all children were harassed and tortured; and all women were teased, molested and raped. A significant portion of population faced the burnt and heat of militarization for no fault. Thus every individual and every family in Kashmir has been engulfed in the militancy inferno and became the victim of harsh militarization. It also dehumanized the Kashmiri society at large. No individual or group in Kashmir could afford to avoid this dehumanizing effect of militancy and militarization.

7. The above social situation became the immediate and sole background on which this study or these studies were based. So, this book reveals the entire social background which determined the present social developments in Kashmir. In this context, it presents the empirical view of social reality existing in the Kashmiri society. In essence, it stands for sociological and scientific presentation of social facts and social realities of militancy and its long-term and short-term social implications experience by Kashmiris in the Kashmiri society.

8. The first chapter of this book deals with introduction of the theme of the book in terms of immediate past of the Kashmir problem; post-1947 social and political developments; different perceptions of the Kashmir problem; views about social impact of militancy; context, focus and major objectives of this study/these studies. The second chapter has been devoted to explain the methodology/methodologies adopted in the course of scientific and sociological research. The chapter delineates the social background of militancy in Kashmir in terms of indianization of Kashmir, negation of Kashmiri identity, demographic manipulation, economic baselessness and downfall, educational backwardness and cultural deprivation in the Kashmiri society. The fourth chapter analysis major sociological implications of militancy and militarization. In this regard, the talks about topics such as cumulative and human loss in Kashmir, nature of economic collapse in tourism, hotel, handicrafts, horticulture and other sectors,

migration of KPs and other demographic processes, an finally mental and physical health deterioration. The fifth chapter explains general sociological implications, especially dimensions of demographic transformation; changes in the institutions of family, marriage and kinship; conflict and treatment of women; nature of social deviance and social disorganization; and cultural problems and changes created due to militancy. New social trends which have emerged in the Kashmiri society after conflict got introduced has become the theme of 6th chapter. In this connection, important social trends such as emergence of late marriage, no marriage, disability, domestic violence against women, increasing number of suicides, emerging juveline delinquency, and crimefull situation in the valley. The identification and analysis of the problems of prime victims of militancy and militarization has been discussed in the 7th chapter. Finally, the last chapter focus on the existing crucial social problems and need for their immediate solution in terms of formulation and implementation of social policy in Jammu and Kashmir state.

9. In totality, this book stands for scientific and realistic presentation of basic realities, problems, issues created due to militancy and militarization in Kashmir. It has specifically concentrated on identification, explanation and analysis of complex and dangerous social situation arising out of the processes of militancy and militarization. It also concentrated on the critique, conclusion and suggestions for support, relief, rehabilitation, programme formulation-implementation and specific help network for the needy victims of violence in the valley.

10. The fact that there are different perceptions of these problems has been upheld in this book. Some important versions of every problem and issue has been presented within an objective and scientific framework. Our attempt in this regard has to present a perception of the locals proms and issues which has the features of objectivity, scientificity, realism, humanism, academic orientation and practical relevance. Generally, all perspectives of various problems have been presented with their critique and relevance and academic standard.

11. Every statement, proposition and argument has been presented with the support of credible, authentic and primary source official and unofficial support. Thus the data and statistics released by governments of India and Jammu and Kashmir have been widely

used. But, at the same time, the statistics provided by unofficial NGOs and other credible organizations and institutions has been utilized liberally. This has made our presentations non-refutable.

12. It is also important to mention here that all statements and arguments in this book have to be seen in proper situational and time context. It is because all papers were written over a period of 4-5 years and themes and data belong to that particular context. This orientation provide proper, realistic and relevant context to all findings in the book.

B.A. Dabla

ACKNOWLEDGEMENTS

All papers in this book were written over a period of 4 - 5 years in and some of these were published in different journals, magazines and newspapers in different countries of the world. I feel thankful to all these for publishing some papers.

I also feel thankful to Gawhar Ahad who helped in the processing the computer typing of this book.

My family members, Iffat, Ambreen and Shariq, showed a lot of patience during the writing and typing of this book. I remain grateful to all of them.

Lastly, I thank my teaching and non-teaching staff members of the department who proved helpful in one or the other way during the preparation of this book.

B.A. Dabla

CHAPTER 1

INTRODUCTION

(I) KASHMIR: THE POLITICAL ENTITY

Kashmir represents the territorial unit of Jammu and Kashmir [JK] state composing of five different regions of Kashmir valley, Jammu region, Ladakh region, Pakistan Administered Kashmir [PAK], and Baltistan. At the time of partition of the Indian sub-continent in 1947, the political future of Kashmir could not be decided finally mainly because of the role played by Maharaja at that time. Subsequently, he acceded to India temporarily with the political support of Kashmiri nationalists.

Thus, in late 1947, 2/3rd of the Kashmir territory came under India, 1/3rd under Pakistan and some parts were grabbed by China. The total area of JK state is 80,900 sq. miles, PAK [called Azad Kashmir– AK] 4,144 sq. miles and areas of Ladakh, Baltistan and Gilgat 63,553 sq. miles.[1]

The total population of Kashmiris, living inside and outside its territories, is about 15.5 million: 10.1 million in JK, 4.5 million in PAK, and 1.5 million in different countries of the world.[2] While Kashmir region has 97 % Muslim majority population, Jammu and Ladakh regions have Hindu and Bhuddist majorities respectively.[3] The minorities in Kashmir are composed of Kashmiri Pandits [KPs], Kashmiri Sikhs [KSs – less than 2 %] and Kashmiri Christians [KCs – less than 1%][4] The Muslims in Jammu and Ladakh regions form 41% and 27% minorities respectively.[5] On the whole, Muslims constitute 99 % and 67 % in PAK and IAK respectively.[6] While Urdu and Kashmiri [and Gojri] languages are common languages in JK, Urdu language stands as the sole dominant language spoken in PAK.

The entire territory of Kashmir is mountainous in the Himaliyan and Karakram range. The Kashmir valley stands distinctly for its exclusive scenic beauty which has compelled visitors and tourists to call it "a paradise on earth" and "Switzerland of Asia".[7] But, not many visitors and writers have focused upon the unparalleled poverty, extreme political domination, massforced labour and cruelties-brutalities perpetrated upon local inhabitants of the 'earthly paradise' by its alien rulers in the last 2 – 3 centuries.

(II) POLITICAL BACKGROUND OF THE KASHMIR PROBLEM

[i] The historical fact stands with a lot of evidence that Kashmiris lived under alien rule continuously for more than two centuries in pre-modern times. During this entire period, they were in general treated like animals and lived a sub-human life. The horrible phenomenon of *Begaar* actually dehumanized them. Mughal, Afghan, Sikh and Dogra dynasties ruled them like colonial powers and feudal masters and they were not allowed to involve in any political activity. In fact, state during this long period was 'class in itself' and treated others, both natives and non-natives, as they needed them. In brief, extreme form of cruelty, inhumanity and discrimination was made against the local inhabitants.[8]

During this difficult period of history, Kashmiris in general could not show active resistance as they were completely disarmed after every alien rule. But, at the same time, they did not surrender abjectly. They showed continuous and organized resistance against alien forces and kept their identity intact. But, when repression, exploitation and inhumanity crossed limits, they rose in revolt several times.The Srinagar Silk Factory Worker's protests in April 1865 reflected clearly the mass sentiment against political suppression, economic exploitation, discrimination, anti-Muslim and anti-Kashmiri policies of these rulers. In these protests, 28 people were massacred by the Dogra army.[9] An eminent historian of Kashmir characterized this organized protest as "the first in the history of class struggle in India."[10]

On the other hand, the world around Kashmir was changing rapidly and radically. While India's freedom movement was at its peak, the Muslim League [ML] was also expanding its support base. Post-revolutionary situation in Soviet Union was emerging as a leading example, while the socialist ideology was gaining ground in India very fast. While the *Khilafat* was abolished by the Turks[11], the movement for its revival failed in India. At the same time, this situation made strong impact on Kashmiris who had left the place and were living in different areas, cities and towns of undivided India. They started raising consciousness of people about problems in Kashmir and working for the interests of all Kashmiris.[12] These developments related to Kashmir had a positive impact on the people of Kashmir, especially on their political orientation and political culture. The impact of exogenous factors on the indigenous situation has been characterized by the author as *neubramization.*[13]

[ii] All these developments inside and outside the state had a positive impact on the political activities of Kashmiris and encouraged them to rise in revolt against the feudal, inhuman and discriminatory practices imposed on them by alien rulers. This situation of political subjugation on the one hand and increasing political aspirations of people on the other hand, created a situation which gave rise to the leadership of Sheikh Mohammad Abdullah [SMA] and his movement. He and his movement [Muslim Conference – MC at that time] were primarily and essentially representing the political sentiments and objectives and their urge for struggle against the feudal rule. In this way, SMA and his party got valid political ground against the tyranny of Dogra Maharaja. Representing people's political sentiments and aspirations, when he caught hold of a Dogra solider [in order to stop him from beating a Kashmiri *taangawala* in Srinagar], this act was considered highly symbolic, revolutionary and historical and conveyed a clear message of political assertion on the part of Kashmiris.[14] Subsequently, he became a popular leader, developed charisma and achieved the status of legendry figure. The first, organized, systematic and politically directed movement of 1931 started in this context which is considered as the first movement of Kashmiris for their total emancipation. In actuality, this movement determined the future course of political developments in Kashmir.

[iii] SMA and his movement did not pose potential threat to the Maharaja only, but to the traditional-religious leadership in Kashmir also. This leadership had partly and unconsciously colloberated with the alien rulers and got discredited. In this situation, the new leadership, which was young, modern, secular and politically-ideologically

oriented, started replacing the old leadership which was age-old, religious and politically-ideologically not clear. In the aftermath of 1931 movement, MC, under the collective leadership started the movement for stopping discrimination against local Muslims, treating them as equal citizens, and recruit them in civil services like KPs and Indian Muslims [IMs].[15] This movement was Muslim-oriented not because it was communal but because only Muslims were discriminated and suppressed in the state. On the other hand, non-native Muslims and native KPs were made 'part of the ruling class'. The political, ideological, economic and social developments at that time led to highest degree of political participation of people in Kashmir. This situation made the environment congenial for conversion of MC into National Conference [NC] in 1938 and formulation –adoption of *Naya Kashmir Programme* as 'the future ideological guide'.[16] This document is considered as first radical political document in India which talked about land to the tiller.[17] While the former act branded the freedom movement as "secular" and provided the platform to non-Muslim to join it, the latter provided ideological basis and political rationale to introduce famous radical reforms, especially the 'Land to Tiller Act' in 1951.[18]

[iv] After all these developments, the "quit Kashmir" movement [19] was launched by Kashmiri nationalists in 1946 to dislodge the Maharaja. In the following year, partition of the Indian sub-continent took place and two independent states of Pakistan and India were created on 14th August and 15th August, 1947. All princely states acceded to India or Pakistan. Even Junagarh and Hyderabad were made to accede to India. The only case which remained undecided was JK state ruled by the Hindu Maharaja, while majority of people were Muslims. In this background, the Dogra ruler wanted to maintain distance from both India and Pakistan. In this regard, he developed understanding with Pakistan under "stand-still agreement".[20] But, the entire situation changed when the Pakistan-supported tribal's raided the state. This made the Maharaja and his family unsafe and, in desperation, he approached India for military help which was provided happily. This led to the accession [temporary] of Kashmir to India but with a condition that peoples consent will be taken after conditions are normalized. The Indian government and leaders made clear promises in this regard.[21] SMA and his party supported this temporary accession.

Thus, Kashmir was acceded to India temporarily but later on forgot it. When SMA reminded them about this promise in 1952-53, he was imprisoned for 11 long years. In 1948, India took the Kashmir issue to the United Nation and 'internationalized' it.[22] In this way, Kashmir Problem remained unresolved and still maintains this status.

(III) POST-ACCESSION DEVELOPMENTS IN J&K

In the background of freedom movements in India and Kashmir separately, the temporary accession of Kashmir to India was carried out by the Hindu Maharaja[23] with active political support of KNs on the promise that Kashmiris will be given the "Right of Self-Determination" [RSD] when the situation improves.[24] The KNs under the leadership of SMA took power in JK state in 1947. Since they were committed to secular, and political programme, they carried out efforts at two fronts. On the one hand, they opposed 'two-nation theory' of Pakistan and upheld to build a secular polity in JK state. On the other front, i.e. economic and educational, they introduced radical reforms like abolition of usury system, land to the tiller, free education for all citizens from primary till university. However, local political forces could not carry out this type of basic transformation mainly because of negative attitude of the Indian state. This Indian response finally led to political obstruction of KNs under SMA in 1953. In fact, this first political betrayal on the part of government of India [GOI] can be explained in terms of the reaction of some political groups, feudal classes and KPs which were directly or indirectly effected by these reforms in the state. Thus, the central leadership denied its ideas of democracy and forgot its promises. It imposed its own political leaders and regimes in the state in the following period. These political developments determined series of political processes in the entire period after 1947. These post-accession developments in JK can be characterized as 'identity politics' which revolved around political ideals related to region, religion and culture.

[i] Identity Politics in post-accession period: Identity politics [IP] refers to a phenomenon of politics which is mainly determined by social, psychological and cultural factors. While its causation can be explained in terms of these factors, its implications can also be characterized by the social-psychological-cultural framework. In actuality, IP refers specifically to the political ideals, realities and

objectives related to social and political processes involving wider participation of masses. It particularly reflects in the political dynamics related to region, religion and culture [RRC]. It has been observed in several sociological studies that constant and reciprocal relationship between IP and RRC have many implications for polity and economy and for whole society. One such important implication can be explained in terms of continuous political conflict, both peaceful and violent, between different political units and consequent political instability. [24]

[a] Role of Religion: The Kashmir political problem stands as a clear case of the political dynamics in relation to IP and role of RRC in it. The fact stands that Kashmir problem started in 1947 when political future of the state could not be decided because people were denied their RSD. In this background, religion played a dominant role in post-partition politics in JK. It had two main features. First, it gave rise to constant political antagonism and violent conflict between Muslim-dominated state of JK and Hindu-dominated state of India. Second, it gave rise to a distinct religious political perspective to the problem of Kashmir. Finally, this particular political orientation and confrontration led to the emergence of militancy in 1989 for political independence of Kashmir.

[b] Role of Region: The factor upheld primacy of the territory of Kashmir and Kashmiri-dominated areas of Jammu region. It also opposed imposition of 'monopoly politics' and undemocratic rule from 'Delhi Durbar' and characterized it as 'colonial type rule from Delhi'.

[c] Role of Culture: It was of indigenous and exogenous nature. At the indigenous level, the IP emphasized on the maintenance of local-Muslim cultural traits, especially related to language, dress, traditions, customs, celebrations, attitudes and so on. Though there prevailed cultural, linguistic and ethnic differences at the local level, the local political forces were successful in subsiding [these differences] and posed as a cohesive force. On the other hand, at the exogenous level, local cultural factor played a dominant role. Local political leaders forged a united political opposition to GOI for a longer period of six decades. This reflected specifically in the united opposition to the imposition of cultural traits, Hindi language, devnagiri script, and Hindi films and mass media.[25]

[i] 1947 – 1953: The post-1947 era of IP in JK can be broadly

divided into four inter-related phases. The first phase from 1947 to 1953 was an era of Kashmiri nationalistic fervour and progressive reforms. While the former reflected in accepting special political and constitutional status of JK in union of India, rejection of 'two nations theory, of Pakistan, and opposition to its tribal raids, the latter referred to famous land reforms, abolition of usury system and introduction of free education. The related fact is that all these reforms were implemented successfully and carried out basic transformation among local Muslims after centuries of subjugation and slavery.

[ii] 1953-1974: This phase was the era of political assertion in which political struggle was carried out for the attainment of RSD under Plebiscite Front [PF] political party. The phase started with the arrest of SMA in 1953 and the following period experienced continuous political demonstration on the part of Kashmiri masses to get their political rights. But, GOI responded negatively. It played with legitimate political institutions in this state and imposed several puppet regimes from New Delhi in pure undemocratic style. This deteriorated processes of political modernization and political participation among the local masses. In actuality, the Centre adopted some elite families in Kashmir through which it ruled the state. In the context of denial of RSD by GOI, some minor political violence by Al-Fatah took place in early 1970s.

[iii] 1974-1989: This phase was a political compromise in which political surrender and mass election rigging were demonstrated by the local leadership. The phase started with 'Sheikh-Indira Accord' in 1974-75 which legitimized the surrender of SMA and his party. Neither could he assert nor could get credible political advantage at that time. In reality, this 'historic surrender' can be seen in the backdrop division of Pakistan into two countries in 1971. SMA felt betrayed on the art of his erstwhile colleagues and was compelled to compromise. This sentiment was revealed in his autobiography[26]. After SMA's death in 1982, the leadership vacuum was fully utilized by intelligence agencies and manipulated all political developments, especially elections in JK. The GOI and its agents behaved in such a way that Kashmir seemed like a 'colony' about which all decisions were taken in Delhi.[27] As a result, while legally-elected governments in JK were toppled, rigging in elections became a nationalist and preferred practice. In this way, all illegal and illegitimate political actions in Kashmir were made legal

and legitimate. Thus, democracy could never be experienced in Kashmir, while whole of India was enjoying it.

[iv] Fourth, the situation, mentioned above, provided immediate backdrop to the fourth phase which started in 1989 with armed revolt by Kashmiri youth against the Indian state and subsequent political struggle of Kashmiri masses for their 'Azaadi'. This phase was evolutionary and logical phase in continuity of previous phases. The militancy and militarization in Kashmir must be seen primarily in this context.[28] It follows that when Kashmiri youth were denied their legitimate political right to participate in elections, they were compelled to take up the gun for political purpose. In actuality, when they were denied to participate in assembly elections in 1987 and were 'defeated' even when some of them won, they left IK for PK, got arms training there and came back with arms and launched armed struggle against Indian forces. The Pakistani and other Islamic support to militant movement in Kashmir was secondary and it came later when militancy had established roots. This situation invited the wrath of Indian forces and they launched a full-scale war against militants and civilian population in an alien territory. They committed all war crimes and human rights violations against the local population.[29]

(IV) DIFFERENT PERCEPTIONS

In the long history of 62 years, the Kashmir problem stands still unresolved. It has involved India and Pakistan deeply and made it more complicated. In the prevailing situation, there seems no consensus-based solution which could be operational wholly. In actuality, both India and Pakistan have made the Kashmir issue as a matter of prestige and honour, in some cases life and death. Hardly any scope for realism and compromise is left by them. In the emotionally charged situation, both countries made Kashmir as 'corner stone' of foreign policy and as 'national agenda' in domestic policy. This affected adversely national interests at regional and global level. This determined the nature of their bi-lateral ties, lost political trust and confidence even fought three wars.[30] They became "distant neighbours"[31] with no economic, social, cultural, educational, linguistic, academic, literary and other contacts and emerged as "nearest enemies". In this background, Kashmir emerged as the "most dangerous zone" in the region and the world".[32] Even it was thought that if a 'limited nuclear war' takes place in South Asia, the first possible place for it would be Kashmir.

In this whole process, who suffered? The answer is people of India, Pakistan and Kashmir. In reality, people of Kashmir suffered more than others. They received the bad part of everything. In the situation of non-resolution of this problem, both countries developed their respective perspectives about Kashmir. Of course, Kashmiris too developed their own perspective. Here, we explain these:

[a] *The Indian Perspective*: Immediately after temporary accession of Kashmir to India, the latter's position was that "JK had acceded to India temporarily and people's consent in this regard will be sought once conditions normalize in the territory."[33] However, this position changed with the changes in the world politics. The SEETO and SENTO security pacts of the West with Pakistan made India security-conscious and took it near to the other super power, erstwhile USSR. Thus, from early 1950s, India's position was that "JK is not a disputed territory but an integral part of the country." [34] The rationale provided was that the JK constituent assembly in 1951 ratified the 'accession treaty' with political support of SMA and NC. Though India itself had taken the Kashmir issue to the U.N., it took revised stand that its resolutions are not applicable after 1952 mainly because of non-fulfillment of conditions by Pakistan. All countries of the world did not accept this argument fully but preferred to remain silent because of three reasons. These were first, these countries were not directly concerned with this problem. Second, India had developed democratic credentials at the world level. Third, India had attained the global status due to its leading role in "non-aligned movement".

On the home front, Kashmir issue was made the point of supreme national agenda. After 1951, when India's position changed, Kashmir became an issue of national interest, national honour and solidarity. It was also presented a symbol of Indian secularism and inseparable part [*atoot ang*] of the country.[34] The Bhartiya Janata Party [BJP] [Jan Sangh earlier] and rightist-aggressive parties demanded abrogation of article 370 of the Indian constitution [which ensures autonomy to the JK state], complete integration of JK to India even if demographic changes have to be carried out, and complete integration with the 'Hindu majority culture'.[35] On the other hand, leftist political parties took the stand that Kashmir stands as the part of India and there can be no compromise on this statement.[36] But, they also supported human, political and other rights of Kashmiris which were violated by the Indian government. They categorically opposed suppression and oppression of the masses in Kashmir.[37] Then there were Congress and other liberal political parties which also endorsed the stand about accession which was interpreted as final and irrevocable. According to this party, Kashmir stands as a unit of Indian federal system within the broader framework of article 370 which ensures maximum autonomy to the state. It also presented the Kashmir as an issue of national honour, national unity and solidarity mainly for electoral gains.[38]

[b] *The Pakistani Perspective:* On the other extreme, the Pakistani position regarding Kashmir remained consistent. It maintains from the beginning that Kashmir stands as a disputed territory because of India's illegal and immoral hold over it. The main Pakistani argument was since partition of the sub-continent in 1947 took place on communal lines, Kashmir, the Muslim majority area, must accede to Pakistan.[39] Pakistan without Kashmir was incomplete, it maintained.[40] Two statements were repeated by Pakistan which were "Kashmir stands as the life-line [*shah-rug*] of Pakistan" and "Kashmir will become Pakistan certainly".[41] Pakistan was aggressive in introducing the Kashmir issue in all international for a and presenting it as an "Islamic issue" in the Muslim world. While it was upheld that Pakistan provides all moral, diplomatic and political support to the freedom movement in Kashmir, it emphasized on the implementation of UN resolutions and political aspirations of the people for the just and final solution of Kashmir problem.

At the same time, there was offensive and aggressive approach to the Kashmir problem in Pakistan. There was no scope of discussion, argument, disagreement, and difference. All political parties and organizations, representing various groups, supported this Kashmir policy without any slightest deviation. As happened in India, nobody in Pakistan could dare to differ to this policy as it was very easy to dub him/her as 'anti-national', 'foreign agent' and 'Indian sympathizer'. Thus, all political parties supported the state-sponsored policy on Kashmir.[42] In actuality, the ruling classes in Pakistan as well as India pursued their political interests on the façade of Kashmir. In this way, political elites in both countries exploited people's political sentiments.

However, in the recent past, it was observed that there is change in this mindset of politics among intellectual and influential sections of society in both countries. As a result, they developed relatively realistic and pragmatic approach towards Indo-Pak problems in general and Kashmir problem in particular. They include individuals and groups representing media, academics, and civil societies of Pakistan and India which have a lot of social-cultural similarity than dissimilarity. [43]

The perception of these distinctive citizens is really different. They emphasize the commonality of interests and similarity of roles and impact of peace and development of these two near-but-distant neighbours. It was on the appeal of these seniors in both countries that ruling classes agreed to initiate peace initiatives in South Asia. They argue that India and Pakistan have done enough damage to each other's interests in last 62 years and now they must resume discussion and dialogue about peace, development and future survival. They talk in terms of reconciliation, compromise and mutuality in the Indian sub-continent. In the case of the resolution of Kashmir problem, they stress on new approach and new orientation in the changed world situation in order to evolve a realistic, comprehensive and ever-lasting solution.[44] It was in that context that, during President Parvez Musharraf's time, the two countries were very near to the resolution of the problem.[45]

[c] *The Kashmiri Perspective:* All Kashmiris have no uniform or joint perspective about the Kashmir problem. In actuality, while they share some ideas and ideals, they reveal moderate to extreme differences. So, they have different perspectives about Kashmir problem and its resolution which we analyze here.

The perspectives of nationalist political parties: The largest nationalist political party in JK, Indian National Congress [INC], upholds the position that Kashmir's accession to India stands final and irrevocable . All constitutional and legal acts imposed on the state by the central government after 1953 were needed for the purpose of national integration. But, at the same time, it maintains that the ideal relationship between JK and union government must be within the constitutional framework of article 370 which ensures the state an autonomous status. The important fact about this party is that it never got people's mass support and so it remained politically paralyzed. While its electoral gains were managed through manipulated and rigged elections, its governments were imposed and ordered from New Delhi.

For a common Kashmiri, the leaders of this party were 'agents of Delhi' and worked against 'independent character of Kashmir'.[46]

The other nationalist political party in JK, JS – BJP, was all against Kashmiris. It opposed the Congress for benefiting the local Muslims. From the very beginning, it opposed article 370 of Indian constitution. In 1952, it started an agitation against, what is characterized as, two prime ministers, two presidents, two constitutions, two flags in one country.[47] They even wanted to change the dominant Muslim character of the state.[48] But, the hard fact is that this party never got political basis in Kashmir, even not among KPs. Its influence was limited to the Hindu-dominated Jammu belt which it always favoured at the cost of Kashmir valley. In this way, it communalized the situation in Jammu primarily for electoral gains.[48a]

The major regional political parties included JKNC and JKPDP [Peoples Democratic Party]. While the former has historical roots and is descedent of historical freedom movement of Kashmir, the latter has recent origin and is the product of political accident-reaction in the recent past. These two parties have been involved in extreme political completion and conflict primarily for electoral gains. Despite political differences, these parties share many 'basics of Kashmir problem'. They agree on 'irreversibility' of the accession, and Kashmir as the integral part of the country. Besides, both parties have provided leaders and actors in the process of national integration. In the present situation, both parties pose as the "protector of Muslim interests" in the state, which they have never proved. Functioning within the framework of Indian constitution, while NC upheld the ideal of "autonomy", PDP presented the idea of "self-rule". Both these types of political system are presented for resolution of the Kashmir problem by these parties. While "autonomy" is explained in terms of rights and powers given to this state by article 370 of the Indian constitution, it provides semi-independent status of the state with union of India wherein the latter's powers are limited to currency, communications, defencse and foreign affairs.[49] The party leaders uphold that the autonomous character of JK was robbed by the Congress regimes through legislative actions like extension of jurisdiction of Supreme Court of India, Election Commission of India, Auditor and Comptroller General of India. They demand that all these revisions must be repealed and ideal pre-1953 position must be restored as early as possible.[50]

On the other hand, PDP presented a theoretical ' vision document' on the name of "self-rule", the central focus of which is to give people in Kashmir and other regions also the right to rule themselves through federal political structure-organization. It refers to a federal type of JK state in which each region and both parts of Kashmir – IAK and PAK – will be represented in joint legislature. While it emphasizes on demilitarization, soft LOC and borders, it stresses on joint trade and economic ties.[51]

On the other extreme stand pro-*Azadi* political parties and groups which demand total independence of Kashmir from India and Pakistan. Their perspective is based on the proposition that India enslaved them in 1947 mainly because of power position at that time. They characterize JK as the "occupied territory".[52] They argue that forgetting the self-determination promise and ignoring the international opinion, India followed a rigorous policy of "indianization" and attempted to make JK like any other state, totally dependent on central government.[52] The central government has succeeded in this to the maximum extent. They put forward a serious critique of Congress regimes in JK and role of central government vis-à-vis the state. They say that despite suppression, repression and material motivation, the central government never got Kashmiris' confidence and support. While all their political regimes were "puppet regimes" which always danced on Delhi's directions, all elections after 1947 were rigged. All the Congress regimes were corrupt and never got people's support. In fact, these were so corrupt and inefficient that they could not work even for national integration. In addition, these regimes and their performance made tremendous dis-service to the cause of India in Kashmir. Thus, the pro-Azadi groups characterize the Indian rule over Kashmir as "colonial" and feel Kashmir as its "colony".[53]

While these groups are unanimous in their criticism against India, they have less unanimity in their political ideas, ideals, objectives, and programmes. They have no clear vision of political future and no consciousness about contemporary political realities in the region and world. While majority of groups in the *Hurriyat Conference* have pro-Pakistan orientation, minority of groups have pro-independence orientation. In this situation, these groups are divided which has led to their cronic disunity. In reality, disunity among different factions seem intrinsic and endemic.[54] It was in this context that the chief of

United Jehad Council had to issue a warning to desist from this behaviour or leave the field for youngsters.[55] It is argued by their opponents that if there prevails sincerity of cause/objectives, it should have created political unity which has not happened so far. This factionalism has also been interpreted in terms of strategy on the part of various competing groups to follow their individual or group interests rather than of the collective interests of Kashmiri Muslims.[56]

Both factions of *Hurriyat [Geelani and Mirwaiz]* are theoretically committed to the political ideal of Azadi from India and then people's decision about future of Kashmir will be accepted. It means accession to Pakistan or independence and option of is out of question. It is important to note here that both these factions have different ideological and religious orientation, but they agree on the peaceful political struggle for attaining Azadi.[57] Generally, the media has dubbed the 'Geelani Hurriyat' as extremist and 'Mirwaiz Hurriyat' as moderate.[58] A point of basic importance is that neither faction of *Hurriyat* has been able to project its political ideology and future vision with clarity and specificity. They oppose everything India stands for but fail to convey their political agenda in future Kashmir. Even their political objectives and agenda in writing are not available. In this situation, the political leadership of the *Hurriyat* has remained ineffective in regard to the fulfillment of the supreme goal of *Azaadi.*

The second important organization of pro-*Azaadi* group is Jammu and Kashmir Liberation Front [JKLF] having several factions. This organization has international character and is committed to complete independence from India and Pakistan through peaceful political struggle. It has kept the armed struggle option open. It presents the idea and concept of independence with solid contents, arguments, clarity and specificity. It also presents a liberal, independent, secular and democratic future of Kashmir. It has published enough literature in this regard. It stands for a united state of Kashmir composing five units of Kashmir valley, Jammu, Ladakh, PAK and Balistan.[59]

The third and most important component of pro-*Azaadi* groups is composed of various militant groups and organizations working for independence of Kashmir through armed struggle. All these groups are religious oriented and motivated and they characterize their political/ armed struggle as *Jehad* in which they can pay even by their lives.

The ideal objective of these militants is simple, i.e., establishment of the ideal Islamic state and society in the form of *Khilafat* through peaceful as well as armed struggle. The members of these cadre-based Organizations do not have sufficient knowledge of political realities in the region and world. They are also ignorant of the background of Kashmir problem. However, some top-level and medium-level members stand highly educated with professional degrees and have expertise in warfare and war technology. The majority of militants and activists associated with these groups have the perception that Hindus of India have occupied Kashmir they want to throw there out think militancy.[60] They have hardly any perspective on political, economic, social, cultural and other issues. These organizations have published many books and booklets which explain their ideas and opinions.[61]

(V) IMPACT OF MILITANCY: THE VARYING VIEWS

The fact stands with a lot of empirical evidence that processes of militancy and subsequent militarization had deeper, larger and wholistic impact on the Kashmiri society. In actuality, it engulfed the entirety of societal dynamics in its inferno and made its impact felt in all sectors and all sections of society. These implications were deeper because all social institutions, inter-relationships, processes, and all fields of life, especially economy, social structure, polity, culture, education, language, psychology, demography, health, development and literature, got involved and effected directly and indirectly. Thus, it may be inferred that reality related to militancy can be observed in totality of these factors partly because these are widespread and partly because these are necessarily related to each other.[62]

In this regard, two main arguments are presented by the local intelligentsia, academicians, professionals, experts and others. The first argument pleads that social implications of militancy need to be analyzed in the broader context of the whole situation after 1947 in the state. The proponents of this view feel that it will provide a broader view and long-term perspective for emerging social issues and problems in Kashmir. They argue that many developments in JK started after 1947 and in the process of evolution-maturity, these got changed, revised and distorted. They give two supportive points in their favour. First, this perspective will provide entirety and totality of situation to be studied. Second, every development in the Kashmiri society cannot be solely related to militancy. It follows that this situation prevailed even before militancy started and could have continued even in non-militancy situation. So, it seems highly purposeful to study all social developments with their origin, initiation, nature and so on. They present the social themes of 'violence against women', 'domestic violence against women', and 'criminal violence against women' in this regard.

The second argument says that social implications of militancy were specific and particularistic and can only be realistically explained and assessed in the limited time-frame of two decades. This approach will enable to develop proper and specific conclusion about these implications. The upholders of this view believe that this perspective will help in objectivity, specificity, realism and comprehensiveness in the explanation/analysis of implications. They put forward the case of the study of widows, orphans and half-widows who are the product of particular type of situation. In this regard, they believe that it seems highly needful and purposeful to study these groups in the limited background of last two decades of militancy.

We feel that both these theoretical and methodological arguments are partly correct because they have many elements of social realism and social reality. On the one hand, the first argument emphasizes totality, entirety and comprehensiveness of the approach/perspective. On the other hand, the second argument divulges the importance of specificity, particularity, direct-limited concentration of the approach/perspective. Thus, these two arguments do not stand conflictive and parallel but are complementary and accommodative. These are also supportive and reciprocal in nature and implications.

In the preceding context, we intend to follow both arguments, approaches and perspectives and utilize positives of both and negative of none. Thus, while the former view will provide us entire period after 1947, the latter will specifically concentrate on two-decades period of militancy. Both these frameworks will give us holistic, realistic and comprehensive nature of social implications of militancy in Kashmir.

Another relevant point needs explanation at this stage. It is about adoption of disciplinary or inter-disciplinary orientation in this study. Keeping in view limitations of the disciplinary approach to social phenomenon, especially change, mobility and development, I feel compelled to adopt multi-disciplinary approach in explaining/analyzing social implications of militancy.

(VI) CONTEXT, FOCUS AND RELEVANCE OF THE STUDY

[i] As is clear from the previous sections, the social implications of militancy and other social developments in the recent past have effected every section and sector of society and at all levels and in all dimensions. These grave implications gave rise to a situation which can realistically be characterized as 'the crisis situation'. Some of these dangerous implications have been identified in the psychological, social, economic, demographic, cultural and political fields. This provides essential and immediate context in which we intend to identify and analyzse specific sociological implications of militancy.

[ii] In the preceding context, this sociological study will specifically focus on the following sociological concerns:

[a] Nature, dimensions and consequences of the processes of social change and development in JK from 1947;

[b] Nature and dimensions of causes and consequences of the processes of militancy and militarization in the Kashmiri society;

[c] Highlighting the local ideas, ideals, views and perceptions about these sociological concerns;

[d] Identification of various local social problems and social issues in present-day Kashmir; and

[e] Suggestions about formulation, implementation and rehabilitation of militancy victims in Kashmir.

[iii] We can imagine about short-term as well as long-term fall out of these socially-damaging and culturally-degenerating implications of militancy in the Kashmiri society. In general, the observation of this situation reveals that these implications are proving devastating, especially in the cases of problems related to juvenile delinquency, crime, sexual promiscuity, prostitution, social pathology-apathy, dehumanization, unemp-

loyment, corruption, drug addiction, moral waywardness, discrimination, violence, late marriage, no marriage, social disability, increasing number of orphans, widows and half-widows.

From any/every point of view, this situation needs to be controlled and finally negated for achieving social-cultural emancipation and establishing just social order. But, on the other hand, there seems no governmental or non-governmental organized, planned and systematic efforts in this direction. Further, there is not sufficient consciousness among influential sections of society about this crucial cause. So, there is no question of any consequent action in this regard. In this situation, there seems an urgent need to make objective, scientific and comprehensive study of this volatile situation in order to understand and analyze it and suggest practical and realistic suggestions to effectively control and negate these acute social problems.

(VII) OBJECTIVES OF THE STUDY

In the context of whole explanation made in all sections, this sociological study will follow the below-mentioned academic objectives:

[i] To carry out a critical analysis and objective assessment of the dynamics of processes of social change and development in the state of J&K in the post-1947 era in general and during past 2 decades of militancy is particular.

[ii] To have a detailed scientific and sociological investigation about major and minor social implications [causes and consequences] of militancy and subsequent militarization in Kashmir for last two decades and relating these implications with on-going social developments in the state from 1947 onwards;

[iii] To identify and analyze in the sociological framework the actuality of social problems and issues in the Kashmir valley [mainly as a result of the social implications of militancy] with strong empirical evidence and statistical support; and

[iv] To make presentation of rational, scientific and realistic suggestions for formulation and implementation of various plans, programmes and schemes for overall welfare and

rehabilitation of militancy victims, especially widows, orphans, half-widows, youth and other women and children.

NOTES AND REFERENCES

1. See M.Y. Saraf, *Kashmiris Fight for Freedom* [Lahore, 1977, Ferozsons].
2. *Voice of Kashmir* [London], 1992. In fact, no independent survey or census has been carried out in this regard. These figures are based on the estimates in 1990s.
3. *Census of India,* 2001.
4. *Census of Jammu and Kashmir,* 2001.
5. *Ibid.*
6. See Saraf, *op. cit* and Census of India, *op. cit.*
7. While the former characterization has been done by famous Mughal emperor, *Shah-e-Jahan, and* rulers in India, the latter characterization was done by several Western visitors-tourists and colonial administrators in Kashmir.
8. See Robert Throp, *Kashmir Misgovernment* [London, 1865].
9. See *Greater Kashmir* [Srinagar], 29th April 2010.
10. Reported in Ibid.
11. See Dr. B. A. Dabla, *Ideology, Polity and Society in Modern Turkey* [Aligarh, 1988, A.M.U.].
12. See W. R. Lawrence, *The Valley of Kashmir* [London, 1895]; P. N. Bamzai, *Modern History of Kashmir* [New Delhi, 1973]; and G.M.D. Sufi, *Kashmir,* 2 Vols. [New Delhi, 1969].
13. See Dr. B.A. Dabla, *Working Women in Kashmir [*Jaipur, 1982, Rawat].
14. The author heard many stories about this incident from his elders.
15. See Saraf, *op. cit.;* G.H. Khan, *Freedom Struggle in Kashmir* [New Delhi, 1984]; and Quyum Rafiqi and M. Yasin, eds. *History of Freedom Struggle in J & K* [New Delhi, 1987].
16. See Manzoor Fazili, *Socialist Ideas and Movements in Kashmir* [New Delhi, 1980, Euroka].

17. *Ibid.*
18. *Ibid.*
19. See Khan and Rafiqi, *op. cit.*
20. This was largely believed among elders and activists in Kashmir. They used to say that there was a written document also in this regard.
21. See 'Instrument of Accession Document' signed by Maharaja Hari Singh and political representative of govt. of India in 1947. See also text of the speech made by Jawaharlal Nehru in Srinagar in 1947 on the issue of accession.
22. See Sisir Gupta, *Kashmir and Indo-Pak Relations* [New Delhi, 1978], See also UN documents related to Kashmir, India and Pakistan.
23. See details of accession, *op. cit.*
24. See Nehru's speech, *op. cit.*

24a. See B.A. Dabla, "Identity Politics and its Impact on Development; the Case of Kashmir", paper [unpublished] presented in 11th NWISA annual conference in University of Kashmir, Srinagar in September 2009.

25. See B.A. Dabla, "Role of Region, Religion and Culture in Economic Development: The Case of Kashmir", paper [unpublished] presented in 35th All India Sociological Conference at University of Kashmir, Srinagar in October 2009.
26. Sheikh Mohammad Abdullah, *Aatesh-e-Chinar* [New Delhi, 1987].
27. See B. A. Dabla, "Ethnic Plurality and National Integration in India: A Study in Kashmir" in *Sociological Papers on Kashmir*, Vol. I [Srinagar, 2010, Jay Kay Books].
28. See B.A. Dabla, "Sociological Dimensions of Kashmir Problem...", paper in Nyla Ali Khan's forthcoming book on "Kashmir ..." from the U.S.
29. See B.A. Dabla, paper, *op. cit.* [no. 24].
30. See Sisir Gupta, *op. cit.*
31. See Kuldip Nayyar, *Distant Neighbours* [New Delhi, 1977].

32. See concerned reports in international press, particularly New York Times, which has given details about U.S. official statement.

33. This was reiterated by Jawaharlal Nehru in a public meeting in Srinagar in 1947. See text of the speech, *op. cit.*

34. See foreign policy statements of India after 1952 published in national and local press.

34a. See speeches and statements of national leaders in this regard published in the national press repeatedly.

35. See B.J.P. constitution and other political documents. See also statements and speeches of BJP leaders, especially of A.B. Vajpai and L.K. Advani.

36. See the national press reports, particularly in *Patriot* [New Delhi], in this regard.

37. *Ibid.*

38. See constitution and other political documents of the Congress party. See also manifestoes which it released at the time of every election.

39. See official statements of Pakistan Foreign Office in Islamabad. See also speeches and statements of different political parties in that country.

40. *Ibid.*

41. *Ibid.*

42. Both countries' national press have reflected this situation.

43. See Reports in the local English and Urdu press, particularly *Rising Kashmir* [Srinagar].

44. *Ibid.*

45. See former Foreign Minister of Pakistan's [2002 – 2007] statement that "India and Pakistan had agreed to an interim agreement on Kashmir worked out through backdoor diplomacy ... by virtue of this...Kashmiris could have got independence in social, economic and political affairs." Later on, a military general of that time confirmed this report. See statements in *Greater Kashmir* [Srinagar] 28th April and 29th April 2010. On the other hand, former Indian intelligence –

RAW- chief also confirmed these reports and alleged that India lost a good chance to solve the Kashmir problem. See *Srinagar Times* [Srinagar] 20th May 2010.

46. See the local newspapers in this regard.

47. It is said about JK state which has still separate flag, constitution and unusual legislative powers.

48. Both, BJP and Congress have used communal tactics for electoral gains and were successful, first Congress and now BJP.

48a. See the local media reports, especially during and after 2008 elections.

49. See "Autonomy Document" prepared by N.C. in 1980s. The party uphold it despite its rejection by the parliament of India.

50. *Ibid.*

51. See "Self rule Document" published by P.D.P. in 2008.

52. See statements and speeches of pro-freedom leaders published in local English and Urdu daily newspapers.

53. See their literature in Urdu language published from JK and PAK.

54. The portrayal of this disunity is common feature in the local press. For critical remarks see also Hashim Qureshi *The Undenieable Truth* [Srinagar, 2010] and *Kashmir Ke Talakh Haqayiq* [Srinagar, 2010]. This disunity was noticed by every sensitive mind. A journalist in London, working for a review of a South African Film, got in mind similarities between the hero of movie and behaviour of Kashmiri politicians whom he had observed. He made the following comment on their behaviour that "the film can serve as a food for thought for Kashmir politicians who it seems do not have the time to rise above personal likes and dislikes. Their egos seem to have become far bigger than their own selves. Their rigidity in even recognizing each other's existence is hampering the people of Kashmir." See Daily Telegraph [London].

55. *Greater Kashmir [Srinagar],* 17th March 2010.

56. *See* these critical views in local newspapers particularly –

Srinagar Times [Cartoon];

- *Aftaab [Khazir Wulur Ke Kinarey];*
- *Greater Kashmir;*
- Rising Kashmir.

57. See publications of both factions of *Hurriyet Conference* published in Kashmir.
58. See national and local press.
59. See J.K.L.F. publications in Kashmir, India, Pakistan and other countries of the world.
60. See literature of these organizations in Urdu.
61. *Ibid.*
62. These views have been presented by experts, professionals and academics in the valley in their informal debate about short-term and long-term implications of militancy in Kashmir.

CHAPTER 2
METHODOLOGY

This book is composed of the writings of the author written in last three years and some before that. Though their objectives within the broader framework of sociology are same, their focus and methodology are not same. In reality, different methods and techniques have been used to study the concerned topics. In all papers in this book, the grand and general 'scientific method' was applied in order to examine, explain, analyze and interpret the existing social phenomena sociologically.

I. APPLICATION OF SCIENTIFIC METHODS AND TECHNIQUES

At the outset, the theoretical and empirical aspects of different topics were examined in detail in order to know about their nature, dimensions, variables, features and so on. The formal-focused areas of the topic, relevance-context of the topic, and identification of major-minor objectives of the topic were highlighted. Subsequently, the universe-unit of study was clearly identified with sociological features. Following these steps, particular methods and techniques were explained in terms of their relevance. In this regard, questionnaire, interview, direct-participant observation, content analysis, survey and case study methods/techniques were presented and applied with their characteristic features. The suitability of a particular method/technique was also established. This was followed by selection and presentation of representative/random sample with its nature of composition and sociological variables.

After doing these table exercises of methodology for topic of study, detailed empirical investigation through fieldwork [in case of questionnaire and schedule] or direct-participant observation [in case of particular study] was carried out. In some other cases, study of primary-secondary sources and case-content studies were undertaken. After collecting information from written sources and statistical data from respondents and documents, these were aggregated, classified, tabulated, and explained-analyzed in accordance with sociological theory methodological framework and major themes and objectives of the study. After all these methodological exercises were over, we were in a position to arrive at findings and reach to logical conclusions.

II. METHODOLOGY OF RESEARCH PAPERS

This book is composed of research papers, reports and briefs of author's books written at different times during the period 2006-2009. The research papers included as mentioned below:

- 2007 Militancy and its Social Impact
- 2008 Social Background of Militancy
- 2008 Multi-dimensional Implications of Militancy
- 2008 Demographic Transformation-Manipulation
- 2008 Social Policy in JK
- 2009 Indianization of Kashmir
- 2009 Economic Baselessness in JK
- 2009 Cumulative and Human Loss in Kashmir
- 2009 Increasing Crime Rate in Kashmir
- 2009 Psycho-social Life of Half-widows in Kashmir
- 2009 Conflict and Gender Violence in Kashmir
- 2009 Educational Backwardness in Kashmir
- 2010 Background and Perceptions of Kashmir problem
- 2010 Mental and Physical Health Deterioration
- 2010 Social Deviance and Social Disorganization
- 2010 Phenomenon of 'Never Married' in Kashmir
- 2010 Rise of Disability in JK

- 2010 Emerging Juvenile Delinquency in Kashmir
- 2010 Social Pathology in Kashmir
- 2010 Suffering Children in Kashmir
- 2010 Raped Women in Kashmir
- 2010 Kashmiri Youths – A Generation Lost

Broadly, these papers can be divided into two categories on the basis of methodology adopted during the course of research. The first category is data-based papers category. The distinctive features of these papers are that these are wholly based on official/unofficial statistical details. This data is based on primary and secondary sources. While the primary source data refers to data taken from census reports of both, governments of India and JK, and official reports, information and statements, the secondary sources include unofficial reports and information, non-governmental reports and statistical information and mass media reports. These sources were further supported by books, research papers, articles and other relevant written sources. The explanation/analysis in these papers is mainly statistical. The hypothesis, propositions and conclusions have been drawn in an objective, scientific and logical way. In general, the sociological framework and perspective in these papers remains objective and critical. The sociological assessment of these papers has been carried out through sociological investigation in its holistic framework of theory and ideology.

The other category of research papers, known as 'observation-based category', is based on methodology related to direct, indirect and participant observation. At the initiation, the relevant concepts, related to the topics of studies, were taken from sociological literature and explained contextually. After highlighting dimensions and features, these concepts were applied in our cases. All major findings and propositions in these papers are based on scientific field investigation. These were supported by information provided in primary and secondary sources and documents like books, journals, megazines, newspapers, official statistics, governmental and non-governmental reports, surveys and so on. Subsequently, the sociological analysis was carried out as was done in the case of first category of research papers.

III. METHODOLOGY OF OTHER STUDIES – BOOKS

These sociological studies were carried out by the author at different times.

The details in this regard follow:

[i] 2007 Sociological Implications of Pandit Migration in J&K.

[ii] 2008 Domestic Violence against Women in Kashmir.

[iii] 2009 A Sociological Study of Widows and Orphans in Kashmir.

[iv] 2009 Life Conditions of Child Labourers in Kashmir.

[v] 2009 Cultural Developments in Kashmir.

These studies stood for detailed sociological investigation on the concerned topics. The brief of these studies have been presented in this book. The specific attempt was to convey all major propositions, findings and conclusions of the books properly, correctly and contextually. The methodology adopted in these studies have been explained in detail in all these books.

IV. METHODOLOGY OF SOCIAL SURVEYS

This book is composed of the reports of four social surveys carried out by the author at different times, the details of which follow:

[i] 2001 Suicides in the Kashmir Valley

[ii] 2003 Changing Marriage Patterns in Kashmir

[iii] 2009 Emergence of Late Marriage in Kashmir

[iv] 2010 Changing Marriage Practices in Kashmir

These social surveys were provided the same treatment as that of sociological studies. Methodology of every survey has been mentioned in detail in every survey report. It seems necessary to mention here that these survey reports were solely prepared by the author and presented in full.

V. OTHER METHODOLOGICAL FEATURES OF SURVEYS

The methodology adopted during writing research papers and

survey reports and other presentations had certain methodological features which are mentioned below:

[i] The overall theoretical-thematic framework was sociological in nature and in perspective. All sociological concepts, theories and methods were utilized to analyze concerned situation, issues and problems. Again, all topics which were studied by the author were completely "sociological concerns" in terms of their themes. The theoretical as well as empirical aspects of studies were sociological in content and perspective.

[ii] The topics of all these presentations deal with different sociological concerns. The theories, themes and methods have all been given sociological treatment. The grand sociological theme's runs through all these presentations.

[iii] The situational focus of all these presentations have been the contemporary KMS living in JK state. At the same time, academic efforts have been carried out to present the locals' perspective about various issues and problems. Their views and opinions have been highlighted objectively. Moreover, relevant methods and techniques have been adopted to arrive at proper and logical conclusions.

[iv] Many presentations have significant portions of official reports and statistics and census data. But, taking into consideration their negative academic credibility, these governmental sources have not been accepted totally. The unofficial reports and statistical data have also been used and analyzed to know the reality and correct version of the concerned social phenomenon.

[v] Last, but not the least, the time-factor in all presentations seems important. Since these papers were written at different times and in different situations, there is minimum possibility of some repetition and variation in the findings. But, that has to be seen in the time context or factor context.

CHAPTER 3

SOCIAL BACKGROUND OF MILITANCY

The emergence of militancy in Kashmir in 1989 has been explained in terms of political developments in chapter 1. Here, we explain some important sociological factors which contributed directly or indirectly to the militancy conditions in Kashmir.

I. INDIANIZATION OF KASHMIR

[i] Forgetting all promises of RSD to Kashmiris and in contravention of the constitutions of JK, the Indian leadership carried out systematically a forceful, rigorous and one-sided process of political integration of the state to India completely. All formal and informal, constitutional-unconstitutional, and democratic-undemocratic political decisions were taken to follow the grand objective of Kashmir's total integration in to the national mainstream of India.[1] This process started with amendments in constitutions of India and JK on the part of GOI. It was aimed at to extend the jurisdiction of Indian laws/institutions/organizations to Kashmir, which was against the essence of article 370 of Indian constitution and spirit of JK constitution. These imposed changes reflected in the change of name of *Sadre Riyasat* [President] and *Wazire Azam* [Prime Minister] into *Wazire Aala* [Chief Minister] and Governor respectively, extension of jurisdiction of Supreme Court of India, Election Commission of India, Comptroller General of India and so on. All this was done with active support of Delhi-imposed political regimes in JK state. The extension/imposition of these laws could hardly be resisted

by these unrepresentative regimes which led to clear violation of autonomous status of JK guaranteed in article 370.[2]

[ii] The grand process of Indianization was pursued in economic field too by adopting a policy of making Kashmir completely dependent on the Indian economy. This dependence increased further when neither Indian nor foreign private sector could invest in Kashmir mainly because of its disputed status and, consequently, no economic infrastructure could be developed here. Educationally, all Indian courses and syllabi were introduced in all schools, colleges and universities in order to orient the young Kashmiri generation to the national mainstream of India at the cost of Kashmir's particularistic stream. At the same time, the GOI adopted an aggressive policy of imposing the dominant Hindu Culture on Kashmir. While the Congress party was soft on this issue, non-Congress political parties, particularly Bhartiya Jan Sangh and now Bhartiya Janta Party, were very vocal in forceful imposition of Hindu culture, especially Hindi language.[3]

[iii] The process of Indianization was followed even in the field of demographic transformation. The political leadership of India followed a 'demographic agenda' of changing the majority character of Muslims in JK state. It was successful in reducing the majority character of Muslims from 80% in 1941 to 68% in 1961 to 63% in 2001.[4] It seems important to note here that, in the context of preceding political, economic. Cultural, educational and demographic efforts, the process of Indianization in Kashmir proved a process of 'Hinduization'[5] which was resisted by the Kashmiri masses strongly and consistently.

II. NEGATION OF KASHMIRI IDENTITY (KI)

[i] The fact stands with empirical evidence that KI within the broader whole of Indian sub-continent stood as a distinctive identity with prominent political, religious, cultural and other features.[6] The GOI from 1947 continuously attempted to negate this particular identity, de-emphasize its religious dimension and distort its meaning. In this connection, conscious efforts were carried out in three specific ways.

First, it started with formal and informal efforts to de-emphasize and distort the religious aspect of this distinctive identity. Second, more emphasis was laid on plurality of cultures, ethnicity and communities represented by Jammu, Kashmir and Ladakh and these were put in opposite of each for electoral gains. Third, though plurality of identities at macro level [i.e. Jammu, Kashmiri and Ldakhi identities] and micro level [i.e. at religious and cultural level] stood as social-political realities in JK, these became the instruments to throw the religious dimension into background. The Indian leadership followed this strategy continuously from 1947 for its political gains.[7]

III. DEMOGRAPHIC MANIPULATION

[i] One of the crucial developments of grave political Implications was related to demography which refers to "population dynamics, its causes-consequences, its varying compositions, death and birth rates and human migration."[8] This change crudely reflected in continuous decrease in Muslim proportion in total population of JK and constant erosion of Muslim majority character. The following details about Muslim proportion of total population in past 8 decades reveal this fact:

S.No.	*Census year*	*Muslim proportion to total population in JK*
1.	1941 [esti.]	80.00 %
2.	1951 [esti.]	70.00 %
3.	1961	68.00 %
4.	1971	65.50 %
5.	1981	64.00 %
6.	1991 [esti.]	63.00 %
7.	2001	62.50 %[9]

This downward trend in population also reflected in the upward 8.00 % increase in Hindu-dominated Jammu region and simultaneous 8 % decrease in the Muslim dominated Kashmir province in last 60 years from 1941 to 2001.[10] These demographic changes occurred in Kashmir against established principals and rules of population dynamics. During 2 census decades of 1971-1981 and 1981-1991, while the decadal growth rates at the national level were 23.86 and 21.34, these rates in JK were 30.34 and 29.04[11]. Despite the fact of lower level of population growth at national level and higher level at state level, the state's majority community does not follow this pattern. This follows that either population figures given in the census are not correct or have been manipulated.[12]

[ii] It was in that context that local intelligentsia, especially professionals, maintained that these and other such population data has been consciously manipulated under official patronage for the political objective of changing the existing population in Kashmir. This core proposition was supported by three evidential points. First, when in mid-1980s, protests and campaign against population manipulation was organized in Srinagar, the local government ordered a mid-decade census in some districts in the state. The preliminary results of that census were found different from the results of 1981 census.[13] Second, at the same time, the Chief Minister of JK made a statement about the practice of population manipulation saying that "the census data has been manipulated against Muslims by the concerned agencies."[14] Third, the GOI, during BJP rule, confirmed that talks were held with the Israeli Foreign Minister about change in existing demographic situation in Kashmir.[15] Though the government was criticized by the opposition for this practice, it necessarily meant that Israeli help was sought in changing the Muslim character of JK as Israel has got such experience in Palestine.[16]

IV. ECONOMIC BASELESSNESS

[i] The accession of Kashmir to India had certain implications which proved economically disastrous for Kashmir as a whole. the first such implication was closure of natural-historical trade routes of Jhelum Valley and Silk roads and, subsequently, dependence on sole unnatural and highly-dangerous Jammu-Srinagar highway. While the former implication denied Kashmir's access to South and Central Asian markets, the latter expanded and strengthened economic dependence of Kashmir on Indian markets only. The latter also proved highly

damaging in terms of human loss [as thousands of fatal accidents took place on this road] and material loss [in terms of wastage of time, money, material, especially fruits]. Moreover, this road usually remains closed for one or two days a week on an average during the winter season and Kashmir remains cut off from the world by road during that period. On the other hand, the central government has not extended the railway connection to Kashmir even after 62 years of independence.[17]

[ii] The second major economic implication was that KMs could not rise in any major economic sector. The service sector under central and state governments in the state was dominated by KPs, Indian Hindus [IH] and Indian Muslims [IM][18] In that situation, local Muslims were represented by 2-3 % of total number of central employees.[19] The private organizations-agencies, private-public undertakings and autonomous bodies in JK made systematic discrimination against KMs. It was after 1950s and 1960s that KMs were recruited in JK at lower and middle positions and their number not equal to their population proportion.[20] It seems important to note here that no KM could think of serving in any government or private office in any part of India in the context of political antagonism raised against them.

[iii] The third implication was felt in economic situation in which traditional as well as modern economic sectors such as agriculture, tourism, handicrafts, forests, horticulture and floriculture could not come up as organized and modernized economies in terms of technological improvement, profes-sional-trained expertise, efficient management, long-term economic policy and so on. In fact, these sectors still remain backward and underdeveloped. This situation can be explained in terms of two main factors. First, no Indian or foreign investor was ready to invest in Kashmir as it was considered a "disputed territory". Even GOI and many of its agencies-organizations could not take risk of investing in Kashmir in large sums and for longer period. Second, consequently, no workable economic infrastructure for all economic sectors could be developed here. This made the Kashmir economy a 'baseless' and 'faceless' economy.[21]

[iv] Despite the fact that KNs introduced and implemented radical economic reforms in 1952-53, no revolutionary change was observed in agrarian sector in Kashmir. In reality, essence and implication of these reforms were negated by political actions of GOI. Though land was distributed among landless at large, it gave birth to new classes, especially the 'orchadist elite'.[22]

[v] The fourth implication was adoption of policy of discrimination against Kashmir region on the part of GOI in the field of development planning, its programmes and schemes. The other aspect of this phenomenon was positive discrimination for Jammu region. Systematic, official and continuous efforts were carried out in various ministries in GOI to allocate more funds, facilities, resources and other benefits to Jammu at the cost of Kashmir.[23] The worst form of this discrimination reflected in transferring unspent funds of Kashmir region to Jammu region, which many governments have acknowledged in state assembly.[24] Another related implication can be explained by saying that constant political uncertainty and instability in Kashmir didn't give enough time to attempt seriously long-term planning for development in JK. In actuality, all political regimes could never concentrate on the nature, objectives and strategy of economic development and its core sectors.[25]

[vi] All these implications of economic baselessness on KMs at large led to a 'situation of poverty' more than other communities in the state. According to a survey, conducted in 2009 by the Economic and Statistics Department of J&K government, the state had a total of 24.21 lakh persons belonging to the 'below poverty line' [BPL] status, which includes 26.14 % rural and 7.96 % urban population.[26] In this BPL population, the highest incidence of poverty in population in the state was among Muslims in comparison to other religious communities. The survey gave the figures in this regard as mentioned below:

Muslims 24.57 per cent

Bhudhists 24.50 per cent

Hindus	18.14 per cent
Sikhs	07.51 per cent
Christians	03.12 per cent[27]

V. EDUCATIONAL BACKWARDNESS

[i] As the fact stands, free education from primary till university stage was introduced in JK from 1952. *But, KMs have been benefited least. As there was near-total illiteracy prevalent in the state before 1947,* it has not gone above 40-45% which shows minimum increased in literacy in last 63 years. Those who got maximum literacy benefit belonged either to KPs or other sections of local population. The former maintained 100 % literacy status and improved quality and variety of their education. The following data about literacy reveals clearly slow growth in Muslim dominated districts in JK during the decade of 1991-2001:

Literacy Rate in JK, 2001

S.No.	*District*	*Literacy rate [%]*		
		Total	*Females*	*Males*
1.	Kupwara	26.83	40.80	53.55
2.	Baramulla	31.42	44.57	56.29
3.	Srinagar	48.11	59.31	68.99
4.	Budgam	26.60	39.54	51.23
5.	Pulwama	34.93	47.35	58.87
6.	Anantnag	31.51	44.10	55.56
7.	Leh	?	62.24	71.98
8.	Kargil	40.96	58.21	73.58
9.	Doda	28.35	46.92	63.56
10.	Udhampur	39.89	54.16	66.43
11.	Poonch	35.30	51.07	65.41
12.	Rajouri	44.14	57.65	69.64
13.	Jammu	68.75	77.30	84.92
14.	Kathua	53.92	65.29	75.73

Source: Census records of JK state, 2001.

The above statistics clearly reveals that literacy improvement of KMs was lowest in comparison to its national and state level averages.[28] It also reveals that KM women had the lowest literacy rates.[29] According to another official reports, the Muslims in the state had only 47.00 per cent literacy in 2001.[30] In addition, KMs experienced lowest level of enrolment and highest level of dropouts at all stages of education in last 3 decades.[31] They also got least representation in professional, technical, other modern and higher educational fields. The entire educational situation, discussed here, can primarily be explained in term of KMs' political involvement in post-accession political uncertainty and instability.

VI. CULTURAL DEPRIVATION

[i] The accession of Kashmir to India gave rise to a situation in which KMs got out of 'Islamic social-cultural whole' and aligned them with Hindu culture and civilization which had least similarity with it. Sociological and anthropological consequences of this change were observed at large and they felt dissociated from their cultural roots and imprisoned in an alien culture. The nationalist leadership of Kashmir showed no awareness about this religious-cultural aspect at the time of accession.

[ii] From the cultural point of view, the accession snatched the status of majority from KMs and gave them the status of minority, especially in the fields of religion, culture, language, and region. As minorities suffer in all situation and in all fields in India,[32] the KMs too suffered from this backwardness. Sociologically speaking, the KMs in post-independent India proved a 'double minority' of religious and cultural nature. In both these fields, they faced continuous domination and discrimination at the hands of the representatives of Indian state. The nationalist leadership of Kashmir could not visualize this situation in future India. They could not see Indian social reality that though constitution of India stands for secularism and democracy but society of India stood completely neither for secularism nor for democracy.

[iii] Throughout post-independence period, KMs faced a strong

process of cultural assimilation launched by institutions, organizations and agencies of GOI. This was done under the patronage of and with active support of extreme [Hindu] nationalist political parties, communal bureaucracy and administration. All these Indian leaders never accepted ideas and ideals of *Kashmiriat*. They rather negated it or destroyed it. This process was further intensified by 'indianization' and 'hinduization'.[33] While the former was meant to integrate all KMs in to 'national mainstream' at the cost of local, regional, religious and cultural identity, the latter, equated with 'sanskritization' was aimed at forceful imposition of Hindi language, culture, rituals, customs ceremonies, life style and so on. The glaring example in this regard may be that though there are no Sanskrit listeners in Kashmir, Radio Kashmir, Srinagar broadcast 5 minutes news bulletin daily in its premier morning channel.[34]

NOTES AND REFERENCES

1. B.A. Dabla, "Impact of Indianization on Muslim Kashmir" in Sociological Papers on Kashmir, Vol. I, [Srinagar, 2010, Jay Kay Books].
2. B.A. Dabla, "Ethnic Plurality and National Integration in India" in Ibid.
3. B.A. Dabla, *op. cit.* [no.1].
4. B.A. Dabla, "Demographic Changes in Kashmir", *Radiance* [Delhi], 2nd January 1994; *News From India* [New Delhi], 21st March 1994; *Kashmir Times* [Jammu], 2nd April 1994.
5. B.A. Dabla, "Hinduization in Kashmir", *Dalit Voice* [Banglore], 1st April 1994.
6. B.A. Dabla, *op. cit.* [no. 2].
7. B. A. Dabla, "Ethnic Plurality and Problems of Nation-building: The Case of Kashmir Problem" in *op. cit.* [no. 1].
8. B. A. Dabla, *op. Cit.* [no. 2].
9. Census of India, 2001 and Census of Jammu and Kashmir, 2001.
10. *Ibid.*
11. *Ibid.*
12. B.A. Dabla, *op. cit.,* [no. 4].

13. *Ibid.*
14. *Ibid.*
15. *Ibid.*
16. *Ibid.* See also "Census 2011 ...", *Kashmir Life* [Srinagar], 18 May 2010.
17. *The Times of India* [New Delhi], July 2009.
18. *Bashir-ul-Haq,* "Unfortunate Muslims of Kashmir", *Radiance* [Delhi], 8th April 1979 and Mohd. Nazir, "Hindu Rulers and Muslim Subjects: Job Division", *Conveyor* [Srinagar], Vol. 1, no. 4, November 2009.
19. *Ibid.*
20. *Ibid.*
21. See comments of economic specialists in *Greater Kashmir* [Srinagar], 29 March 2010.
22. See K.Gopal Iyer, "Agrarian Reform and Rural Transformation in J&K" [paper presented in the annual conference of NWISA at University of Kashmir, Srinagar in September 2009.
23. B.A. Dabla, *op. cit.* [no. 7].
24. *Ibid.*
25. *Ibid.*
26. *Greater Kashmir* [Srinagar], April, 2010.
27. *Ibid.*
28. B.A. Dabla, "Demographic Changes in J&K", SRC Newsletter, University of Kashmir, Srinagar, 2nd January 2002.
29. *Ibid.*
30. *Kashmir Life* [Srinagar], April 2010.
31. See B. A. Dabla. "Impact of Conflict Situation on Women and Children in Kashmir: A Study of Two Districts" [Report prepared for 'Save the Children' in 1994-95.
32. *See Report prepared by Justice* Rajinder Sachhar Committee in 2001 and presented to the government of India. Its findings revealed extremely backward status of Muslims in all fields of life, especially in education, employment, in all states.
33. See "Impact of Indianization....", *op.cit.* and "Hinduization...", *op.cit.*
34. *Ibid.*

CHAPTER 4

CRUCIAL SOCIOLOGICAL IMPLICATIONS OF MILITANCY

I. CUMULATIVE HUMAN AND MATERIAL LOSS

[i] The militancy in Kashmir eddected all sections of society and all sectors of human life. Lakhs of innocent and common people were killed, injured, tortured and made disabled-handicapped. Most of the local elders were abused and dishonoured repeatedly, all local youth were brutally treated, all local children were harassed-tortured, and most of the local women were teased, molested and raped. Thousands of residential houses and business establishments were burnt or destroyed. Other valuable properties worth billions of dollars were lost. In brief, the militancy brought a devastating and catastrophic effect in totality in the entire Kashmiri society, especially in the fields related to large-scale economic destruction, widespread social disorder and disorganization, educational backwardness, mass psychological depression, physiological and mental health deterioration, mass humiliation, extreme type of helplessness, degenerated cultural aggression, political deception and domination, and extreme cronic social problems such as deviance, crime, suicides, drug addiction and erosion of values–norms, which were experienced by majority of members of the Kashmiri society.[1]

[ii] The fact is that no survey or census has been carried to find out the total number of people who have been killed in the period of last 20 years. In actuality, no official or unofficial systematic and scientific documentation of these people has been done. However, there are different claims and estimates

in this regard put forward by different sources. While pro-freedom source claim a large number of people were killed in the armed conflict between Kashmiri militants and Indian security forces in Kashmir, government sources give lesser or least number of such people. Non-governmental, human/civil rights groups, civil society and NGOs have also given their estimated figures.[2] Finally, military and para-military security forces have given details about death of their personnel in the conflict situation in Kashmir. These statistical details are varying in extreme form and reveal their partiality, biasness, manipulation and were printed/circulated with political and military objectives. Here, we present these different estimates about the number of people killed in the conflict:

- Pro-freedom and militant sources 1,00,000[3]
- State and central government sources 60,000[4]
- Security-intelligence agencies sources 40,000[5]
- NGOs, Civil society, human-civil rights groups 80,000[6]

The average-mean of these various estimates is about 70,000 which stands as the minimum figure of casualties during last 20 years of armed conflict in Kashmir. It follows that at least 3,500 common people were killed per year and 292 people per month during last two decades.[7]

In addition, the official sources have provided officially the following number of deaths among Indian military, para-military and state police personnel during the armed conflict in Kashmir:

- Military personnel 3,000[7]
- Para-military-security personnel 6,000[8]
- JK police personnel 7,000[9]

But, an annual report of the Union Home Ministry for the year 2009-10 points out that total number of 18,465 persons [13,775 civilians and 4,690 security forces] were killed during the period 1989 – 2009.[10] It was also revealed officially in the parliament by the Union Home Ministry that 1,754 persons were killed and 5,589 persons were injured only due to grenade attacks and bomb blasts during the last 20 years.[11] Nearly total number of civilians killed in the armed conflict in Kashmir were local Muslims. However, the government revealed that 219 KPs were also killed in the conflict.[12]

[iii] As a result of this situation, a large number of orphans, widows and half-widows were given birth in the valley. According to a survey conducted by the author in 2000 [and revised the estimated in 2009], the total number of widows in Kashmir was about 32,400 and orphans 97,200 – 1,29,600.[13]

[iv] Moreover, there are about 10,000 cases of half-widows whose husbands are missing after they were taken by the security forces. These cases are referred as cases of "imposed disappearance". The Association of Parents of Disappeared Persons [APDP] have documented most of these cases which have also been published.[14]

[v] Among other factors, the militancy factor in JK contributed to huge number of local and young disabled persons in one or other form. The population of these disabled persons in JK was as is revealed from the following table:

Table 4.1

Disabled Population in JK, 2001

S.No.		*Total/sex*	*Rural*	*Urban*
1.	Persons	3,02,670	2,29,718	72,952
2.	Males	1,71,816	1,29,443	42,373
3.	Females	1,30,854	1,00,275	30,579

Source: JK Census, 2001, JK Government.

These disabled persons in JK total population had following types of disabilities:

- Disability in seeing 3,02,670
- Disability in speech 2,08,713
- Disability in hearing 7,693

- Disability in movement 37,965
- Mental disability 24,879[15]

This number and proportion of disabled persons in JK stands higher than its national average and in comparison to the states of Himachal Pradesh, Chandigarh and Karnataka.[16] This higher proportion can only be attributed to the militancy situation.

II. MILITARIZATION AND ITS SOCIAL IMPACT

[i] In the broader sense, the concept of "militarization" is explained by Ronald Simbulas as is the process of using the military…to suppress the people's just demands for a humane society. It logically connotes human rights violations by the physical presence or even saturation of soldiers…a situation which, to the general perception, implies and results in coercion … The main pretext of militarization is the achievement or maintenance of 'political stability', 'national security' or other similar goals, but whose real purpose is the maintenance of the regime in power.[16]

Militarization at the global level is systemic in the sense that it reinforces militarization at an international level where both northern and southern states participate in a global military order. On the other hand, militarization's domestic variables includes not only direct violence against civilians by the military but also gendered abuse such as rape and molestation of women.[17] But, considering the limits of state military power at domestic level, Mary Kaldor notes that "Russia cannot control Chechnya, Israel cannot control the Palestinian territories. India cannot control Kashmir."[18]

Both these aspects are rooted in a cosmology of 'nation' and 'national' power that endorses the exercise of coercive, centralized force in domestic and foreign affairs. However, military and nuclear consolidation without, and political consolidation through military means within has not translated into security or strategic advantage to the Indian state. It has almost eliminated domestic challenges to the state. In this regard, Seema Kazi observes that fortified by military and nuclear power, the Indian state seems unassailable; yet, as the tragedy of Kashmir so vividly demonstrates, an extraordinarily 'powerful' state backed by the world's fourth largest military, can hold on to Kashmir only through brute force, even as its formidable 'power' is spectacularly unsuccessful in eliminating what Daniel Barenboim appropriately terms 'the problem inside'.[19]

The militarization also symbolizes the imitation and replication of western ideas of "military power" that have shaped and defined independence elite interests in developing countries.[20]

[ii] Kashmir stands for the gravity of crisis that originates from using the armed/security forces as an instrument of dominant political power and domestic repression. In this connection, Bonner says:

"In the name of fighting secessionist militants, those responsible for governance of this great country are themselves hitting at the very foundations of our democratic republic .... A republic dost not last by enforced submission of its people at gunpoint. It has just the opposite effect." [21]

Emphasizing the same theme, Kazi comments :

"Kashmir is part of a larger crisis of the Indian state that is neither incidental nor transient but a symptom of centralized tyranny whose collective discontents are negotiated through military means. This crisis has serious implications not just for citizens, but also for the military. When the latter battles citizens in Kashmir or, for that matter, in Manipur, Mizoram, Assam or Nagaland, it raises serious questions regarding the legality and morality of the state. The violation of citizens' civil and human rights by an institution that is meant to protect citizens underlines the crisis."[22]

She also maintains that use of the army as a proxy for civil governance represents political failure on the part of the state, exacerbated by legislative sanction for Indian soldiers to kill any number of citizens. Thus, despite a formal civil-military separation, the military has come to play a direct role in domestic and other affairs of the state. This stands as the emerging trend threatens the functioning and continuity of all, especially political and democratic institutions in the Indian society. Thus the need is to make a clear and fundamental distinction between the role of the state and functioning of the military on the other, which will help in establishing a real and actual democratic institutional framework in India.[23]

[iii] In the specific context of the Kashmir problem as an issue,

not only between India and Pakistan but between government of India and people of Kashmir, it is argued that a plural concept of 'nation' and 'identity' is premised on a commitment to nurturing multiple communities and identities, where no one particular community or identity is privileged over the other's. Regarding re-imagining Kashmir in the broader social-political background of India, she maintains:

"Democracy in Kashmir would mean that its formal, participatory dimensions – involving elections at the local and state level – are complemented and augmented by its rights for Kashmiris – namely, freeing Kashmiri civilians from violence and harassment from the police and the military, the revocation of repressive legislation, the end of unlawful killings, arbitrary searches and detentions, the restoration of Kashmir's judiciary, the protection of civil rights, including the right to freedom of speech and assembly, freedom for Kashmir's citizens to travel within and beyond state borders, the promotion of free press, and last, but certainly not least, the initiation of a process of public accountability for Kashmir's human rights tragedy."[24]

Emphasizing the need and role of 'demilitarized vision for future' about the entire state of JK, she identifies its implications clearly. In this regard, she makes the following observation:

"Taking both as a point of departure, the Indian state should envision a democratic and non-national vision based on recognition and respect for Kashmiri identity, and Kashmiris' desire to chart a political future free from central control and dominance. This is not to formulate a 'solution' to the crisis [itself an ongoing debate …] but to envision a future based on Kashmiri aspiration rather than territorial."[25]

[iv] It was reported in 1990 that there were about 1,50,000 Indian soldiers stationed in India, i.e. about 17 soldiers per square mile and one soldier for every group of 17 civilians.[26] Subsequently, an independent estimate in 1994[27] put these soldiers' number in Kashmir to 4,00,000 which was estimated between 5,00,000 t0 7,00,000, i.e., one soldier for every 10 civilians.[28] The former Deputy Chief Minister of JK informed the state legislative assembly in 2006 that there were more than 6,67,000 security forces in the state for a population of

12 million.[29] In 2007, the Indian army sources gave the figure [in this regard] of 3,37,000 army personnel in JK, i.e. one trooper for every 18 persons.[30] In this way, Kashmir was made "the most heavily militarized zone" in the region and world. It was essentially in this explosive context that the United State's State Department's top official characterized Kashmir as the "most dangerous spot in the world".[31]

The militarization had not political, military and strategic implication only. In actuality, it has effected all sections and sectors of the Kashmiri society and thus influencing the whole life of Kashmiris involving social, cultural, psychological, economic, educational and other fields. While former type of impact has been observed in detail, the latter type of impact has neither been identified nor explained.[32]

[v] The military-civilian relationship throughout India has remained tensionful and conflict-oriented leading often to violent clashes between the two parties. Several studies in different states of India have confirmed this proposition. The reasons for these clashes have generally been related to the military personnel's rude and immoral behaviour, especially with females.[33] Same is true about the Kashmir situation, particularly after militancy started there. In the Kashmir case, there is an added dimension. It follows that jawans of Indian military and security forces in Kashmir behave like "alien force in an alien territory" and consider the entire local population as "political and military enemy". This mind-set of security forces has not changed despite their two decades stay in JK. This image has rather strengthened in recent years. As a result of this psychological orientation, the overall behavior of these forces towards the local population has been antagonistic, arrogant, offensive and humiliating.[34] In this background, the local population see the Indian military-security forces as "occupational forces" which have no similarity and sympathy with the local population.[35] This has also been well established and documented by many national and international human-civil rights organizations.[36] This abnormal relationship has completely adverse effects on the Kashmiris as well as the forces. The military-civilian relationship seems "spoiled" and hurts the basic national interest and national image in Kashmir.

[vi] Militarization created serious obstacles and constraints for the normal functioning of all societal institutions in Kashmir. In the case of family, all processes related to the maintenance-continuity of 'social environment', 'socialization', and 'personality formation' could not operate fully and continuously mainly because of the behaviuor of forces vis-à-vis locals. At the same time, traditional values and norms and roles-statuses could not be maintained and saved for next generations of Kashmiris. The traditional marriage practices and kinship-patterns were exposed to a situation, created by the security forces, in which they faced a serious threat. In many cases, these practices and patterns could not be practiced fully in presence of security forces.

[v] Side by side these problems, militarization gave rise to many psyclo-social problems. Prominent and most damaging among these are dreaded psychological problems and diseases such as mass depression, tension, anxiety, stress, suicidal tendencies and PTSD. While it was reported that most of the members in every family in Kashmir valley suffer from depression and stress problems, tension and anxiety has emerged as a permanent phenomenon in Kashmiri social life.[37] According to an empirical study of this author, about 2,000 – 2,400 suicides have been committed by young, male-female, and urban-rural Kashmiris.[38] The experts here feel that this can easily be related to the inhuman treatment, rude behaviour, torture and harassment, security checks, crack-downs, search operations, imposed disappearances and general anti-Kashmiri sentiment on the part of Indian security forces.[39] Other related problems can be identified as least desirable socialization, least social control, least respect and following of the patriarchal-parental authority, and negative attitudes and behaviour pattern. These problems have also led other problems like deviance, delinquency, violent behaviour and major-minor crime inside and outside family environment.[40]

[vi] The most dangerous implication of militarization was felt in the increasing trend of violence against women [VAW] which has crossed all limits in the recent years.[41] All women, young and old, faced all types of violence including eve-teasing,

molestation, domestic violence, harassment, torture, rape and murder.[42] The recent phenomenon of 'criminal violence' against women is symptomatic.[43] The fact stands with a lot of empirical evidence that these heinous crimes against the Kashmiri women were started in an organized way by the security forces during crackdowns, security checks and so on.[44]

[vii] It has been observed that militarization has proved against the attainment of education by the local children. In many rural areas of Kashmir, many students, particularly girl students, had to drop out of schools due to security-related factors. It happened in the background in which the security forces either took over the school building forcibly or security picket was established near to the school.[45]

[viii] Militarization imposed heavy economic losses on the local traders and businessmen because security forces occupied forcibly the orchard lands, agricultural lands, business establishments and so on.[46]

[ix] Militarization has given rise to the phenomena of cultural exclusiveness and cultural isolation of the security forces. In the pre-militancy days, the local Muslims used to participate in the religious festivals and other cultural occasions of KPs in the valley, but now local can even think in terms of participation in religious-cultural occasions. This also led to the processes of mutual antipathy in place of [positive] mutual interaction and to 'cultural misunderstanding' in place of 'cultural understanding'.[47]

[x] Last, but certainly not the least, militarization in Kashmir had many negative political implications which, in the long run, hurt the cause of peace, reconciliation and conflict resolution of the Kashmir problem.

III. THE ECONOMIC COLLAPSE

[i] *The Economic Impact: Poverty:* The overall impact of militancy can be seen from details about prevalence of poverty, in terms of number of people living below poverty line [BPL], in JK which were released recently by the state government.

According to details in this official report, the Muslim in JK stand as the most poor community in comparison to other religious communities in the state.[48] This economic debacle has been experienced primarily because of militancy conditions.

[ii] *Development Planning:* Since political instability, uncertainty, militancy and militarization dominated the entire period, there was hardly any serious effort of formulating and implementing planned programmes and schemes in the state. Special development planning for short-term objectives had a serious setback. Even if annual and five year plans were prepared on paper for the formality sack, these could not be implemented properly and realistically. The government of JK informed the State Legislative Assembly on 21st August 2009 that 80 % of funds of 'Prime Minister's Reconstruction Programme" could not be utilized since its launch in the state during 2004-05. It said that only Rs. 6,367 crores were spent out of Rs. 30,000 crores.[49] It was reported, and not denied by the government, that planned funds were not utilized in Kashmir region and were shifted to Jammu region and spent there.[50] Moreover, it led to lesser plan allocation to Kashmir province in comparison to Jammu province though population of the former was more than the latter. This reflects clearly in the plan allocations to Kashmir and Jammu regions in recent years.[51] This situation also reflects in the per capita investment pattern in the state. The following table makes it sufficiently clear:

Table 4.2

Per Capita Plan Investment in JK [Rs.]

Year	*Jammu*	*Kashmir*	*Ladakh*
2002-03	2041.87	1752.16	4000.00
2003-04	2269.22	1948.19	4304.82
2004-05	2652.91	2311.18	4867.19
2005-06	3707.20	2854.72	5678.25

2006-07	3092.12	2559.61	5856.63
2007-08	3948.39	3313.43	4266.02
2008-09	4798.39	4060.48	5052.84[52]

It may be argued that in the above-mentioned way, there was a kind of institutional and planned discrimination against Kashmir province which could neither be highlighted nor removed because the local political leadership was involved in the militancy-militarization situation.

[iii] *Economic Growth:* In this period of two decades, the economic growth was made equal to the national growth rate. Some local media agencies quoted an average of 4% or less growth rate for this period.[53] In this context, we may argue that some economic growth, even affluence-type, was noted by some politicalelite business families and upper sections of middle class. While political elite families got money from various political, intelligence and government sources, business families accumulated wealth through their business operations at national and international level. Again, government employees of higher and middle cadre got regular salary without any break, the entire small business in all sectors was taken over by local businessmen after 1989 which gave them tremendous monetary benefits. But, the social reality related to this situation was that some families got benefited economically at the cost of large number of families which suffered from economic depression. The apparent symbols of affluence, palatial houses and new cars in Srinagar must not ignore basic poor economic conditions of huge majority of population in Kashmir. The related fact is that the degree of exploitation has increased significantly in all economic sectors, especially handicrafts, tourism, child-women labour, agriculture and horticulture.[54] The common features of exploitation in these sectors are lesser wages and more work, especially for artisans, children and women, in rural as well as urban areas.

[iv] The net economic impact of the developments related to militancy was characterized as "catastrophic" in all sectors.[55]

In simple terms, it reduced considerably the number of working days and hours and stopped new economic initiatives and opportunities. In fact, it reduced to rumbles the existing economic infrastructure in the valley and government and private sector together could not revive it fully. According to an unofficial survey, the Kashmir economy had to face a loss of more than 60,000 crores of rupees mainly as a result of strikes [called by pro-freedom political parties to protest against the state and central governments] which were observed for 120 days in a year [on an average] and about 4,000 days in last 20 years.[56] It also quoted this financial loss in the economic fields of transport, commerce, trade, auto-vehicle industry, horticulture, floriculture, zafran and other industries.[57] According to the president, Federation of Chambers of Industries, Kashmir [FCIK], the total number of shut-downs, including curfew period, since September 1989 is more than 1,800 days and the minimum loss incurred amounts to 1,80,000 crores.[8] He also calculated the loss of per day contribution to GDP as 66 crore rupees during this entire period.[59]

[v] *Unemployment:* Other crucial economic problem which emerged during this period was 'unemployment'. It has been observed that, during last twenty years, a large number of Kashmiri youths got education in general, higher, professional, technical and other modern specialties inside and outside state. On the other hand, these educated and qualified youths were not recruited in state services in significant numbers mainly because of blanket ban on recruitment by the government. The natural result was in the huge accumulation of skilled, semi-skilled and professional, technical and general educated unemployed youth in all fields. According to the latest official registration of unemployed youth in JK in December 2009, the number was 5,50,000 males and females.[60]

[vi] *Impact on Tourism and Handicrafts:* Due to the factors of militancy and consequent militarization, two core sectors of Kashmir economy nearly collapsed. It follows that all individuals, groups and communities directly or indirectly related to tourism and handicraft sectors suffered extreme

loss and some families came to even zero economic level. Since tourists stopped coming to the valley after 1989, the occupancy rate in many hotels and houseboats came down to 20%. As a result, the concerned individuals, groups and families, especially belonging to the *Hanji* community, had to suffer lifetime economic loss. Similarly, all tourism-related occupations and personnel such as taxi-transport operators, *shikarawallas,* retail sellers, footpath vendors, handicraft and other shopkeepers, and other seasonal-occupational personnel had to face same situation.[61] The extreme sufferers in this field were artisans and workers doing the basic handicraft work. In the absence of tourists in the valley, the local retailers could not sell handicraft items in the local market. They were compelled to sell their manufactured-prepared items to the local middlemen and wholesalers on much cheaper rates. The latter sold these items on much higher rates in national and international markets. Thus, exploitation of the former led to huge profits for the latter at the cost of former. The latter were also benefited by the foreign currency benefits given by the central government.[62]

[vii] *Impact on Agriculture, Horticulture and Floriculture:* During last two decades, traditional and new crops could not be grown and maintained properly. If there was not any significant deterioration or loss there was not any improvement also In reality, the production in agriculture, horticulture and floriculture fields was not improved at all. The fact reveals that production in all these fields showed a downward trend. This could not be avoided in the militancy and militarization conditions.[63] One important reason for this was forcible occupation of land by security forces in JK that didn't allow local villagers to work on their lands. While the Union Defence Ministry says that 5.86 lakh kanals of land was occupied by security forces[64], the state government maintained that these forces had occupied 10.54 lakh kanals of land.[65]

More important is the point that governments which were awfully busy with the threats posed by militancy, could neither get time nor environment to enhance and improve the production in the fields. In this situation, there was large scale shift of agricultural-horticultural land for the construction of houses and other establishments. Though illegal, the government could not stop this practice till date. Moreover, new areas of floriculture could not be developed on realistic basis. When the government started it without proper scientific planning, it proved counter-productive. The establishment of Indira Gandhi Tulip Garden in Srinagar stands as a glaring example in this regard.[66]

[viii] *Neglect of Core Sectors:* In.the situation of political instability and insecurity in the state, no serious developmental planning could be carried out. Consequently, the government could neither identify preferred development sectors and areas nor could pursue specific programmes and schemes for development objectives. The glaring example of this treatments reflects in the 'power generation' sector and area of 'rail connectivity' with the country. As the fact stands, 'power generation' stands a basic and important component in the development of the state. But, the political engagement of the state government didn't allow the local leaders to convey the importance of this sector. As per a report published in a local daily, JK government accepted its complete failure to tape water resources in JK.[67] Thus, the state faces serious handicap for industrial and urban growth and its impact on the quality of life.

The power situation in terms of availability of electricity for 6 – 8 hours per day for all winter months reveals the extreme suffering of local people. This has happened due to negligence of this sector on the part of local leadership.[68] Though the state can generate 20,000 megawatts of electricity, only 2318.70 megawatts has been exploited both in state and centre sector.[69] The state has 6 hydro electric projects under its control. The rest have been taken over by the N.H.P.C. which generates 17 megawatts in JK and pays 12 % royalty to the state.[70] It seems ironical that the state purchases the electricity at exorbitant rates from the same electricity which the NHPC produces in the state.

[ix] *Rail Connectivity: The rail connectivity* between Kashmir and rest of country stands as the basic requirement for realistic integration and overall development of the state. But, this has not happened even after 62 years of independence. This is not because it stands impossible but because of half-hearted efforts, financial constraints and absence of political will on

the part of central leaders. The recent decision of the railway ministry to scattle the national project in JK with rest of India speaks the real story in this regard.[71]

IV. MIGRATION AND DEMOGRAPHIC LOSS

[i] After militancy started in Kashmir in 1989, there was a shock-like situation in the entire valley. It was probably because completely non-violent people of Kashmir were witnessing what they had not expected or desired in their lifetime. The minorities in Kashmir, especially the KPs, felt extremely threatened as they felt security conscious. In some cases, particular individuals and families of KPs were threatened also. In that situation, the KPs decided to migrate at mass level.[72] Though many locals tried to persuade them not to opt for this disastrous action, but this community level decision of KPs could not be changed. As a result, thousands of KP families migrated to Jammu, Delhi and other cities of India.[73] At the earlier stage, migration was carried out by KPs only, but in the following period, KMs and KSs too migrated to Jammu due to militancy conditions.[74]

It is generally argued that KPs migrated at mass level solely because they felt threatened in the militancy environment. This seems correct and logical proposition. But, at the same time, there are other factors which contributed significantly to the process of migration of KPs from Kashmir. These factors include encouragement of the then state administration to migrate while imposing curfew restrictions during the day time and to provide extra-ordinary arrangements [like camps, tents, electricity and day-to-day need items and hospitality arrangements]. In that situation, majority of KPs left Kashmir in hurry and left most of their belongings in their houses.

In this way, their geneuine security concern was exploited by the state administration led by its Governor, Jagmohan.[75] Though this fact has been highly politicized, the reality is that he and his administration in Srinagar misled KPs in order to motivate them to migrate at the cost of their traditional relations with KMs.[76] Even some KPs, after migrating to Jammu, informed the local media about these designs of the Jagmohan administration.[77]

[ii] According to official reports, the total number of migrants in 2003 was 1,81,280 with 36,256 family households. The central government gave the information to the Lok Sabha in July 2002 about the number and households of migrants as mentioned below:

Category of Migrants	**Number**	
Households	*Total*	*Members*
1. Total number of migrant households	56,246	2,81,230
2. No. of migrant households at Jammu	34,305	1,71,525
3. No. of migrant households at Delhi	19,338	96,690
4. No. of households at other places	2,603	13,015
5. No. of migrant h. holds in camps Jammu	4,778	23,890
6. No. of migrant h. holds at other places	238	1,190[78]

These migrants had the religious affiliations as mentioned below:

Kashmiri Pandits	1,65,000 [91.01 %]
Kashmiri Muslims	8,000 [04.41 %]
Kashmiri Sikhs	8,280 [04.56 %][79]

[iii] As is clear from the above pattern of migration, it took place in certain phases mentioned below:

First phase	1989-1992	40% of the total
Second phase	1993-1999	50% of the total
Third phase	2000 onwards	10% of the total[80]

While in the first stage, near-total number of migrants were KPs who migrated mainly to Jammu and Delhi, second and third phases had the migrants of all communities, KPs, KMs and KSs who left for different cities of India.[81]

[iv] In the year 2010, the Union Home Ministry gave figures about total number of Kashmiri migrant families as 59,542 which composed KPs and KMs.[82]

[v] In March 2010, the state government gave information to

state Legislative Assembly that a total number of 38,119 Kashmiri families were registered in Jammu with the official relief organization. Their religious composition was as follows:

Kashmiri Pandits	34,202 families
Kashmiri Muslims	2,168 families
Kashmiris Sikhs	1,747 families.[83]

These Kashmiri families were living in different cities of India. The detail is on follow;

Delhi	19,338 families	H.P.	11 families
Haryana	924 families	Chandigarh	14 families
Panjab	319 families	Uttrakhand	57 families
U.P.	222 families	M.P.	43 families
Tamil Nadu	01 families	Karnataka	38 families
Maharashtra	208 families	Rajasthan	48 families[84]

[vi] There are other estimates and figures given by unofficial sources. According to various KP organizations, there are 3,00,000 – 5,00,000 pandits and about 2,00,000 are "displaced".[85] Since these organizations have not carried out any census or survey, these estimates have no academic credibility and stand for 'political propaganda'.

[vii] Majority of these KPs [and KMs] families are now settled in different cities and towns of India mainly because they were highly qualified in all fields of education and got all sorts of jobs in government as well as public sector in the country and abroad. But, many among them, especially elders, still want to return to Kashmir. It is the inner desire which they would like to fulfill during their lifetime.[86] Our finding in this regard was that while elder KPs have still the desire to return back to Kashmir, youngsters and children do not think on these lines. While all youngsters got involved in different profession, occupations and other economic activities in different cities of India, school-age children have hardly any emotional or material commitment to Kashmir.[87]

[viii] In response to an advertisement about return of KPs to Kashmir, "as many as 4,440 applications have been received

from the families which wish to return to the valley under the policy of return and rehabilitation of Kashmiri migrants."[88] Among these applicants, 1,682 families are still in possession of immoveable assets in Kashmir valley. So, the main source of motivation for returning back to Kashmir seems economic.[89] These applications were received from the inhabitants of following Kashmir districts:

Srinagar	1,237	Anantnag	1,140
Baramulla	462	Budgam	431
Pulwama	359	Kulgam	283
Shopian	150	Ganderbal	98[90]

[ix] The problems which the KPs and other migrants faced outside Kashmir were all important. But, the most important among them was 'accommodation'. Just after the migration from Kashmir, the migrants were provided temporary accommodation with all necessary facilities in the migrant camps in Purkhu, Muthi, Mushriwalan and Nagrata.[91] Subsequently, while some migrants shifted to rental accommodation or to their own houses/quarters, others left for their families settled in different cities of India. But, a large number of migrants, especially from rural areas and lower classes, had no alternative to stay in sub-human conditions of these camps. At the time of author's study in 2003-04, the KP migrants were living in following types of accommodation in Jammu:

	Self constructed houses	12.00 % of the total
-	JK Govt. flats	30.00 % of the total
-	Rented flats/houses	13.00 % of the total
-	One room set in camps	30.00 % of the total[92]

[x] *Left-over Property:* The second important problem for KPs at the time of migration was related to their moveable and immoveable property which they left in Kashmir unprotected and without any local custodian. In fact, they were misled by conveying to them that they have to come back shortly, so there was no need of taking all moveable-immoveable items with them. However, some KP families took these items with them. In the valley, most of these properties remained unsafe.

> But, after some time, while some houses and lands were taken over by security forces for accommodation and operations, some local elements also picked up the belongings in these houses. Thus, many "migrant houses" in the valley were damaged, looted and burnt by these two opposite elements.[93]

In the meantime, the return of KPs to the valley got delayed again and again. From the emerging developments in Kashmir, many KPs got the impression that their return to the valley will take a long time. So, they started selling their property on cheaper rates. Another reason for selling property in Kashmir was that many KPs had settled or wanted to settle outside Kashmir. This was done through the agents' network, called 'drals' who did this work by following the relevant legal procedure.[94] As per the realistic reports, the KPs property was sold in 3 stages as mentioned below:

First stage [1989-1992]	14 % houses and 7.00 % land
Second stage [1993-1999]	28 % houses and 20 % land
Third stage [2000-2004]	36 % houses and 28 % land[95]

However, when this 'sale phenomenon' increased heavily, the local Kashmiris objected to this. In this wider context, the JK government went to Supreme Court of India and pleaded for stopping these 'sale deeds" in the national interest, which it did through a judgement.[96] Though it stopped the practice at mass level, it continues in clandestine ways. In general, it is estimated that about 40 – 50 % KPs have sold their lands and houses in legal or illegal ways in the Kashmir valley.[97]

[xi] *Migrant Camp Life:* Another grave problem for KPs at the time of migration and afterwards was related to worst conditions in migrant camps in Jammu. After the visit of these camp's the author observed as follows:

"Some camps are like slums in which the KP migrants live a miserable life in sub-human conditions, especially in hot-summer months. These living conditions can be characterized as 'worst'. They don't have sufficient basic facilities like drinking water, electricity, living space and health facrlities. Though most of these camp areas fall within municipal limits, they lack basic urban facilities. There are common bath-rooms and open latrines which creates a lot hygienic problems. The meager financial relief provided to migrants by the government was not paid in time and regularly. Even rations and other essential commodities were not provided continuously. In one room accommodation, children could hardly make a serious study. It was found that there were many unemployed youth living in the camps. This situation had led to problems of deviance, delinquency, crime and drug abuse. The camps were exposed to various offences to women and children. They were completely insecure. They also faced the problem of privacy which was not available to them one room accommodation. This effected the psychological and sex behaviour of migrants.[98]

[xii] *Diseases and Health Problems:* Just after migrating from Kashmir to Jammu, many K.P. migrants, especially children and women and elders, were exposed to extremely different environment. This had damaging effect on their health. Our investigation in this regard revealed that many diseases emerged among the KPs, the details of which follow:

Cardiac/heart related diseases	30.00 – 45.00 % of KPs
Neurological diseases	25.00 – 35.00 % of KPs
Hypertension and related diseases	40.00 – 60.00 %
Blood pressure and related diseases	45.00 – 65.00 %
Depression and related diseases	47.00 – 65.00 %
Mental health problems	30.00 – 40.00 %[99]

The migrants living in the camps face extreme difficulties in the performance of normal sex behaviour. It was reported that migrants faced different degrees of disturbance in sex performance up to 60.00 – 100.00 %.[100]

[xiii] *Mental Health Problems:* The migration and its immediate implications had directly affected mental health of KPs/ Prominent among these psychological disorders were stress, strain, tension, trauma, phobia, schizophrenia, depression, and PTSD. According to our investigation about these problems, depression and stress figured at the top with 78–80% among migrant KPs. Other psychiatric problems prevailed among 55% among the same.[101]

[xiv] *Family and Marriage:* [a] Before migration, KPs, used to live in joint families in rural areas and nuclear families in urban areas. However, the process of migration of KPs from 1947 onwards initiated a process of change whose direction was from joint to nuclear family. Our investigation in Jammu revealed that while 75–80% families were of nuclear type, 20–25% families were of nuclear type.[102]

[b] The migration of KPs changed their attitude towards the marriage practices of 'endogamy' and 'exogamy'. In fact, there emerged a big question regarding their marriage with outsiders, i.e. non-Kashmiri Hindus belonging to all parts of the country. Our investigation in this connection got following responses from KPs:

Yes	84–90 % [males]	60–70 % [females]
No	16–33 % [males]	28–48 % [females]
Partly Yes, partly No	64–80 % [males]	34–42 % [females]

Thus, the KPs, males as well as females, got approved their marriage with insiders and outsiders simultaneously.

[c] However, there was no change in relation to the factor of caste, i.e. the Brahmin caste. Our investigation in this regard divulged that 100% response was in favour of marriage within this higher caste, though it didn't prove successful in all cases.[104]

[xv] *Culture and Language:* After mass migration of KPs to Jammu took them away from their original cultural ethos and were formally detached from its system, there was temporary downfall in the 'cultural contact and interaction' between KMs and KPs. In the changed circumstances, certain degree of cultural change was adopted by KPs at that time. This was considered necessary in a different cultural environment. However, majority of KPs at that time followed some practices of Kashmiri culture without any break, which included the following:

- Traditional dresses of males and females;
- Kashmiri salt tea in the morning and afternoon;
- Kashmiri dining habits;

- Kashmiri entertainment patterns;
- Kashmiri music, dance and arts;
- Kashmiri language;
- Kashmiri lifestyle, especially attitudes and behavior patterns.[105]

[xvi] The Kashmiri language faced absolute decline among KPs from 1947 onwards in general and after mass migration in 1989. It clearly reflects in the information gathered by this author during his study in 2003-04 about the number of KPs who have dropped the Kashmiri language in terms of speaking and writing. This information shows a significant number of KPs have stopped Kashmiri writing and speaking after 1947 and after 1989 migration also. The details follow:

Grand	*parents*	*parents*	*children*
Till 1947	100.00 %	100.00 %	100.00 %
Till 1989	90.00 %	80,00 %	45.00 %
After 1989	90.00 %	80.00 %	20.00 %
Till 2004	90.00 %	60.00 %	02,00 %
Till 2010	70.00 %	30.00 %	01.00 %[106]

After 1989 migration, this process of dropping out of Kashmiri language increased and intensified because more potential factors were working now. As a result, this trend effected the entire cultural life of the KPs outside Kashmir.

V. MENTAL AND PHYSICAL HEALTH DETERIORATION

[i] **MENTAL HEALTH:** [a] "There is more to good health than just a physically healthy body: a healthy person should also have a healthy mind." This is how a mental health expert introduces this concept.[107] He says that aspects of mental health can be considered when "a person with a healthy mind should be able to think clearly, should be able to solve the various problems in life, should enjoy good relations with friends, colleagues at work and family and should feel spiritually at ease and bring happiness to others in the community."[108]

At the same time, he explains mental illness as "any illness experienced by a person which effects his emotions, thoughts or behaviour, which is out of keeping with their cultural beliefs and personality, and is producing a negative effect on his life and the lives of his family."[109]

[b] Regarding the mental health conditions existing in Kashmir valley, he mentions :

"The mental damage wrought on the collective psyche of Kashmiris is resulting from the decades of instability and violence in Kashmir, gradually appears to be tearing at the social fabric of the community. Violence or threat of physical violence seems to have had a significant effect on the mental health of people in the region."[110]

He also presents some of the important findings of M.S.F.[111] sponsored study about 'mental health status' of 2 rural districts of Kashmir valley. He writes that in the period between 1989-2005, nearly 1 in 10 people had lost one or more members of their immediate family because of violence. Second, almost half of the respondents felt occasionally or never safe. Third, they had lost one or more extended family members. Fourth, about 50 % of respondents admitted to having entertained thoughts about ending their life.[112]

[c] In general, Kashmiris at large lived a non-violent life. But, when violence [and state sponsored violence] became order of the day, its impact was felt deeply. Accordingly, the violent incidents such as armed encounters, cross-firing, killing at random, torture of youth and children, rape and molestation of women after 1989 had serious effect on mental and physical health in Kashmir.[113] It certainly led to mental health deterioration in all groups, classes and communities and in all areas. Explaining the psychological disorders in Kashmir in last 20 years, a local analyst observed:

"Living a life of uncertainty and darkness for 60 long years – even longer than that – is a human catastrophe. A lack of certainty about the future is breeding sick mind in Kashmir. A lack of direction is breeding a strong sense of pessimism. Perpetual insecurity is breeding newer kind of disorders, which are impacting people's genes. Psychological disorders are manifesting in psychological problems....we are passing on adapted abnormalities through our genes to our coming generations too. It is a kind of epidemic..."[114]

[d] The 'depression' is considered as the most important feature of mental health. It has been observed by experts that majority of people in Kashmir face depression at individual and collective level. According to an unofficial expert, every family in the valley has one or more cases of depression due to violence.[115]

Another expert characterized this situation as "mass depression" which has also led to the situation of "extreme type of social pathology".[116] Most of these people take drugs regularly to treat them. According to a survey conducted by Action Aid International [in collaboration with Humanitarian Aid, European Commission] in urban Kashmir in 2000-01, the following features of depression were observed:

- 59.30% males and 39.50% females were suffering from depression and hypertension and these diseases increased in 74% and 68% cases respectively;
- 84% males and 89% females faced extreme type of depression mainly due to violence in the valley;[117]

The Percentage of persons involved in depression and its apparent reasons are mentioned below:

Percentage		**Apparent Reasons**
Males	*Females*	
45.00	27.00	lack of social institutions
50.00	50.00	non-availability of basic amenities of life
46	44	lack of entertainment[118]

It was also found in the survey that 45.00 to 59.00 % male and female respondents faced depression due to the problems like lack of water supply, communications, redressal system, essential commodities, sporting activities and energy sources.[119]

In order to treat depression, some drugs are used constantly. The survey revealed following types of drugs in use in Kashmir at large:

	Anti-depressants	*Tranquilizers*	*Sedatives*
Males	24.80 %	07.76 %	06.07 %
Females	23.30 %	08.40 %	05.40 %[120]

[d] Similarly, stress, strain and tension have emerged other common factors of mental health after conflict got introduced in Kashmir. The perpetual tension was a permanent phenomenon for common people in Kashmir for the last two decades. This was mainly because of continuous harassment and torture by security forces. At the same time, extreme form of stress and strain among large number of local people could not be avoided in a situation in which there used to occur daily armed encounters, cross-firing, bomb-blasts, crack-downs, security checks and identity parades by security forces. Shasha mentions in this regard that "prolonged exposure to stress that the insecure situation has endangered means that the coping mechanism of individuals is impaired or dysfunctional."[121]

[e] Finally, "anxiety" emerged as a grave social-psychological problem in Kashmir after, under counter-insurgency measures, an offensive and aggressive policy of 'catch and kill' and related behaviour of forces was introduced in Kashmir. It created extreme kind of insecurity among all individuals and families. The 'security consciousness' developed in this background contributed to mass-level anxiety among Kashmiris during the 1990s. In those days, usually one was not sure to return back to his/her house safely in the evening when he/she left home in the morning. In that tension environment, torture cases, daily killings and disappearances of Kashmiri youths led to fatal psychological problems related to anxiety and PTSD.[122] An expert in the field revealed that there were thousands of such cases in Kashmir in the past two decades mainly because of impact of militancy and militarization.

[g] In the highly depressing and stressful-strained situation in

Kashmir, a negative but strong trend of committing suicide by young males and females emerged with disastrous consequences. This happened in all age-sex groups, all rural-urban areas, and among all socio-economic classes.[123]

According to one estimate, there have been 18,500 cases of suicide during 1990-2008 in Kashmir, i.e. 954 per year and 81 per month.[124] Another survey carried out by this author gave the total number of those who committed suicide was 12,500 during 1990-2008, which means 658 per year and 55 per month.[125] The prominent conclusions of this survey were as follows:

- 85.71 % and 13.84 % suicides were committed in rural and urban areas respectively;
- Those who committed suicide belonged to 16–25 years age group [76.92 %];
- 26–40 years age group [20.00 %];
- 40.33 % and 59.67 % were married and unmarried persons;
- 60.00 % and 40.00 % cases belonged to literate and illiterate classes respectively;
- 11.96 % of women were pregnant when they committed suicide;
- While 65.20 % women were housewives, 35.00 % women were govt. or private employees;
- Suicides were committed by - consuming different kinds of poison [83.87 %];
- Jumping in the river [06.45%];
- Self-immolation [04.83 %];
- Hanging [03.22 %];
- The apparent [not real] reasons for committing suicide were given as mentioned below:
- Heated-strong argument with parents/husbands 30.54%;
- Strained marital relations 20.96%;
- Extreme poverty and unemployment 11.29%;
- Depression 06.45 %[126]

[h] Other grave problem related to mental health was 'drug addiction' or 'drug abuse' among the younger group of population. It was generally observed in present-day Kashmiri society that a significant number of boys and girls from all groups, classes and communities have got involved in this practice during the militancy times and this continues till date. The school-college-university students have been made the main targets by the 'drug mafia'. According to one unofficial survey, about 35 % of the youths [i.e. every 3rd or 4th] of 16 -35 years age group, both males and females, from rural and urban areas, were found drug addicts in the valley in 2007-08.[127] A realistic and perspective assessment of this situation may be done by saying that one generation of Kashmiri youths was lost to the gun, and another generation is heading towards its extinction due to constant drug abuse. It is generally believed here that, in addition to usual drug network and drug mafia, different intelligence agencies working for clashing political objectives and interests were also actively involved in drug business in Kashmir.

[i] In the prevailing conditions, sex has been exposed crudely and its influence has proved larger in the society leading to the phenomenon of 'sexual promiscuity'. Experts and professionals relate this situation to impact the processes of westernization, modernization and globalization–mass and media-IT. Experts also highlight the contribution of continued conflict situation to this sexual permissiveness and moral wayward-ness. This situation is also characterized as the reaction to the forceful imposition of the strict moral code by some extremist elements.[128]

A social inquiry in the recent past revealed that there has been rise of considerable pre-marital and extra-marital sex activities in all urban areas of the valley. The former can be observed in and around schools, colleges, universities, tutor–coaching centres and most of internet cafes and restaurants. These reports can be confirmed from the tourist resorts [which Kashmir has in plenty], gardens, parks and open-secluded places. These immoral activities can also be seen in light vehicles parked on sides of the road and riding shikaras in Dal Lake. These sexual acts are performed by the local youth consciously, openly and without any guilt or regrets. In the case of extramarital practices, mature, educated, married as well as unmarried people get involved in sexual activities and interact as the situation and intimacy demands.[129] Both these types of sexual behaviour are in clear contradiction with the societal values and norms. It seems important to mention here that with this sexual permissiveness, there has been increasing incidence of violence against women such as harassment, molestation, eve-teasing, and rape.

[j] In the above–mentioned grave mental health situation, there is only one psychiatric hospital in Kashmir for treatment of concerned patients. This hospital does not provide sufficient treatment to patients mainly because of paucity of expertise and latest technology in the field. Though its rush of patients has increased from 40-50 OPD patients per day in pre-1989 period to 200-250 OPD patients per day after 1990, neither its meager staff has been increased nor its obsolete technology has been replaced.[130] Regarding availability of relevant experts and facilities, the experts in the hospital Say that "with increasing incidence of autism among children, dementia among aged and drug abuse among youths in the society, Kashmir faces a risk of having more families burdened with mental ailments in near future."[131] But, on the other hand, "the state of excellence psychiatry department here, sole institution for mental health care in Kashmir, neither has a rehabilitation centre for treating patients nor does it bear requisite manpower to treat them."[132] In this state of affairs, the MSF chief commented that "in Kashmir, community psychosocial services are absent and psychiatric services outside Srinagar remain almost non-existent."[133]

[ii] PHYSICAL HEALTH DETERIORATION

[a] Side by side with mental health problems, physical health deterioration in Kashmir could not be avoided due to conflict situation. Consequently, the normal public health became a dream. In the conflict-ridden society of Kashmir, some dreaded diseases with dangerous implications emerged recently. In an informal estimate, it was revealed that there was a surge in neurological, cardiological, oncological, hyper-

tension and cancer-related diseases.[134] In another report, SKIMS found in a study of 5,000 children that 22 % urban and semi-urban children were suffering from obesity.[135] It was further revealed that "in coming years, the children would be more susceptible to lifestyle diseases like diabetes, cardiac ailments and hyper-tension.[136] Another study of 11,000 people found that 27 % youth in the age group of 25 – 40 years were living in pre-diabetes situation. On the whole, it was observed that there was highest rise in enrolments and OPD registration in the premier medical institutions of SKIMS and GMC.

[b] But, at the same time, there are neither sufficient doctors-specialists-experts nor modern medical technology available in Kashmir to deal with different diseases and to cope with this heavy rush. It was observed that despite availability of some specialists and medical facilities in SKIMS, GMC and other associated colleges, a large number of patients feel compelled to rush to Delhi, Chandigarh, Mumbai and other cities to get quality and specialized treatment.

[c] In general, entire JK faces the same situation. While health care system stands weak and inadequate, the facilities and technology are obsolete and sub-standard. Though it is government's adopted policy, the health care facilities fail to fulfill minimum needs of maximum number of people in a proper and standard way. Thus, it was revealed in a report that while there was 36 % increase of patient influx in GMC, the infrastructure remained same.136 While OPD patients in 1999 were 3,42,751, the number rose to 12,64,006 in 2008-09.[137] According to another report, there has been increase in the number of doctors from 184 in 1950-51 to 2,129 in 1980-81 and 5,847 in 2008-09. Similarly, there was expansion of health institutions from 124 in 1951 to 4,804 in 2009.[138] Accordingly, there is only one doctor for 2,142 patients and a single bed for 1,063 patients.[139] Despite this number of doctors, medical institutions and bed-strength, the state has not been able to provide a minimum, descent and desirable health-care system to the people.

NOTES AND REFRENCES

1. See B.A. Dabla, "Sociological Implications of Conflict Situation" in Nyla Ali Khan's forthcoming book on Kashmir. [U.S., 2011]
2. See Reports etc. [prepared after proper investigation in the field] by various national and international human/civil rights groups, civil societies, and NGOs in this regard.
3. This estimate is presented by pro-Azaadi political parties and militant organizations in Kashmir. These have been broadcast—telecast and published in the local media.
4. These figures have been conveyed by official representatives of JK government and various intelligence agencies in the state and centre at different times at different places in the country. These reports were quoted widely in the local and national media.
5. *Ibid.*
6. See reports, *op. cit.,* no. 2.
7. See figures, *op. cit.,* no. 4.
8. *Ibid.*
9. *Ibid.*
10. See reports published in *Srinagar Times,* Srinagar, 22nd October, 2009.
11. See central government reports published in *Srinagar Times,* Srinagar, March, 2010.
12. See state government reports published in *Greater Kashmir,* Srinagar, April, 2010.
13. B.A. Dabla, *A Sociological Study of Widows and Orphans in Kashmir,* [Srinagar, 2010, Jay Kay Books], p. 22.
14. See A.P.D.P., Srinagar Published reports in this regard.
15. B.A. Dabla, "An Analysis of Disability in JK" *Honour, Srinagar, June 2010.*
16. Roland Simbulan, "Militarization in Southeast Asia" in Asia: Militarization and Regional Conflict, edited by Y. Sakamoto,

Tokyo and London, 1988. The U.N. University and Zed Books.

17. Seema Kazi, *Between Democracy and Nation: Gender and Militarization in JK* [New Delhi, 2009, Women Unlimited], pp. xiv-xv.
18. Mary Kaldorn, "We have to think about the security of individuals rather than the protection of states", *Boston Review,* March-April 2005.
19. Kazi, *op. cit,* p. 192.
20. *Ibid.,* pp. 192-93
21. Arthur Bonner, "The Culture of Caste" in *Democracy in India: A Hallow",* [Washington, *1994,* American University Press.]
22. Kazi, *op. cit.,* p. 195.
23. *Ibid,* p. 197
24. *Ibid.,* p. 201.
25. *Ibid,* p. 202.
26. Reported in *Conveyer,* Srinagar, Vol. 1, No. 4, September 2009.
27. *Ibid.*
28. *Ibid.*
29. *Ibid.*
30. *Ibid.*
31. See B.A. Dabla, "Social Implications of Militarization", *Kashmir Life,* Srinagar, 19th September 2009.
32. *Ibid.*
33. See several studies carried out in this regard by different experts in different states of India.
34. See B.A. Dabla, *op. cit.,* no. 31.
35. *Ibid.*
36. *Ibid.*
37. See opinion of the concerned experts repeatedly published in the local media.

38. B.A. Dabla, *Report on 'Suicides in the Kashmir Valley'* published by Centre for Study of Social *Change and Development, Srinagar in 2000; and 'Rising Graph of Suicides in Kashmir", Honour*, Srinagar, September 2009.
39. *Ibid.* About security officers' behaviour in JK, see also Canadian Embassy official's statement reported in *Greater Kashmir*, Srinagar, 19th May 2010.
40. B.A. Dabla, *op. cit.*, no. 38.
41. B.A. Dabla, "Violence against Women", *Kashmir Life*, Srinagar, 11th July 2009.
42. B.A. Dabla, "Domestic Violence against Women in Kashmir", paper presented in national seminar on "Domestic violence against Women in JK" organized by Lawyers Fraternity in collaboration with I.M.P.A., JK Govt. in Srinagar in October 2009.
43. *Ibid.*
44. B.A. Dabla, "Social Impact of militarization", *op. cit.*
45. *Ibid.*
46. *Ibid.*
47. *Ibid.*
48. Official report published in Greater Kashmir, Srinagar, April 2010.
49. Reported in Greater Kashmir, Srinagar, 22nd August 2009.
50. *Ibid.*
51. See relevant statistics issued by Planning Department, JK Govt.
52. *Ibid.*
53. See B.A. Dabla, "Role of Religion and Culture in Economic Development; the Case of Kashmir", paper presented in 35th annual conference of AISA held at University of Kashmir in October 2009.
54. *Ibid.*
55. *Ibid.*

56. See reports in *Business Edition, Greater Kashmir*; Srinagar.
57. *Ibid.*
58. Reported in *Greater Kashmir, Srinagar.*
59. *Ibid.*
60. *Ibid.*
61. See B.A. Dabla, paper, *op. cit.*, no. 53.
62. *Ibid.*
63. *Ibid.*
64. Reported in Greater Kashmir, Srinagar, June 2010.
65. *Ibid.*
66. As reported in Greater Kashmir, Srinagar, June 2010.
67. *Ibid.*
68. See B.A. Dabla, paper, *op, cit.*, no. 53.
69. Reported in Greater Kashmir, Srinagar, 24th August, 2008.
70. *Ibid.*
71. Times of India, New Delhi, September 2009.
72. B.A. Dabla, 'Social Impact of Militarization', *op. cit.*
73. *Ibid.*
74. *Ibid.*
75. See Jagmohan, *My Icy Turbulence in Kashmir* [New Delhi, 1995].
76. See several reports in the local press, especially citation of letters which were written by KPs from the migrant camps in Jammu.
77. *Ibid.*
78. B.A. Dabla, *Sociological Implications of Pandit Migration in J&K [Srinagar, 2008, Jay Kay Books]*, p.74
79. *Ibid.*, p. 75.
80. *Ibid.*, p. 77.
81. *Ibid.*
82. *Greater Kashmir*, Srinagar, 14th March 2010.

83. *Ibid.*
84. *Ibid.*
85. *See Panun Kashmir's* argument that KPs are not migrants in their own country. They prefer to call themselves as "displaced persons".
86. See B. A. Dabla, *op. cit.,* no. 78.
87. *Ibid.*
88. G.K. Srinagar, *op. cit.,* no. 82.
89. *Ibid.*
90. *Ibid.*
91. B.A. Dabla, *op. cit.,* no. 78.
92. *Ibid.*
93. *Ibid.*
94. Based on our observations in the Kashmir valley.
95. B.A. Dabla, *op. cit.,* no. 78.
96. See relevant judgement of Supreme Court of India and published in the local English press.
97. This estimate has been conveyed by *Dralz* who have played crucial role in the dealings and got huge financial benefits.
98. B.A. Dabla, *op. cit.,* no. 78.
99. *Ibid.,* p. 90.
100. *Ibid,* p. 91-92.
101. *Ibid.,* p. 92.
102. *Ibid.,* p. 100.
103. *Ibid,* p. 101.
104. *Ibid,* p. 101.
105. *Ibid,* pp. 102-03.
106. *Ibid.*
107. See Vikram Patel, International Mental Health, New Delhi; and Shasha Mathhews, "Of Mental Health and Illness" – I, *Greater Kashmir, Srinagar, 7th April 2010.*

108. Shasha Mathhews, *ibid.*
109. *Ibid.*
110. *Ibid* – II.
111. *Ibid.*
112. *Ibid.*
113. *B.A. Dabla, op. cit.,* no. 1.
114. *A.H. Talib, Greater Kashmir, Srinagar, 19th May 2010.*
115. B.A. Dabla, "Social Impact of Militancy in Kashmir" in *Sociological Papers on Kashmir* [Srinagar, 2010, Jay Kay Books].
116. *Ibid.*
117. "State of Mental Health in Urban Kashmir" – A Report [survey conducted and published by Action Aid International in 2004.
118. *Ibid.*
119. *Ibid.*
120. *Ibid.*
121. B.A. Dabla, *op. cit.,* no. 115.
122. *Ibid.*
123. *Ibid.*
124. B.A. Dabla, *op. cit.* no. 38.
125. *Ibid.*, no. 38.
126. *Ibid.*
127. See M.Phil. Dissertation on 'Drug Abuse in Anantnag District of Kashmir' submitted by Shahzad Wani in the Department of Sociology, University of Kashmir in 2009.
128. See "Emerging Sex Practices in the Valley", *Greater Kashmir, Srinagar, 2008.*
129. *Ibid.*
130. B.A. Dabla, *op. cit.,* no. 115.
131. G.K. Srinagar, 12th March 2010.
132. *Ibid.*

134. B.A, Dabla, *op. cit.,* no. 115.

135. G.K Srinagar, 5th May 2010.

135a. *Ibid.,* 24th March 2010.

136. *Ibid.,* 5th May 2010.

137. *Ibid,* 24th March, 2010.

138. *Ibid.*

139. *Ibid.*

CHAPTER 5

SOCIOLOGICAL IMPLICATIONS OF MILITANCY

[I] DEMOGRAPHIC TRANSFORMATION

[A] SOCIAL DYNAMICS OF MIGRATION IN KASHMIR

Migration essentially refers to the movement of human beings from one place to another. It occurs at the regional as well as universal level and in all societies irrespective of their differences in region, culture, religion, language, social structure, economic and political system. Sociologically, it reflects three primary and crucial features. First, it refers to the movement of human beings from one particular place of residence to another place of residence over a period of time and having certain definite reasons to do so. Second, it includes debasement of unit of residence at one place and subsequent establishment of another unit of residence at other place. Third, it represents the phenomenon which engulfs entire life of people concerned as they change their life-pattern wholly.

The initiation of the process of migration on this globe may be traced to the earliest human beings. The earliest human society may be the society of 'Adam and Eve' and their offspring who had to move from place to place. As has been studied by sociologists, demographers and other concerned experts, human migration had certain causes which can be explained in terms of 'push and pull' factors. While the 'push' factors refer to numerous reasons of migration [which are involuntary in nature], such as search for food, security, favourable climate and safety from various epidemic diseases and calamities, the 'pull' factors point to several reasons [which are voluntary in nature] that include desire for change and improvement in the quality of life.

In the background of human migration from santiquity from one place to another place, certain specific pattern of migration have emerged in human history. Equally important is the fact that these patterns of migration can be related to specific causes. Thus, sociologists and demographers have developed a co-relation between practices and patterns of migration which may be explained as follows:

[i] Climatic – from cold to hot places, hot to temperate places; and from hills to plains.

[ii] Political – from one to another country, near far away.

[iii] Economic – from developing to developed world; and from rest of the world to the Gulf.

[iv] Religious – from rest of the world to Israel; and from India to Pakistan and vice versa.

[v] Cultural – from rest of the world to U.S. and Europe.

[vi] Educational – from Asia and Africa to the U.S. and Western Europe.

It has also been observed that migration had set implications on the migrant as well as host societies. Most important consequences are as follows; first, migration creates a significant demographic change in host societies which reflects in their changing composition and fertility-mortality rates. In Kuwait and Malaysia, migrants have changed the population composition radically. While in the former case, the migrants compose 55 % of the total population, the latter's proportion of migrant Chinese population has gone up to near 50 % of the total population. Second, migration gave rise to plurality of cultures, religions, languages, social structures and, more importantly, ethnicity. The case of ethnic communities in most of the countries in the world reveals this phenomenon. Third, with the growth of plurality, there emerged problems of competition, conflict, control and so on. Fourth, mass migration gave rise to new societies and new civilizations. The case of America is a distinctive example in this regard. The famous sociologist of Iran, Dr. Ali Shariati, concluded on the basis of his study of human societies that all 27 civilizations which are known to the human society today were preceded by the processes of mass migration. In this connection, he cites the examples of Christian, Jewish and Islamic civilizations.

Experts have identified three distinctive streams of migration. First, in the context of change and development at the global level, significant number of people from the developing world migrated to the developed countries in the world, particularly to the United States and Western Europe for economic, educational, social and other material reasons. Majority of such migrations comprised people of higher education, professionals, technicians, and experts in different fields, skilled and semi-skilled personnel. Though the migration initiated in the medieval times, it experienced a sharp increase in modern times.

Second, people from whole of world, developed as well as developing, moved to the tiny state in the Gulf primarily for economic reasons. After oil was discovered in the Gulf in the sixties, the region witnessed large scale migration from Asia, particularly the Indo-Pak sub-continent. The migrants included professionals, technicians, skilled labour, and experts in different fields from developed countries and semi-skilled and unskilled labour from developing countries. While in the former case, the majority of migrants settled in developed countries and adopted their culture partly or wholly, migrants in the latter case stayed there for as short period as possible to adopt the host's culture.

Third, another stream of migration in the contemporary times took place in most of the states in Asia, Africa and Latin America at the time when their colonization ended or was nearing its end. In this type of migration, people migrated within their nation states from rural to urban areas for economic and other reasons. The most important reason for this migration was the colonial-type of development which focused on urban areas at the cost of rural areas to benefit the colonial rulers. This type of migration took place in majority of developing- third world countries and could not be avoided in the environment created by the type of economy pursued by governments in these states. While this type of migration led to rural dependence, continuity of rural under-development and exploitation of rural resources, it also contributed to demographic change, economic inequality and multi-dimensional problems of migrants in urban areas. While majority of migrants in this process settled in urban areas, minority of them either shifted to rural areas or moved from rural to urban areas and vice versa.

In India, a similar situation prevailed in the case of migration after independence. Several types of migration-patterns emerged in post-colonial India. First, linear migration which involved people who moved from rural to urban areas and settled there. Second, cyclical migration which involved people who moved from rural to urban areas and back. This process took place repeatedly. Third, migration from rural-urban areas of one place to urban areas of other place. This involved people who felt compelled to migrate due to political, religious, ethnic and other such factors. The migration of people from India to Pakistan and vice versa in 1947-48 and Kashmiri Pandits from Kashmir to different parts of JK state and India in 1990-91 fit in this type of migration.

The causation of these and other types of migration in post-colonial India can be explained in the rural and urban context. In the rural context, modernization of agriculture led to unprecedented increase in production benefitting significant number of rural people. But, at the same time, this process created the problem of unemployment in rural areas. These rural unemployed people had no alternative except to move to the cities in search of livelihood. In the urban context, various processes of modernization, especially educational and job opportunities compelled the people to migrate. Moreover, the processes of urbanization, industrialization, development of secular, materialistic and individualistic outlook attracted, on the one hand, people from rural to urban areas and, on the other, made preferable for some people to migrate from one to other urban areas.

As has happened in all societies of the world, the Kashmiri society too has undergone this process with far reaching implications. In the ancient times, people of different races came to Kashmir and some of them settled here. In the medieval times, Kashmir experienced the processes of in-migration and out-migration. In the former case, many aliens, especially *Mughals, Afghans, Sikhs and Dogras,* came here as rulers and many of them settled here. Again, thousands of missionaries came from several parts of Central Asia, converted the locals to Islam peacefully and majority of them settled here. In the case of out-migration, thousands of locals had to move outside Kashmir primarily for political reasons. During that period, the locals, both Muslims and Hindus, were compelled to migrate to different parts of India, especially to northern and central India. Pandit

Jawaharlal Nehru and Sir Mohammad Iqbal represented such migrant communities.

In the modern times, the Kashmiri society underwent the processes of in-migration and out-migration. While the former was less significant, the latter was more significant. In the first case, some tiny groups such as several professional-occupational groups, bureaucrats and so on came here and settled here. On the other hand, out-migration started from early decades of the 20th century and that was intensified after 1947. This may explain the out-migration of KPs from Kashmir to different parts of India from early decades of the last century for educational and employment purposes.

The KP community was a near-total literate community and individual of this community was after government job which was not possible in the changed situation at that time. The KPs with their higher technical and professional qualifications, could not be accommodated in the state as it was under-developed at that time. The Kashmiri Muslims [KM] got education from early decades of this century, especially after 1947, and subsequently shared the government jobs with the KPs. In this situation, the process of migration among the KPs intensified from 1947 who settled in different urban areas in India. This explains the phenomenon of the presence of KPs in most of the cities of India on top positions in all fields, especially bureaucracy, education, business and industry.

The phenomenon of KP migration from Kashmir has parallel examples in the Indian society. In Tamil Nadu, the Tamil Brahmins occupied higher status and top positions in the bureaucracy in pre-independent days. As a result of the exploitative role of Brahmin caste traditionally, the Dravida Kazagam [DK] movement started in the 1930s under the leadership of Periyar to destroy the Brahmanic hegemony. Thus, after 1947, all DK parties in Tamil Nadu which came to power there, made efforts to debase the traditional Brahmanic hegemony in the administration. Consequently, most of the Brahmins had to leave the state and settle in different parts of India, especially Delhi.

Kashmir experienced a radical type of migration in 1989-90 when the KPs made a near-total movement to different cities of India, especially in the north. Subsequently, the KMs too migrated, but in lesser numbers. Despite the fact that 90– 95% of KPs migrated from

Kashmir, this was caused mainly by political factors. The religious factor is not primary but co-incidental. The impact of this migration has been negative and disintegrative, though the community opted for this type of migration.

[B] DEMOGRAPHIC CHANGES IN JAMMU AND KASHMIR STATE

Demography is generally used to denote the study of phenomena connected with human population such as its composition, birth, death, marriage and migration. As happened in the broader human society, the population also underwent deeper and wider transformation due to various factors. The Kashmiri society too has faced micro-level as well as macro-level changes in its population in the recent past. Some of these changes are natural caused due to population dynamics and some are imposed or manipulated by interested parties due to various reasons. However, there prevailed a serious feeling among the educated in Kashmir that population figures shown in the census reports were not correct but were manipulated by interested parties in the government.

After 1981 census figures were released in J&K, they showed a strong reaction against these [figures] and held that these were manipulated consciously. The Kashmiri intelligentsia demanded that a fresh and genuine census must be carried out. It was in that context that the then J&K government had ordered for a mid-decade census to be carried out afresh. But, the results of that census could not be made public due to political disturbances in the state at that time and stiff resistance of the non-local bureaucrats in J&K government.

These doubts about census reports in J&K were not baseless. In fact, the Kashmiri intelligentsia was aware about the plans of many political leaders, bureaucrats, professionals and businessmen to change the existing composition of population in JK, which at present was a Muslim majority state. The Bhartiya Janata Party – BJP, an extremist Hindu nationalist political party, position on abrogation of article 370 from the Indian constitution and subsequently change the population composition in JK was glaringly clear in its declared 'Kashmir policy'. This party had not hesitated even to take and accept the advice of the Israeli government and political and non-political leaders of that country in this regard. At the time of his visit to India, Israeli Foreign Minister, Shemon Peres, gave then clear ideas for carrying out this plan to change the dominant Muslim character of the JK state. At the same time, some elements in other political parties in India too upheld like these ideas, but, they preferred to follow this objective silently. The assurances given by the ruling Congress Party leaders in this regard could not be taken for granted. The 'Babri Masjid' case stood an eye-opener in this connection.

The preceding arguments regarding heavy decrease of Muslim population in JK are supported by census figures given in Table 1 below:

Table 5.1

Decrease in Muslim Population in J&K, 1951 – 1991

Year	*Total Population*	*Muslim Population*	
		Number	*Percentage*
1941	2,946,728	....	....
1951	3,253,832 [proj.]	2,277,694	70.00
1961	3,560,976	2,421,463	68.00
1971	4,616,632	3,000,810	65.00
1981	5,967,389	3,789,291	63.00
1991	7,718,700 [proj.]	4,785,594	62.00

Source: Census of India, New Delhi, 1951, 1961, 1971, 1981, 1991.

The table 5.1 reveals crude reality with regard to the decreasing Muslim population in JK in the past five decades. There has been a continuous fall in the Muslim proportion in JK and simultaneous rise in the non-Muslim proportion [especially of Hindus] in the post-1947 period. While the Muslim proportion had gone down by 8% from 1951 to 1991, there had been upward trend in the Hindu proportion by about 7.50% in the same period. If this trend of population continues for few decades more, it may lead to a significant reduction in the dominant Muslim population in JK. This may lead either to the Panjab like situation or Muslims in the state will be reduced to a minority by slight margin. On the other hand, if population of migrants from West Pakistan to Jammu in and after1947 and settled there permanently will be given the status of citizenship in the state [as they have demanded in previous decades], it will also result in significant reduction in the Muslim proportion in JK.

It seems important as well as interesting to know that this heavy decrease in the Muslim Proportion in JK population happened despite the fact that growth rates in the state have remained higher in comparison to average growth rates at all India level. Table 5.2 below clearly reveals that:

Table 5.2

Growth Rates in India and JK State, 1971 – 1991

Year/Decade	*Growth Rates [per 000]*	
	India	*JK State*
1951 - 1961	21.51	29.44
1961 - 1971	24.80	29.65
1971 - 1981	24.66	29.69
1981 - 1991	23.50	28.92

Source: Census of India, New Delhi, 1951- 1991.

The argument that Muslims in JK state maintain higher growth rates corresponding with high birth rates and low death rates which reflect in the relevant census data but not in the final results. The census figures in Table 5.3 reveals clearly higher birth and lower death rates in JK state in comparison to its national record:

Table 5.3

Birth and Death Rates in India and JK State, 1971 – 1991

	India		*JK State*	
Years/Decade	*Birth Rate*	*Death Rate*	*Birth Rate*	*Death Rate*
1971 – 1973	30.30	15.1	32.3	10.5
1980 – 1982	30.08	12.3	31.2	09.0
1986 – 1988	32.01	11.0	32.5	08.2

Source: Census of India, New Delhi, 1971 - 1991.

In the light of above analysis, an important question arises, i.e. whether the continuous decrease in the Muslim population in JK State stands a 'demographic reality' or 'manipulated effort'? The Kashmiri intelligentsia believes in the latter with proper and authentic documentary support. It upheld the position that this has been done consciously under a planned effort and in a systematic way for broader political objectives.

[C] POPULATION CHANGES IN JAMMU AND KASHMIR: 2001

The latest census in the state of JK was carried out in 2000-2001. The main features of this census are as follows:

[i] The total population in the state was 10,069,917 [males 5,300,574 and females 4,769,343], while as it was 77.18 lakhs in 1991, 59.87 lakhs in 1981, 45.16 lakhs in 1971, 35.68 lakhs in 1961, 32.53 lakhs in 1951, and 29.46 lakhs in 1941. The present population in the state constitute 0.98% of the national population which was 1,027,015,247 in 2001. Thus, the JK ranked 19th among 35 states and union territories of the country.

[ii] The census revealed that the decadal growth rate in the state was 30.34 during 1981 - 1991 and 29.04 during 1991 - 2001

respectively in comparison to the national decadal growth rates of 23.86 and 21.34 respectively. Thus, the decadal growth in the state was higher than its national level. But, at the state level, the decadal growth has decreased, though not significantly.

[iii] The sex ratio [females per thousand males] in the population has gone in favour of females. The census revealed that the sex ratio in the state was 900 in 2001, while it was 896 in 1991. However, the sex ratio at the national level was 927 in 1991 and 933 in 2001.

[iv] The density of population in the state had also changed. While it was 77 per sq. km. in 1991, it has increased to 99 per sq. km. in 2001. In contrast, the density at the national level was 267 per sq. km. in 1991 and had increased to 324 per sq, km. in 2001.

[v] The census report revealed that there has been the phenomenal increase in the literacy of males as well as females in JK. Accordingly, the literacy rate in the state was 54.46%, males 65.75% and females 41.82%. However, this rate stands lower than the national literacy rate which was 65.38%, males 75.85% and females 54.16%. It seemed that the state had made considerable progress in literacy. It was 11.83% in 1961, 18.58% in 1971, and 32.68% in 1981. It may be mentioned here that female literacy in the state was as low as 5.05% in 1961and it had jumped more than 8-fold during last 40 years. But, the state had much lower rate than the national average. According to census reports, only one district, i.e. Jammu, crossed the national average by attaining the literacy rate of 77.30%, males 84.92% and females 68.75%. Next to Jammu is Kathua district which had recorded 65.29 % literacy in 2001. On the other hand, the lowest literacy rate was observed in Budgam district which was 39.54%. The female literacy was as low as 26.06%. Same was the situation in Kupwara district.

The official statistics provided in the preceding sections revealed that significant, basic and important changes in different population compositions were experienced in the JK state. While total population in all regions and state at large had increased significantly, the density of population in all regions had also increased proportionately. The male-female ratio in the total population too had undergone change which has gone in favour of females quantitatively. It was because female ratio to the total population and to the males population has increased relatively. However, females ratio in the state stood much lower than the national average. It may not be out of context to mention here that the census data of 2001 released by the concerned government department had no mention of migrants staying in the state, employees of out-state origin, and the KP migrants who have left the state during last two decades.

The census data about literacy situation in the state seemed interesting. Though the overall literacy rate in the state had increased, it had not benefitted all regions equally. While the Jammu region had attained higher literacy rates, Kashmir region showed comparatively poor performance. The Ladakh region had also improved significantly the rate of literacy. This situation of literacy reveals in the following table:

Table 5.4

Literacy Situation in J&K, 2001

S.No.	*District*	*Literacy Rate*	*Literacy Rate [%]*		
Total Population			*Total*	*Male*	*Female*
1.	Kupwara	640,013	40.80	53.55	26.83
2.	Baramulla	1,166,722	44.57	56.29	31.42
3.	Srinagar	1,238,530	59.31	68.99	48.11
4.	Budgam	593,768	39.54	51.23	26.60
5.	Pulwama	632,295	47.35	58.87	34.93
6.	Anantnag	1,170,013	44.10	55.56	31.51
7.	Leh	117,037	62.24	71.98	50.03
8.	Kargil	115,227	58.01	73.98	40.96
9.	Doda	690,474	46.92	63.56	28.35

10.	Udhampur	738,965	54.16	66.43	39.89
11.	Poonch	371,561	51.07	65.41	35.30
12.	Rajouri	478,595	57.65	69.64	44.14
13.	Jammu	1,571,911	65.29	75.73	53.92
14.	Kathua	544,206	65.29	75.73	53.92

Source: Census Records of J&K state, Srinagar, 2001.

The dismal performance of Kashmir region in the field of literacy reveals glaringly in the above table, especially in Srinagar, the summer capital and largest city in the state. Budgam and other districts in this region have also shown poor performance. This situation can be explained in terms of the long-term implications of conflict situation prevailing in Kashmir for last two decades.

[II] CHANGES IN FAMILY AND MARRIAGE PATTERNS

[A] FAMILY IN KASHMIR BETWEEN TRADITION AND MODERNITY

The celebration of 1994 as the "International Year of the Family" by the United Nations reflects crucial, basic and universal importance of the fundamental social institution of family at the global level. In fact, this primary social institution directly contributes to the maintenance and continuity of existing social order in all societies irrespective of their differences in culture, region, religion, polity, economy, social structure and so on. Thus, the role of family in the broader society has provided much-needed stability in the traditional set up. However, in the recent past, the family in the whole world, particularly in the Western societies, was exposed to various processes of modernization such as industrialization, urbanization, migration, educational advancement, demographic shifts, mass media exposure, democratization, secularization and new cultural adaptation. This situation, directly and necessarily, affected structure and function of family in traditional setup. While this process was complete and radical in the Western societies, especially the American society, it was partial and marginal in the Eastern societies in Asia and Africa. In this broader context, the Indian sub-continental society too underwent certain degree of transformation vis-a-vis family.

This complete or partial change in family at the global level created various problems in the Western and Eastern societies which included disorganization of institutional structure of society, disappearance of family as a sacred value, downfall of traditional patriarchal authority, emergence of sexual permissiveness [pre-marital as well as post-marital], heavy increase in abortions and divorces and fast rise of tension, deviance, conflict and violence. These and other problems generated a grave crisis, more in the West and less in the East, which endangered even the survival of existing social order. It was in this background that the U.N. wanted to raise consciousness about basic functions of family and initiate formal and informal actions in this regard. Though the Kashmiri society still maintains traditional form of family and kinship, certain changes in this field have been experienced by various groups and classes. Consequently, some crucial problems have also been observed.

Sociologically speaking, the Kashmir society in general may be categorized as a 'traditional society' which maintains the joint family system, composing three or more generations, living in the traditional environment. The relationship pattern between members of family is on set pattern and senior-most male member of family retains the patriarchal authority. This family is patrilineal in nature [in which descent is traced from the father's side] and patrilocal in character [according to which the bride joins the family of the bridegroom after marriage]. In most of the cases, this also stands as the composite economic unit. This type of family is associated with monogamy [a practice according to which one male marries more than one female in his life time. It also maintains 'endogamy', a custom according to which marriage takes place inside one's own kin, clan or caste group. It generally maintains the traditional cultural ethos and transmits the particular cultural heritage from one generation to another generation through the processes of socialization and internalization. These features of traditional family in Kashmir have been explained in some other studies of this author.

As has happened in many traditional societies, the traditional Kashmiri family too has undergone a significant degree of transformation. Special mention may be made about changing pattern of structure and function of family. In the changing situation, while joint structure of the family is paving the way for the emergence of its nuclear structure, the functional primacy of family is going into the background very fast. The former may be observed in the speed rise of nuclear families in cities and towns of Kashmir, the latter reflect in deeper and wider impact of many processes like pervasive impact of mass media. Consequently, the nuclear family is becoming a norm among urban educated people and middle classes. Similarly, the primacy of family as the sole socializing agency, especially for children and youngsters, has been robbed by other agencies such as school, mass media and peer groups.

This pattern of social transformation concomitantly gave rise to certain crucial and complex problems in the Kashmiri society. In this context, the first mention may be made about disorganization of authority structure within families and kin groups. The supreme and sacred patriarchal authority of the family-group has been seriously questioned. This has resulted in the breakdown of traditional type of control mechanism which has directly contributed to deviance, lesser control and violence in the present-day Kashmiri society. Thus, the concept of family as the sole determining agency for socialization has ceased to exist. This change created many problems for all, especially for youth, women and children.

Second, the change in family created serious and complex problems for women, especially working women, who work outside their homes on regular and remunerative basis. Special mention may be made about adjustment problems for women, dual role of women [one at home and other in office], tension situation for women, intra-sex and inter-sex conflict, and more possibilities for deviance and divorce. Many such problems have been analyzed by this author in his book entitled *Working Women in Kashmir.*

Third, this family change has affected the traditional pattern of marriage. While marriage practices associated with endogamy, exogamy, polygamy, and monogamy have changed partly, marriage customs related to age at marriage, payment of 'mehr', dowry and so on have undergone significant degree of change. In actuality, the 'marriage market' in Kashmir has changed in quality, content and implications. It faced a serious crisis mainly due to late marriage, higher amount of demanded dowry, bargaining on the amount of '*mahr*' and other problems. It has also increased the intensity of harassment and torture of married girls in their in-laws families. In this context, the possibilities of divorce have increased relatively. In this kind of environment, the 'aging' has started becoming a problem to be taken seriously.

However, it must be made clear that the above-mentioned problems have not emerged in the extreme form when compared to such problems existing in societies outside Kashmir. The rationale of this argument lies in the fact that the Kashmiri society still functions within the traditional framework in which family ties and kinship relations are still intact or have not been disturbed radically. The processes of development and modernization have not given rise to inhuman, impersonal, highly individualistic and materialistic society. Thus, the structure of joint family may have been changed partly or wholly, but, the traditional functions of this family still continue. Similarly, there may be a lot of post-marital tension and conflict in the family unit, but declaration of divorce is still rare in rural as well as urban areas. In reality, it is generally abhorred in the Kashmiri society. Even second or third marriage, religiously allowed, without proper reason is considered 'undesirable' and 'objectionable'.

The above analysis of the Kashmiri family in terms of its changes and problems clearly reveal that while some of its functions have undergone serious change, other features still exist partly or wholly. This phenomenon may be characterized as 'continuity and change' in the Kashmiri society. Sociologically, this situation may be explained by saying that family in Kashmir functions in between 'tradition and modernity' but its direction is certainly towards modernity.

[B] KASHMIRI FAMILY BESIEGED STRESSFULLY

The problems of family have emerged at regional, national and global levels and need serious attention on the part of concerned experts, organizations and states. In actuality, most of the family problems seem the direct or indirect impact of broader and deeper social transformation which reflects in the processes of modernization such as cultural exposure, effect of electronic mass media, modern education, industrialization, urbanization, secularization, individualism, materialism, demographic shifts and changing social structure. In this social context, family problems emerged as 'change co-relates' in developing societies. The Kashmiri society too has undergone these processes of transformation partly or fully. Consequently, it has given rise to some acute family problems in this society. In this chapter [a] we will identify and explain some major problems which have emerged in Kashmir in the recent past.

[a] *Practices of Child-bearing and Child-rearing:* One of the crucial problems faced by the Kashmiri family was related to traditional practice of having large number of children. Due to economic and non-economic factors, it has become difficult, even in upper class families, to maintain a family of large number of children. It has been observed that generally children in large number have not been provided all basic needs of life such as diet, clothes, medicines, education, entertainment and other necessary daily expenditure. Even if these children get these needs fulfilled by their parents/guardians/elders, their quality of life stands highly questionable. Moreover, at the societal level, a large number of these children do contribute to the failure of welfare programmes meant for them.

The other problem is related to the practices of 'child-rearing'. This problem stands as the direct effect of change and extension in the traditional role of women in Kashmir. Traditionally, the Kashmiri women's role was limited to or revolved around their homes. In the present situation, when they go out regularly for most part of the day for earning, the first casualty of this situation is child/children who have to stay at home alone or with relatives for the whole day. In majority of cases, children stay with mother's parents or other near relatives. This kind of socialization of baby children creates problems in their upbringing, personality development and social attitudes and behaviour. In this situation, children hardly get time and attention from their parents, which they need most at this stage of life. The condition of school-going children in this regard stood 'pathetic'. While they are regimented in their schools, their emotional and psychological needs were hardly fulfilled at home because of parents' absence there.

[b] *Role Conflict among Women:* The adoption of new working role of women led to the situation of dual role of women in Kashmir. While they carried out all works at their homes, they also performed all office duties outside their homes. This in-home and out-home

performance effected them adversely. This situation created conflict at two levels, within woman's personality and woman's family. First, woman's work inside and outside home created conflict because she found it difficult to determine the importance, primacy and priority between the 'home work' and 'office work'. Second, she got involved in intra-sex and inter-sex problems within her home. The first type of conflict arose between wife, husband, daughter-in-law and father-in-law. It happened mainly because the [traditional] expectations of husband and father-in-law were not fulfilled as she remains out for most part of the day. The second type of conflict arose between daughter-in-law and mother-in-law and between wife and her husband's sisters. It happened mainly because of feelings of insecurity by mother-in-law and jealousy of sister-in-law.

[c] *Negative Impact of Nuclear Family:* It has been observed by sociologists and other experts that, as a result of broader social transformation, the structure of traditional joint family was experienced significantly. Subsequently, the nuclear family replaced it. This structural change reflected mostly in the functions of family unit. In the context of Kashmir, this change had positive as well as negative implications. Among other problems, most crucial ones are related to lesser family control and, consequently, inviting all sorts of problems. The first can be explained in terms of absence of control of parents over unmarried children in nuclear family. The second refers to a changed situation in which parents and their unmarried children in nuclear family could not carried out all necessary works.

[d] *Challenge to Patriarchal Authority:* In the kind of situation mentioned above, the challenge to the authority of eldest male member of family was logical. If not challenged, this authority was questioned which reduced or negated its legitimacy. Thus, in the changed situation, head of the family [who was usually the eldest male member of the family or clan] lost his reputation and status. With this followed the conscious violations of traditional values and norms. This was further followed by the crisis of the notion of patriarchal authority of the family unit.

[e] *Decrease of Social Control:* In a situation in which authority was challenged both at the ideational and actual levels, social control had to decrease naturally. In this context, this control got delegitimized. It seems important to note here that the bases of social control were

not negated completely. That would have leta total collapse of the existing social system.

[f] *Undesirable Socialization:* In the social situation explained above, the process of socialization, on the one hand, created and legitimized the roles needed in that situation. On the other hand, existing situation determined the thematic and functional basis of socialization. Thus, social conditions and socialization developed reciprocal relationship. In this social milieu, the process of socialization developed undesirable features, some of which are mentioned below:

First, the members of the family, especially elders, faced the problem of lesser social security. When the moral-ethical basis of social relationship ceased to operate fully, there remained very less basis for social reciprocity and collective well-being.

Second, the lesser emphasis on specific social objectives in the process of socialization led to mental wilderness among members of the family, especially belonging to the younger age groups. They lost the social direction and social worldview.

Third, since youngsters in significant number of families have no positive worldview and positive behavioural approach, they lose career orientation and experience lesser chances for upward mobility. They also face the situation related to the phenomenon of generation gap reflecting extreme opposite views and roles.

Fourth, with these developments, the situation of value erosion has emerged, though with its full impact. Thus, it has become easy to deviate from established values and difficult to follow these values.

Fifth, undesirable role models got social approval and were imitated and followed widely.

[g] *Social Pathology:* Number of families faced the features of social pathology such as tension, stress, and anxiety. These features were immediate result of the materialistic situation, which has been created over past few decades. It crudely reflects in the feeling of economic compulsion under which all members of the family were compelled to work to earn more and more. In this situation, all members of the family stay out at their places of work for most part of the day. Consequently, many residential colonies remain deserted and closed during the day time. It has been observed in some colonies that many houses remain locked during the whole day. These people have lesser

time for their children and other near relatives and lesser time for home entertainment.

[C] THE CHANGING PATTERN OF MARRIAGES IN KASHMIR

The most fundamental institution in the human society is 'marriage'. Sociologists have generally explained it in terms of "a socially sanctioned sex relationship involving one or more people of the opposite sex, whose relationship is expected to continue beyond the time for gestation and birth of children." [See *Dictionary of Sociology* by G. Duncan Michell London, 1977, R & K] It has also been explained as a "legally recognized relationship between an adult male and female that carries certain rights and obligations." [Ibid.] The social sanctions of most cultures would imply a stable relationship between two or more individuals. Hence, marriage is not co-extensive with prostitution or any other sexual relationship which is not sanctioned by law, religion or custom.

In the broader social framework, marriage is given the hallmark of social approval, it becomes a social contract; it defines the relationship between husband and wife and between parents and their children; it has to be concluded in public; and it usually receives blessings of religion and culture. The marriage arises from human procreation and rearing of children; from lengthy period of dependence of children on their parents and need for parental care and training; and finally it stands for the combination of mating with parenthood. [Ibid.]

Every human society in the world has developed certain particular and distinctive practices related directly to the institution of marriage. This is essentially needed for stability and continuity of this basic and central institution in the wider social context. But, at the same time, certain changes occur in these traditional practices mainly due to deeper and wider processes of social transformation. For example, broader changes like shift of human society from primitive to modern stage and development of human society from primitive to agricultural to industrial stage have effected certainly the practices of marriage qualitatively as well as quantitatively. In brief, wider processes of transformation such as industrialization, modernization and urbanization create new material conditions in which emerge new marriage practices necessarily. This has happened in world societies and has also been experienced partly or wholly in the Kashmiri society.

Traditionally, the marriage in Kashmir was characterized more by the feature of endogamy than exogamy. While the former refers to the practice of marriage within one's own family-kin-occupational group, the latter refers to the practice of marrying outside this social circle. The former included families, clans, occupational communities and other social groups. The 'cross-cousin marriage' [especially on reciprocal basis] can be referred to an ideal case of endogamous marriage. In actuality, the endogamous groups in Kashmir included Sayyids, Khans, business classes, occupational communities, sects and so on. While 'endogamy' was considered as desirable, preferable, valued and sometimes unavoidable, 'exogamy' was viewed as undesirable, avoidable and sometimes attracted negative sanctions including punishment.

Now, this situation has changed qualitatively as well as quantitatively mainly due to cumulative impact of various processes of social transformation. In the present-day social environment, 'endogamy' has lost the obligatory and preferable character. In practice, it has been divested of all its important features. More importantly, it has lost its primacy which has been shifted to education, economic position, social status and related factors. In this situational context, one may marry within his/her endogamous group, it may not be essentially for family/clan/occupational group considerations, but for economic, educational, social, cultural and other relevant considerations. This pattern of exogamous marriage has emerged significantly in all classes, groups and communities in Kashmir. A rough estimate based on the study of invitation cards in the valley revealed that a dominant majority of boys and girls, i.e. about 67%, married outside their respective endogamous groups. This clearly reflects a sharp decrease in endogamous marriages and a sharp increase in exogamous marriages. A crucial aspect of latter type of marriage is the exogamous circle which has also crossed conventional boundaries.

In addition to other factors , mentioned earlier, the 'culture contact' has played a decisive role in this change, especially among middle and lower classes. Consequently, some Kashmiri boys and girls have married [and some settled] not only out of their areas out of the valley only but out of state and out of India too. Though their number is insignificant at present, but this number is increasing fast.

In the traditional Kashmiri society, the hyper-gamous and hypo-gamous marriages were in vogue. While the former meant the practice of marriage in which the boy belonged to the upper caste and girl to the lower caste, the latter referred to the practice of marriage in which boy belonged to the lower caste and girl to upper caste. While the hyper-gamous marriage was very common, the hypo-gamous marriage was not common at all. However, the religion of Islam did not favour either type of marriage. In reality, Islam stood for an egalitarian social order and negated and debased all types of caste stratification. But, at the same time, Muslims in Kashmir have inherited some caste practices from pre-Islamic past even after conversion to Islam. It was in this context that, in Kashmir, Sayyids and Khans were considered as upper castes and occupational groups as lower castes.

However, there were no 'out-castes' in that society. In that situational context, Sayyid-Khan boys married non-Sayyid-Khan girls in general, but opposite type of marriages were negligible. In fact, these were considered undesirable and were not normally practiced. In case of violation, the couple had to face social sanctions.

However, as a result of wider processes of change in Kashmir in the recent decades, these types of marriage were emerging very fast. The processes of occupational mobility [wherein large number of families have adopted different from their traditional occupations] and consequently improved their economic and educational status and social mobility [especially the process in which, after improving economic and educational status, many families adopted new and upper caste names in place of their old and lower/middle caste names] have made hyper-hypo-gamous marriages highly irrelevant and undesirable. Moreover, they have lost much-needed social legitimacy in the changed environment. Thus, the hyper-gamous marriage has lost considerably its primacy and it has been shifted to economic, educational and other related factors.

Now, at present, this marriage may take place apparently, but it may not be necessarily for conventional considerations. On the other hand, the hyper-gamous marriage takes place on non-traditional considerations.

The traditional marriage in Kashmir in the past was characterized with features of patri-locality and matri-locality. While the former referred to a practice of marriage in which the bride was taken to the groom's household at the time of marriage and settled there after marriage, the latter meant opposite of it, i.e. groom went to the bride's household and settled there after marriage. It has been observed that near-total number of people practised patrilocality and only some families practiced matri-locality. In fact, in the latter case, the groom was called *Khane-Damad* and usually he was compelled to enter into such matrimonial relationship for personal or social reasons. In the present-day situation, this type of marriage hardly exists except in some exceptional cases. On the other hand, the patri-local marriage has continued and become essential in case the couple intends to establish a new nuclear family unit after marriage.

Another important feature of marriage in Kashmir was related to monogamy and polygamy. While the first referred to a type of marriage in which a male married to one female at a time, the latter meant a type of marriage in which a male married to more than one females at a time. Another related type of marriage was polyandry which referred to a practice of marriage in which one female married to more than one males at a time and it was not in practice at all mainly because Islam has banned this marriage.

Traditionally, Kashmiris in general were monogamous in character. This characteristic feature still continues but with certain significant changes in it. Since Islam has allowed marriage with more than one woman at a time [with certain particular obligations and limitations] some people have married with one/two/three/four [maximum limit allowed by Islam] at a time for personal, psychological, social, health, economic, political and other relevant factors. In the present-day Kashmiri society, monogamy stands as the most dominant type of marriage. It applies to all classes, groups, communities, sects and other social collectivities.

While the decadal census figures convey this view, several surveys have also confirmed this view. According to a survey about 'Women in Kashmir Valley' carried out by this author in 1999, the polygamous-monogamous character of marriages in the valley revealed as recorded in the following table:

Table 5.5

Details about Number of Women Married to Men, 1999

S.No.	*Number of Women Married*	*Number of people*	*Percantage of the Total*
1.	01	3173/4800	66.10
2.	02	138/4800	07.87
3.	03	19/4800	00.89
4.	04	02/4800	00.04
5.	No response	1468/4800	30.50

Several other practices related to marriage [*Nikkah*] were found changed partly or wholly. Some new practices of marriage were also observed. First, in the basic process of mate selection, the role of the concerned boy and girl has increased tremendously and that of their parents had decreased relatively. In majority of cases, marriage was not possible without getting approval of both partners. The criteria in the male selection has also changed considerably. While in the past, the primary criteria and significant factor in the male selection was endogamous standing/relationship. In the changing situation, the primary focus has shifted the factors of education and employment at the personal level and social and economic status at the group level. Concomitantly, the degree of pre-marital interaction between the mates has increased to the maximum extent. This was observed more in urban areas than in rural areas.

It was found that consent of both partners of marriage was taken necessarily and in public. This practice provided equal status to both partners and engaged them in the Islamic framework of rights and obligations. It was found that, in general, amount of *Mahr* was paid in part or full at the time of marriage by the bridegroom to the bride in urban as well as rural areas. A detailed sociological study about "Problems of Women in the Kashmir Valley" carried out by the author 1998-99 revealed that more than 50% bridegrooms paid the amount of *mahr* in part or full at the time of marriage. This was not the practice in the past. However, about 20% bridegrooms got the part payment delayed. In practice, this meant no payment in future. This was done partly because of poverty and partly because the amount of *mahr* was determined much higher than the economic status of the boy and his family.

It was generally observed that post-marital life was characterized with more conflict and less consensus. Consequently, there was less adjustment and more maladjustment among the newly-married couples. It was more visible in urban than in rural areas. This situation necessarily led to the progressive disintegration of joint family structure and concomitant emergence of nuclear family structure. The changing social situation added many more problems for newly-married couples, especially in the cases where partners were employed and had to go to their offices regularly. This also created serious problems of children in these families.

Traditionally, divorce in Kashmir was very negligible. This social situation existed despite the fact that religiously it was allowed and polygamy was in vogue, though in very less number of cases. In the changing environment, though some cases of divorce were noticed, but, in totality, the practice was negligible. In this situational context, the above-mentioned study about problems of women in Kashmir carried out among 5,000 local women stands highly relevant. It revealed that 1.79% married women were divorced in the valley. It is essentially in this context that the practice of divorce was considered as "undesirable" by vast majority of people and was practiced only in the situations of compulsion and 'no return'. Moreover, strong social opposition was observed in cases in which women were divorced on unjust reasons. It also seems important to note here that life of divorcee does not become extremely miserable as was the case outside Kashmir. While most of them remarried, some of them got social security from the primary matri-kins. In the same way, majority of the widows got married and established their family unit afresh.

It was observed that, in general, the practice of dowry was in vogue, but with a difference. While outside Kashmir, boys or their families demand it from the girl's families, the practice in Kashmir is different qualitatively. Here, girls demand it from their parents and take with them to the groom's family at the time or after the marriage. It may be said that this practice made hardly any difference for parents, especially for the girl's parents. They have to give or pay for all major items of dowry.

The amount of dowry ranged from Rs. 20,000/- to lakhs of rupees, depending upon the economic position of the girl's families. It was revealed in the above-mentioned survey that the dowry was given in near-total cases. It was considered even more crucial than *mahr* in some cases. It was also reported that, in cases where dowry was not given or was not given sufficiently by the girl's parents, the post-marital life of the couple was characterized by conflict and instability for some time. The items of dowry demanded by boy's family included the following items:

Gold items	99.00% cases
Cash	67.00% cases
Crockery items	60.00% cases
Household goods	88.00% cases
Furniture-furnishing items	29.00% cases
Gift-bank cheque	43.00% cases
Copper, steel, glass, plastic sets	35.00% cases
Fridge and Cooler	42.00% cases
Washing machine and water purifier	51.00% cases
Steel almirahs and bedding	47.00% cases
CTV/VCP/Recorder	48.00% cases
Scooter	19.00% cases
Car	00.50% cases
Clothes	89.00% cases

One of the basic, important and unavoidable practices of marriage in Kashmir was the exchange of gifts between boy's and girl's families among all classes, castes, communities and groups. In actuality, it has emerged as the necessary co-relate of various marriage practices. It starts from the match-making function and continues till the last function related to marriage partners. The gift exchange takes place in Kashmir and in other societies too in the religious, cultural, economic, rural-urban and other relevant factors and context. In marriage situation in Kashmir, this practice has developed the feature of reciprocity, which means that every gift has to be reciprocated properly which implies that every gift has to be given back in terms of quality or quantity. Thus, a costly gift has to be reciprocated by equal or more costly [and not less costly] gifts and less costly gifts have to be reciprocated by equal or relatively more costly gifts. This gift exchange and reciprocity provide necessary continuity, stability and equality in the marital relationship.

'Wazwan' stands as the famous Kashmiri cuisine which is composed of about 20 non-vegetarian dishes [all based on meat] prepared differently by special cooks on marriage and other special occasions. In actuality, all sections of Kashmiri society have become addicted to all delicious dishes of 'wazwan'. The practice of its preparation on important domestic occasions, especially the marriage, is in vogue among all families, groups, classes and communities. Till the recent past, it was prepared within the reasonable limits in terms of quantity. But, the recent changes in Kashmir has effected this practice badly. A rational argument was put forth by the locals that many preparations of 'wazwan' have crossed the limits of decency and normal consumption. It was simply because toc much of its consumption in compelling situation led to health abnormality and its share wastage. Moreover, repeated consumption of its highly spicy and un-hygienecally prepared dishes affected the system of health negatively. This criticism became more relevant when the wastage of 'wazwan' unused food was presented as a 'status symbol'.

The most important aspect of changing practices of marriage in the valley was related directly to the impact of conflict situation of the last 20 years. The most crucial impact of this situation was felt in the shortage of suitable and qualified boys in the primary marriageable age group which falls between 20 and 32 years. This situation has arisen mainly because a significant number of boys belonging to this age group have died, injured or disabled or have joined the militant groups. This has certainly effected the marriage practices, especially related to endogamy-exogamy, hyper-gamy, hypogamy, patrilocality and matrilocality. In the pre-militancy situation, there used to be more qualified and eligible grooms available for girls. But, the reverse situation has emerged now. In fact, this phenomenon has emerged in all post-war situations in all societies. Even after the first and second world wars, one of the problems which concerned societies faced was lesser number of eligible boys for more number of girls in the 'marriage market'. In this situation in Kashmir, girls had to suffer. When they didn't get the suitable matches, they had to opt for 'compromise choice'. If they didn't adopt this choice, they had to opt for later marriage or no marriage at all. Thus, general age of marriage has also gone up significantly.

One of the major social implications of militancy was that girls of the militants, dead or alive, such as their sisters, daughters, cousin sisters and other female relatives suffered a lot. In actuality, they lost the chance of getting "good, equal and choicest" boys. Though marriage with girls of militant families has not emerged as a taboo, they were considered undesirable and were often avoided. This was done because of the reasons which included harassment on the part of security forces and pro-government militants and the feeling that these families could not pay the dowry.

Another crucial implication of the militancy was felt by the emergence of huge number of widows and orphans, whose number has been estimated by the author as 32,000 and 96,000 respectively [see authors book entitled *A Sociological Study of Widows and Orphans in Kashmir*]. The study revealed that these two groups lived in pathetic and miserable life conditions, especially in the fields of education, living accommodation, income, health, social ethos, psychological traits and so on. It was generally observed that these widowsdon't marry and live the life of widow for the sake of their children and their development.

This situation demands necessarily positive and immediate response not only on the part of government agencies-organizations, but also on the part of non-government agencies and organizations. These organizations need to work not only in formal sector, they need to develop a strong social movement with two major social responsibilities. First, they have to work for development of very positive social environment which will emphasize as well as legitimize the marriage with the girls related to militants' families. Second, they have to carry out systematic, organized and continuous efforts to make the marriage of these suffering girls a broad-day reality. Moreover, widow remarriage, allowed under Islamic rules, must also be emphasized, so that the widows remain no more dependent and disadvantageous members of society.

[D] CHANGING PRACTICES OF MARRIAGE IN KASHMIR

Every human society in the world has established certain particular practices related to marriage. These are known as 'traditional" practices of marriage. These play a specific role for the basis, maintenance and continuity of the institution of marriage. In fact, these work for the social system. However, the related fact is that these traditional practices of marriage have undergone certain degree of transformation. It has happened mainly because of large-scale implications of the processes of change and development in all societies of the world.

The preceding propositions regarding change in marriage practices may be applied to all developing societies, including the Kashmiri society. It follows that all traditional marriage practices in Kashmir are exposed to the forces of change and are giving place to new practices. Thus, the practices related to polygamy are reducing and that of monogamy are increasing. Similarly, the patri-matri local marriages are replaced by neo-local marriages. It has been observed that there seems a clear direction in this pattern of change from traditional to non-traditional-/modern type of marriages. As the sociologists maintain that there are certain specific causes and implications of this change, this phenomenon leads to changes in the nature, types, dimensions, and other practices related to marriage.

In the above sociological framework, this survey was carried out in the Kashmir valley with the following objectives:

[i] To enquire about actual change in the traditional practices of marriage in the valley of Kashmir;

[ii] To study the causes and consequences of this type of change in marriage practices; and

[iii] To determine about the direction of this type of change.

The focus of this survey had three aspects. First, it was carried out in the sociological framework and analysed with sociological features. Second, it surveyed the relevant marriage practices which were in vogue in the valley at that time. Third, it concentrated on broader Kashmiri community giving representation to all its groups and classes. Hardly any compromise was made with the quality of data collection and data analysis. Efforts were made by supervisors of the survey to make it flaw-less research. But, there is little possibility of an error or interpretation as the entire fieldwork was carried out by the second year students of M.A. Sociology.

1. METHODOLOGY

[a] ***Universe:*** The universe of this survey was the Kashmir province of Jammu and Kashmir state which was composed of ten administrative districts of Srinagar, Ganderbal, Budgam, Baramulla, Bandipora, Kupwara, Anantnag, Kulgam, Shopian and Pulwama. All districts were covered by giving representation of 250 respondents to each district.

[b] ***Methods and Techniques:*** The main method/technique used for carrying out this survey was the questionnaire. In fact, a detailed questionnaire was formulated which included all necessary details, topics and themes. The questionnaire was of stratified nature and had open-ended and fixed-choice questions. Simultaneously, the participant observation proved helpful as it helped to get correct and original information.

[c] ***Sample:*** The total sample of this survey composed of 2,500 representative respondents selected from all districts of the Kashmir province at 250 per district. They were selected on the basis of following sociological criteria:

- Sex [male and female];
- Age [3 age groups of adolescent, younger and old];
- Education [literate and illiterate];
- Income [3 groups of higher, middle and lower income];
- Marital status [married, unmarried and divorced-separated]; and
- Demography [rural and urban areas].

[d] ***Field Investigation:*** After formulating the questionnaire, research investigators of this survey were trained in the relevant methodology. These investigators were M.A. Final students of Department of Sociology. Then these student investigators were sent to all districts, tehsils and blocks in the Kashmir valley. This enabled them to collect the total and representative information.

[e] ***Data Processing:*** The data collected from the field was aggregated first at the individual level and then at the collective level. This was followed by tabulation and analysis of data by individual and group of student investigators.

[f] ***Report-Writing:*** In this way, the investigators reached to the stage of report-writing which they did under the supervision of the supervisors.

Since the entire field work and the following research work was carried entirely by student investigators, one must be conscious of its limitations.

2. FINDINGS OF THE SURVEY

[I] MONOGAMY AND POLYGAMY

[a] ***Proportion of Monogamous and Polygamous Marriage Practices:*** While a monogamous marriage means a practice in which an individual male marries a single female for the life time, the polygamous marriages refers to a practice in which a male marries more than one female in his life time. The religion of Islam has allowed the latter type of marriage [with certain conditions] and limited the number to four only. The survey revealed that while the proportion of monogamous marriage practices was 83.90%, that of polygamous marriage practices was 08.20%. It follows that monogamous type of marriage stands highly dominant in the present-day Kashmiri society.

[b] ***Status of Second/Third/Fourth Wife and Her Household:*** The survey found that percentage of more than one wife was as mentioned below:

II	wife	15.56%
III	wife	06.59%
IV	wife	04.70%

These wives live in the joint or nuclear/separate household. The details follow:

household	Joint family household	nuclear/separate family
II wife	83.81	17.19

III wife	36.33	11.71
IV wife	18.79	....

[c] **Wife's Belonging:** Usually the second, third and fourth wife belonged to close family/kin background. It reveals in the following details about belonging of these wives:

- Wife/wives belong to your family/clan 31.37%
- .... caste 29.34%
- .... occupation 15.39%
- .... group/class 20.56%
- .... other affiliations42.84%

[d] **Reasons for Polygamous Marriage:** There are set reasons which compel an individual to opt for more than one marriage in the Kashmiri society. Our survey revealed the following set reason/s for more than one marriage:

- Childlessness of first wife 28.09%
- Health problem of wife/wives 27.51%
- Sexual desire of the males 16.36%
- Economic considerations 15.40%
- Death of the previous wife 37.05%
- Divorce to previous wife 29.49%
- Mutual love and affection 07.19%

[e] ***Reasons For Monogamous Marriage:*** At the same time, the respondents of this survey were probed about the monogamous marriage option on the part of males. When they were asked about main reason/s for opting this type of marriage, they gave the reasons mentioned in the following:

-Universal practice of monogamy 22.37%
-Absolute satisfaction 36.93%
-Full care of children 24.68%
-Considered a standard practice 15.26%
-Economic consideration 16.93%
-Stability of the family organization 21.55%

[f] ***Wife's Belonging:*** It was also observed that in case individuals opted for monogamous type of marriage, the wife had some pre-fixed relationship with her husband. Thus, the female partner belonged to the same.

- Class	23.38%
- Caste	23.22%
- Occupation	14.65%
- Group	18.00%
- Other affilia	24.79%

[II] ENDOGAMY AND EXOGAMY

[a] The endogamous marriage means a practice in which an individual, male or female, marries within his/her family/clan/caste/group, while exogamy stands opposite to it, i.e. outside ones endogamous circle. On the whole, this survey revealed that 45.35% respondents practised endogamous marriage, while 54.80% opted for exogamous marriage. This shows a clear trend of the direction of change from endogamous to exogamous practices.

[b] ***Nature of Endogamy***: The survey showed that the nature of endogamy was on the lines/patterns mentioned below:

- Cousin marriage	26.54 %
- Cross-cousin marriage	24.56
- Other relatives	35.06
- Other non-relatives	13.50

[c] ***Reasons/Factors for Endogamy:*** The research investigation revealed the following reasons for going for endogamous marriage:

- Caste-class	25.58%
- Family relationship	43.22%
- Educational qualification	15.29%
- Personality/maturity of indi.	06.60%
- Other factors	03.05%

[d] ***Major Implications of Endogamy:*** The survey identified the major implication of this type of marriage as mentioned below:

-Patronage of parents increased	53.20%
-Family solidarity intensified	18.23%
-Caste consciousness increased	09.40%
-Weakness of financial ties	09.00%
-Employment/individual career	06.14%

[e] ***Nature of Exogamy:*** On the other hand, the practice of exogamous marriage was dominant and was increasing. These marriages had the following patterns:

- marriage outside one's caste	53.06%
- Family	16.31%
- Group	06.08%
- Occupational commu.	10.21%
- Region/area	07.27%

[f] ***Reasons for Opting for Exogamy:*** As in the case of endogamy, the practice of exogamy too had set reasons because of which people opt for it. The following major reasons were found in the investigation:

- Against one's own caste/class membership	26.78%
- Emphasis on educational qualification	14.57%
- Personality and maturity	08.20%
- Experience of family relations	41.93%
- Other reasons	09.96%

[III] *Hypergamy and Hypogamy*

[a] In general, hypergamy means a practice of marriage in which the male belongs to the upper caste-family and female belongs to lower caste-family. The hypo-gamous type of marriage stands for opposite to this type, i.e. female belongs to upper caste and male belongs to lower caste. On the whole, this survey revealed that 22.76 % respondents were involved in

hypergamous practice of marriage, while 14.15 % respondents were involved in hypogamous practice. However, the trend of change shows increasing and decreasing number of hypogamous and hypergamous practices respectively.

[b] ***Wife's Belonging:*** The upper-lower caste status of females can be explained as mentioned below:

- Hypergamy – women generally belong to lower family-clan 03.28%
- .... caste 05.13%
- .... occupation 20.17%
- .... class/group 12.21%
- .... other affili. 59.19%
- ***Hypo-gamy*** – Women generally belong to upper family-clan 07.71%
- .... Caste 07.11%
- .... Occupation 13.35%
- .... Class-group 14.60%
- .... other affili. 57.18%

[c] ***Justificatory Factors:*** Both these practices of marriage have respective justificatory factors. Our survey identified the below-mentioned factors:

Justificatory Factor	Hyper-Gamy	Hypo-gamy
- Weakening of caste application	29.32	24.03
- Destiny	11.26	11.75
- Social solidarity	03.44	02.70
- More respect for brides/grooms	04.45	06.80
- Love marriage	04.29	05.29
- Prescribed by religion	61.00	05.90
- Other responses	26.11	31.88
- No response	14.27	10.36

[IV] RULES OF RESIDENCE

[a] The rules of residence are directly and necessarily related to the practices of marriage. In fact, there seems inverse relationship between the two. Thus, on the basis of rules of residence, we can identify three main practices/types of marriages in Kashmir. These are:

-*Patri-local Marriage:* A practice of marriage in which the bride leaves her household after marriage and goes-settles in her groom's household;

-*Matri-local Marriage:* A practice of marriage in which the groom leaves his household and sttles down in the household of the bride; and

-*Neo-local Marriage:* A practice of marriage in which the couple leaves their respective households and establish a new nuclear household.

On the whole, this survey revealed that these practices of marriage were in vogue in Kashmir in the following proportion:

-	Patri-local marriage	64.21 %
-	Matri-local marriage	07.31 %
-	Neo-local marriage	28.50 %

[b] ***Reasons for Patrilocal Marriage:*** As is clear from the data, the patri-local practice of marriage seems the dominant type of marriage. It has specific reasons which include the following:

- Lone son	6.47%	Economic reasons	09.60%
- Responsibility towards parents	42.70%	Social obligation	04.60%
- Family traditions	06.76%	Respect in society	01.96%
- Brothers in family	01.20%	Religious obligation	03.94%
- Male superiority	02.98%	Personal satisfaction	01.21%
- Solidarity in family	00.15%		

[c] ***Implications of Patrilocality:*** The practice of patri-locality had several social implications, especially the following:

- Family-increase in social solidarity	59.56%
- decrease in social solidarity	12.16%
- interference in social affairs	12.43%
- creating division of labour	13.35%
- increase in child care	02.46%
- Society-harmony	65.93%
- no response	13.43%
- social control	02.71%
- no effect	09.02%
- negative effect	08.88%
- individual more responsibilities	43.58%
Less responsibilities	29.89%
Status gained	02.16%
Satisfaction	20.15%
Social security	00.86%
Less privacy	06.34%

[d] ***Reasons for Matrilocality:*** In the case of matri-locality, our survey found following reasons:

- No brother in family	07.00
- Death of parents	04.32
- Poverty	24.70
- Parental choice	05.00
- Lone daughter	23.14
- Love marriage	02.03
- Destiny	01.60
- To gain authority in f.	01.50

[e] ***Impllications of Matrilocality:*** The following specific social implications were observed among respondents of this survey:

- Family organization-increased	38.87%
- Strengthened	50.12%

- Stability	10.39
- Family life-more respect	57.94
- Less respect	41,10
- Inheritance rights-property inherited	71.70
- Prop. snot inherited	14.49
- No response	13.51
- Gender inequality-male domination	37.68
- Female domination	19.97
- Equal status	42.34

[f] ***Neo-local Residence:*** After the marriage, a significant number of couples usually establish a new household away from their respective parents. This increasing-decreasing trends were noted as follows:

- Scarcity of space	01.60	- Family disorganization	41.99
- Death of parents	06.52	- Education of children	05.16
- Job reasons	06.81	- Separation by consent	13.40
- Already living separatel	00.83	- Destiny	02.06
- Support of tradition	02.69	- More freedom	02.25
- Religious permission	01.50	- Love marriage	02.35

[g] ***Neo-local Implications:*** Finally, this survey identified the major implications of the establishment of neo-local household units by married couples and details follow:

- Parental authority-strengthened	40.00%
- Increased	43.00%
- Continued	15.60%
- Disorganization -increased	39.43%
- Decreased	16.22%
- No disorganization	42.75%
- No response	15.07%
- Cultural-increased	49.40%
- Decreased	14.21%

- Continued	09.30%
- No response	27.00%
- Traditional ethos-diluted	28.20%
- Continued	47.98%
- Increased	06.39%
- Vanished	23.41%

[III] CONFLICT AND VIOLENCE AGAINST WOMEN IN KASHMIR

It is generally believed that the traditional society of Kashmir about 70 or more years back was absolutely a crime-free society. In that society, dominant majority of population had neither witnessed nor heard about any major crime committed by members of the same society. But, the same society today stands at its opposite extreme and stands criminalized. We all are first-hand witness to this phenomenon of the emergence of minor and major crimes, especially violence against women, in the Kashmiri society. This has happened in 4-5 decades in a particular social context with specific factors contributing to its continuity and dynamics.

Broadly speaking, this alarming situation has emerged in the valley in the background of two distinctive processes of modernization and militancy-militarization. The first set of factors were directly related to the processes of modernization, particularly urbanization, industrialization, cultural-media exposure, migration, educational attainment, secularization, materialistic orientation, value-free environment, moral degeneration and so on. This has happened in all other developing societies and has also happened in our society. Thus, the situation of inequality, competition, conflict and anomy has led to what is characterized as 'domestic violence against women'.

In this situation, mainly due to education and employment, women in general developed 'dual role' in society, one at home and other at office. In the process of adopting new role and status, they exposed themselves to new problems which have been given the name of 'domestic violence'. While at home, they faced problems like competition, conflict, jealousy, discrimination, harassment, dowry-demand, post-marital discard, mental and physical torture, dowry deaths, psychological problems and so on. This violence against women was not only the intra-sex affair but inter-sex affair also. It follows that violence was committed against women not only by men but against women by women also. In actuality, in many cases, men have proved prime protectors of women.

On the other hand, processes directly related to militancy and militarization have unleashed a wave of violence against societal groups, classes and communities, especially their women. While misuse of the gun by militants led to series of violent acts against women, the state-sponsored gun in the hands of military and para-military forces led to all sorts of excesses against women, including abusing their chastity, dishonouring them, and their molestation and rape. The former kind of violence had no social, legal and political legitimacy, while the latter kind of violence seemed in a way legitimized by draconian laws like 'Disturbed Areas Act' and 'Armed Forces Special Powers Act'.

It has now been established that violence against the Kashmiri women, especially the rape, has been utilized by Indian security forces as a weapon to impose collective punishment, shame or dis-honouring Kashmiri Muslim women. This argument has been well presented by a recently published book entitled "Militarization and Gender in Kashmir' written by Seema Kazi. Moreover, the fact stands with strong evidence that molestation and rape against women in Kashmir was started in an organized way by these forces. The rape incidents in Kunan Poshpora, Trehgam, Kupwara and at other places stood as 'telling examples' in this regard. The gruesome incident of rape and subsequent murder of Assiya and Neelofar in Shopian represented the climax in the wave of violence against women in Kashmir.

Thus, both sets of processes and factors created a situation of violence against women which seemed difficult, if not impossible, to reverse completely. For women, it was immaterial who the criminal or offender was, local or non-local? They became victims of security, militant and local forces which were equally involved in the 'gender aggression' and overall degeneration of culture. In reality, they were repressed and suppressed by indigenous as well as exogenous elements. In this situational context, there emerges the need to initiate collectively the processes of 'humanization' to negate the very processes of militancy and militarization.

[IV] SOCIAL DEVIANCE AND SOCIAL DISORGANIZATION

Social Deviance: The concept of 'Social Deviance' is primarily related to the behaviour of violation of established values and norms. It is concerned with infrequent and dysfunctional behaviour of individuals and groups – breach of norms and rules which are regarded as necessary to coherent and harmonious social order.[1] It refers to those situations in which social behaviour is in disapproved direction.[2] In strict sense, it applies to any behaviour which is not consonant with their expectations and norms for individual conduct which are shared and recognized within social system.[3] It specifically refers to crime, delinquency, drug addiction, suicide, illegitimacy, prostitution, marriage breakdown and vagrance.[4] Deviance is also explained in terms of violation of religious values and as social stigma.[5]

Social Disorganization: Social organization refers to interdependence of parts which is an essential characteristic of all collective entities, i.e. groups, communities and societies.[6] These interdependent parts are explained in terms of relationship among roles; values, norms and beliefs; sub-groups within a large unit, institutions; and tasks and objective activities. When there is breakdown in this social interdependence, disorganization takes place, though it varies in different situations.[7]

Most often, the social structure remains intact till there is no serious erosion or radical change. So, when any sort of serious change takes place, it generally leads to social disorganization. In this situation, while established relationship patterns change, social roles and institutions also adopt new form. Thus, roles and institutions don't play normal functioning, they become dysfunctional. Individuals don't follow authority and order. Different units of society get disjointed, no established relationship continues, no cohesion and solidarity exists, and no social goals are achieved.[8] In this way, social disorganization encourages and makes it easy to deviate from established roles and to violate values and norms.[9] Most of these features can be applied to the Kashmir situation.

Disorganization in Kashmir: When the conflict got introduced and effected the Kashmiri society at large during 1990s, it shook the basis of social order and the process of disorganization was established through formal and informal actions of individuals and groups. This process in actuality threatened the entire social order and its moral basis. However, it could not reach to its extreme because of the role of some societal factors. Thus, minimum degree of harmony, unity, coherence and consensus was evolved which saved the Kashmiri society from complete breakdown.

In-family Disorganization: The disorganization occurred in two major areas, i.e. in-family and out-family. In the former case, most-affected areas of disorganization were processes of socialization-internalization; personality formation and evolution of its desirable traits; conscious and deliberate deviance, abuse and violation of the patriarchal-parental authority; established-legitimized patterns of role and status; de-legitimization of religious values and norms; deliberate deviance from ideal-positive attitudes and behaviour at child-younger stage; establishment of desirable child-bearing, child rearing practices; and ideology of irresponsibility, offence, and negative worldview.[10] Commenting on this situation in Kashmir, especially related to children, a social analyst observed :

"Children nowadays have grown arrogant, abrasive, and impolite, what we call in Kashmiri 'bhotepheor'. Some people may go as far as calling the generation X as uncultured."[11]

Out-family Disorganization: In the out-family situation, perpetual conflict introduced disorganizing effect on roles, institutions, inter-relationship and entire social order. The whole society got engulfed in this effect and was exposed to the consequences of social deviation and social disorganization. First, the entire range of social roles of father, mother, teacher, relative, neighbor, colleague, friend and others were exposed to the offensive and threatening environment in order to negate their operational implications. In this way, these roles were opposed, challenged and discredited among the youth, especially in the schools. Consequently, the general behaviour of children and youth became atrocious. Second, the conflict introduced conscious efforts and elements to discredit basic institutions, especially family, school and religion in order to stop their operational functioning. This worked partly and for some time only. While family environment and authority was restored shortly, school established its control after a brief lull. Again, marriage practices revived after a brief stop and deviance-violation of religious values could not continue for long. Thus, the relevance and credibility of social and religious institutions was continued without heavy damage. Third, the conflict in Kashmir introduced elements of antagonism and conflict in all fields, in all dimensions and at all levels. This gave rise to new type of material relations and proved disorganizing in implications. Thus, Kashmir turned into a social order which had never existed here. Fourth, in this situation, the whole existing social order got disturbed whose main features included deviance, delinquency, crime, violence, drug addiction, depression, tension, suicides, mental abnormality and so on. The entire situation analyzed here reflects the changing roles, institutions, processes, inter-relationships and so on.[12]

[V] CULTURAL PRACTICES AND PROBLEMS IN KASHMIR

1. **Cultural Encounters:** Sociologically, it has been observed in all human societies that culture has most often faced other cultures in the processes of cultural interaction, cultural assimilation, cultural domination and cultural antagonism. In this way, a particular culture has encountered other cultures, especially in the modern times and during the western colonial rule in Asia and Africa. Though equitable and reciprocal relationship in the cultural life was possible in the colonized countries, the western powers treated them as their "colonies" and enforced their culture forcefully. At the global level, knowledge, science and technology and other factors were fully utilized to carry out the cultural domination. But, in the post-colonial period, though the local-indigenous cultures in Asia and Africa emerged, maintained and asserted, they faced serious challenges of modern life which had effected their youth significantly. In this situation, the youths had developed specific ideas, attitudes and behaviour vis-avis modern way of life.

2. **The Kashmir Situation:** In this situational context, the Kashmiri youth also faced some challenges of modern life in the field of culture, especially from the initiation of the last century. These challenges were responded in a specific way and with a specific orientation. The positive and negative

cultural ideas, attitudes and behaviour pattern led to the evolution of youth's perception towards modern challenges related to knowledge, science, technology, religion, culture, language, education, economy and so on. In the post-independence era, this perception got strengthened further, especially with long-term and short-term implications of the processes of modernization and development. Subsequently, the youth's perception in Kashmir was partly changed and partly re-defined due to the emergence of armed conflict in Kashmir in 1989.

3. **The Study:** It was generally observed in Kashmir that, in the recent past, while there was erosion of some traditional Kashmiri culture in social life, some prominent features and ideal traits of the Kashmiri culture such as tolerance of all religions, plurality of various cultures, respect for different ideas and ideologies and completely non-violent approach and behaviour in social ethos were violated and abused. These social developments distorted the ideal Kashmiri culture and even dehumanized the cultural ethos. In this situational context, an evaluation study was carried out in 2005 among the Kashmiri youth about its changing perceptions of cultural issues. This study was sponsored by CROKSY in order to evaluate its educational and cultural programmes for student youth in Kashmir.

4. **Methodology:** The universe of this academic study was the valley of Kashmir composing of all six districts of Anantnag, Baramulla, Budgam, Kupwara, Pulwama and Srinagar. The study was specifically carried out in 68 selected high/higher secondary schools spread in these districts. The main methods adopted for this study were questionnaire and interview. Three questionnaires were made for student youths, their teachers and their advisors. The last category of respondents were interviewed also. The fieldwork in all districts was carried out by trained investigators among the highly representative sample of 340 student youths, about 55 from each district. The sample composed of 50–50% male-female ratio and 60-40 rural-urban ratio. The data was collected scientifically, aggregated and tabulated, and, subsequently,

analysed sociologically as per the themes and objectives of this study. Finally, conclusion was drawn scientifically.

5. Some Sociological Findings:

5.1. *Kashmiri Cultural Messages:* The respondents in this study conveyed the following particular messages of the Kashmiri culture:

Table 5.6

Cultural Messages about Kashmiri Culture

S.No.	*The Cultural Messages*	*A [60]*	*B [60]*	*B [50]*	*K [60]*	*P [60]*	*S [50]*	*Total [340]*
1.	CM-01	52	42	50	42	47	50	28 [84.70%]
2.	CM-02	53	46	48	46	49	48	290 [91.76%]
3.	CM-03	59	55	50	48	50	50	312 [91.76%]
4.	CM-04	42	40	46	36	48	44	256 [75.29%]
5.	CM-05	36	46	41	35	42	45	245 [72.05%]
6.	CM-06	49	42	42	40	43	42	258 [75.88%]
7.	CM-07	50	49	46	48	47	47	289 [84.41%]
8.	CM-08	45	48	43	42	49	44	271 [79.70%]
9.	CM-09	55	50	47	50	52	50	305 [89.70%]
10.	CM-10	54	52	50	51	53	50	310 [91.17%]

A stands for Anantnag

B stands for Baramulla

B stands for Budgam

K stands for Kupwara

P stands for Pulwama

S stands for Srinagar

CM-01 You should maintain the Kashmiri identity.

CM-02 You should uphold the Kashmiri personality traits.

CM-03 You should study all about Kashmir, especially its past.

CM-04 You should use Kashmiri language at home and in school.

CM-05 You should emphasize oneness of the Kashmiri culture.

CM-06 It must help you to solve today's problems.

CM-07 It must help you to build a just and human social order.

CM-08 It must help you to understand the negative role of political leaders.

CM-09 It must help you to understand the plural nature of our society.

CM-10 It must give clear ideas about secular character of the Kashmiri society.

5.2. Knowledge about Composite Character of Kashmiri Culture.

Respondents conveyed the responses regarding composite character of Kashmiri culture as reflects in the following table:

Table 5.7

Knowledge about Composite Character of Kashmiri Culture

S.No.	*Response*	*A*	*B*	*B*	*K*	*P*	*S*	*Total*
01.	Yes	45	41	37	35	40	38	236 [69.41 %]
02.	No	15	19	13	25	20	12	140 [30.58 %]

This response, especially at No. 2, may be explained in terms of two factors. First, since most of these students belong to the age group of 10-166 years, they had hardly any opportunity to interact with non-Muslim Kashmiris, particularly the Kashmiri Pandits.

Second, since they hardly visited areas outside Kashmir valley, they could not encounter the non-Muslim Kashmiris. Some of these youths are completely .ignorant about KPs, their culture, society, and their belonging to the past and present of Kashmir.

5.3. Modern Challenges to Kashmiri Culture in Response to our Question.

Regarding the modern challenges which Kashmiri culture, like other cultures, faces at present, the respondents gave the response which reveals in the following table:

Table 5.8

Response Towards Various Modern Challenges to Kashmiri Culture

S.No. Response to	*Yes/No*	*A*	*B*	*B*	*K*	*P*	*S*	*Total*
1. Sc. & Tech.	Yes	05	06	04	07	05	00	27[07.94%]
	No	55	54	46	53	55	50	313[92.05%]
2. Plurality of relig.	Yes	03	05	05	06	77	02	28[08.23%]
	No	57	55	45	54	53	48	312[91.76%]
3. Plura. of cultures	Yes	03	05	05	06	02	07	28[08.23%]
	No	57	55	45	54	53	48	213[91.76%]
4. Human rights	Yes	05	06	03	07	04	02	27[07.97%]
	No	55	54	47	53	56	48	313[92.05%]
5. Gender discrina	Yes	10	09	06	10	12	07	54 [15.88%]
	No	50	51	44	50	48	43	286[84.11%]
6. Social justice	Yes	09	09	05	08	10	06	47 [15.88%]
	No	51	51	45	52	50	44	293 [86.17%]
7. Environmental Preservation	Yes	00	00	00	00	00	00	00 [00.00%]
	No	60	60	50	60	60	50	340[100.00%]

The explanation of the above table is as follows:

5.3.1. *Application of Science and Technology:* The preceding table shows that dominant majority of 92.05 % students held the opinion that there was no need to guard against the application of science and technology as it poses no threat for the local culture. They argued that since it stands for scientific and material development in the present-day times, the local culture should not become hurdle in this grand process. They also held the view that if the local culture becomes a potential block in the scientific development, there should be deviation from that culture. This they considered desirable and preferable. A significant number of these respondents maintained that science and religion [and culture] are not conflictual, so the opposition to the former's application has no justification. However, a minority of 7.94 % respondents opined that traditional culture [mostly religiously determined] must be guarded against application of science and technology. It was primarily because they consider religion and science mutually antagonistic.

5.3.2. *Plurality of Religions and Cultures:* An overwhelming majority of 91.76% respondents conveyed that they must safeguard the plurality of religions and cultures in Kashmir. This was partly because this plural character stood as most distinguishing empirical social reality in Kashmir and partly because this character stood for essence and need of our time. Other important reasons for this response included the facts such as Kashmiri society has established a tradition of respect, tolerance and accommodation of various religions-cultures throughout its history; maintenance of plural character of Kashmiri identity in all situations; and efforts in the direction of establishing a modern and democratic society. Other considerations for maintaining the plural character of the Kashmiri society were to help in the scientific and other material developments; to reduce conflict to controllable limits; and to help in the process of restoration of peace.

5.3.3. *Safeguarding the Human Rights of all:* Since respect and Maintenance of human rights are consensus-based desirable objective in Kashmir, a huge majority of 92.05% student respondents upheld the opinion that culture has not to guard against them. In reality, the culture provides the required legitimacy to the practices directly and indirectly related to human rights. They said that these rights must be upheld for all groups, communities and classes and in all situations. This topic attains more importance in Kashmir where practices of human rights violations have been recorded in extreme form.

5.3.4. *Practices of Gender Discrimination:* As traditional practices related to gender discrimination are fast disappearing in Kashmir, the majority of 84.11% student respondents conveyed clearly that there prevails no cultural justification for these obsolete practices. Though there have been such practices inn vogue even in the recent past, these have been reduced considerably now. These present achieved status and role of women in present-day Kashmir confirms these propositions. However, a significant number of student respondents, i.e., 15.08%, upheld the view that practices of gender discrimination may not continue in Kashmir, though they justify these practices absolutely. These conservative and lower socio-economic respondents argued that men and women are not equal religiously and culturally and efforts to negate this inequality will prove futile.

5.3.5. *The Ideals of Social Justice:* The dominant majority of 96.17% respondents held the view that the Kashmiri culture has not to guard against ideas and ideals of social justice. They felt that in reality the local culture itself promotes these ideas and ideals in all sections of society, at all level, in all fields, and at all times.

5.3.6. *Environmental Preservation:* 100% student respondents revealed their opinion that the Kashmiri culture emphasizes on the total preservation of environment in the valley. It also opposes environmental pollution in all forms. In the context of heavy environmental pollution of lakes and rivers here, especially Dal lake and Jhelum, and deforestation is opposed strongly. The famous saying of Alamdare Kasshmir –AN POSHE TELE YELI VAN POSHE- is quoted repeatedly everywhere in Kashmir in this regard.

6. Conclusion

The above-mentioned empirical findings lead us to formulate sociological conclusion that while modernity is increasing/expanding, some aspects of tradition are maintained consciously. This situation may be characterized as continuity and change in the cultural context.

As has happened in the cases of all cultures, the Kashmiri culture too was exposed to other cultures and other challenges and it has responded in a particular way. In actuality, this response was shaped by the pattern and intensity of the global or regional challenges and the socio-economic status, religious-political affiliation and nature of interaction between the Kashmiri culture and other cultures.

Finally, the Kashmiri culture responded to the modern challenges in which there was acceptance of all cultural practices which go with the global trends and have necessary contemporary relevance and importance.

NOTES AND REFERENCES

1. S. Duncan Michel, ed., *A Dictionary of Sociology* [London, 1987, R & K].
2. *Ibid.*
3. Gordan Marshall, ed., *Oxford Dictionary of Sociology* [New York, 1994, O.U. Press].
4. *Ibid.*
5. *Ibid.*
6. *Ibid.*
7. *Ibid.*
8. *Ibid.*
9. *Ibid.*
10. *Ibid.*
11. Firdous Baba, "The Poison of Waywardness", *Greater Kashmir,* Srinagar, 13th March 2010.
12. See B. A. Dabla, "Social Impact of Militancy" in *Sociological Papers on Kashmir, 2 Vols. [Srinagar, 2010, Jay Kay Books.*

CHAPTER 6

EMERGING SOCIAL TRENDS IN KASHMIR

[I] EMERGENCE OF LATE MARRIAGE IN KASHMIR

1. *Introduction:* It has been established with a lot of sociological evidence that every human society has decided about marriage at a particular age. It has also been observed that various factors such as cultural, religious, psychological, educational, political, societal, economic, demographic and other factors, contributed to this phenomenon. Thus, at present, we face a situation at the global level in which some societies, especially modernized societies, have developed comparatively higher age of marriage, while other societies, especially modernizing societies, have maintained comparatively lower age of marriage. In this theoretical background, the phenomenon of early and late marriage needs to be seen in multi-dimensional context and sociological perspective.

Sociologically, late marriage refers to a situation in which marriages are generally solemnized much after the normal or average or desirable age of marriage. It varies from late teens to late twenties for males as well as females. This situation generally arises in the context of limitless impact of the processes of modernization. However, in certain situations, a particular factor such as political or economic emerges as the dominant and determining factor for changing the nature, criteria and consequences of late marriage.

The above-mentioned sociological propositions about late marriage can be applied to the existing situation in the Kashmiri society. The impact of multifarious developments during last 60 years related to the practice of late marriage can be explained in two specific points. First, socio-economic and educational-political developments in JK state had radical impact on the practices, rituals, values and norms of marriage, especially related directly to late marriage. Second, more important, politically oriented developments in last 20 years of militancy had further changing impact on the traditional pattern of late marriage in Kashmir. As a result, a situation has been created in which emergence of late marriage seemed as an established fact of life. The sociological analysysis of this crucial phenomenon through various dimensions and factors is the central theme of this survey.

2. *Methodology:* This survey stands primarily as an empirical survey about the phenomenon of emergence of late marriage in the Kashmir valley. No pre-conceived theoretical or ideological framework was used to observe and explain the relevant phenomenon. Among other reasons, this was done to avoid any kind of bias in the findings of the survey. The universe of this survey was whole valley of Kashmir composing of ten following administrative districts:

Table 6.1

Details about the Universe of Survey Undertaken

S.No.	*District*	*No. of Respondents*	*S. No.*	*District*	*No. of Respondents*
1.	Srinagar	225	2.	Anantnag	150
3.	Baramulla	125	4.	Kupwara	100
5.	Bandipora	100	6.	Pulwama	150
7.	Shopian	150	8.	Ganderbal	150
9.	Kulgam	150	10.	Budgam	200

The methods and techniques of data collection in this survey were questionnaire and interview. A detailed questionnaire was formulated for the purpose of collecting primary source information from respondents. It was composed of questions on important selected themes. It had stratified, open-ended and fixed-choice questions, which were filled by trained investigators in the presence of respondents or in absentia. The responses were recorded cautiously in order to maintain originality and specificity of responses.

The sample in this survey was highly intensive and stratified in order to include more groups and communities. It was also highly representative to all relevant collectivities of respondents. The sociological variables became the basis for selection of respondents. These specific variables were identified as sex, age, literacy, income, marital-status and rural-urban status. The total number of respondents in the sample was 1,500 who composed the categories shown in following tables:

Table 6.2

Composition of Age Groups of the Sample

S. No.	*Respondent's Cluster No.*	*Age Groups [no.]*			*Total*	
		00-25 yrs.	*26-40 yrs*	*41+yrs*	*No.*	*Percentage*
1.	01 – 50	18	14	18	50	03.33
2.	51 – 100	13	25	12	50	03.33
3.	101 – 150	13	25	12	50	03.33
4.	151 – 200	12	25	13	50	03.33
5.	201 – 250	13	25	12	50	03.33
6.	251 – 300	16	23	11	50	03.33
7.	301 – 350	18	14	18	50	03.33
8.	351 – 400	13	25	12	50	03.33
9.	401 – 450	13	25	12	50	03.33
10.	451 – 500	06	44	04	50	03.33
11.	501 – 550	13	25	12	50	03.33
12.	551 – 600	12	24	14	50	03.33
13.	601 – 650	13	25	12	50	03.33

14.	651 – 700	15	20	15	50	03.33
15.	701 – 750	20	15	15	50	03.33
16.	751 – 800	13	25	12	50	03.33
17.	801 – 850	13	25	12	50	03.33
18.	851 – 900	20	16	14	50	03.33
19.	901 – 950	17	23	10	50	03.33
20.	951 – 1000	13	25	12	50	03.33
21.	1001 – 1050	13	25	12	50	03.33
22.	1051 – 1100	13	25	12	50	03.33
23.	1101 – 1150	12	24	14	50	03.33
24.	1151 – 1200	25	15	10	50	03.33
25.	1201 – 1250	17	17	16	50	03.33
26.	1251 – 1300	13	25	12	50	03.33
27.	1301 – 1350	16	24	12	50	03.33
28.	1351 – 1400	17	15	18	50	03.33
29.	1401 – 1450	14	26	10	50	03.33
30.	1451 – 1500	18	14	18	50	03.33
Total	442	678	370	1500	100.00	
	29.40	45.20	24.60	100.00		

Table 6.3

Composition of Income Groups of the Sample

S.No.	*Respondent's Cluster No.*	*upto 10000*	*10000 25000*	*Total No.*	*Percentage*	
1.	01 – 50	14	22	14	50	03.33
2.	51 – 100	23	20	07	50	03.33
3.	101 – 150	15	22	13	50	03.33

4.	151 – 200	16	22	12	50	03.33
5.	201 – 250	15	25	10	50	03.33
6.	251 – 300	44	05	01	50	03.33
7.	301 – 350	14	22	14	50	03.33
8.	350 – 400	23	20	07	50	03.33
9.	401 – 450	23	20	07	50	03.33
10.	451 - 500	39	07	04	50	03.33
11.	501 – 550	13	25	12	50	03.33
12.	551 – 600	10	20	20	50	03.33
13.	601 – 650	18	20	12	50	03.33
14.	651 – 700	15	20	15	50	03.33
15.	701 – 750	20	15	15	50	03.33
16.	751 – 800	24	10	16	50	03.33
17.	801 – 850	20	15	15	50	03.33
18.	851 – 900	20	15	15	50	03.33
19.	90I – 950	18	26	06	50	03.33
20.	951 – 1000	27	13	10	50	03.33
21.	1001 – 1050	15	25	10	50	03.33
22.	1051 – 1100	21	26	03	50	03.33
23.	1101 – 1150	24	16	19	50	03.33
24.	1151 – 1200	17	18	15	50	03.33
25.	1201 – 1250	25	15	10	50	03.33
26.	1251 – 1300	20	15	15	50	03.33
27.	1301 – 1350	25	13	12	50	03.33
28.	1351 – 1400	15	25	10	50	03.33
29.	1401 – 1450	25	15	10	50	03.33
30.	1451 – 1500	16	24	10	50	03.33
Total		614	557	329	1500	100.00
		40.90	37.10	21.90	100.00	

Table 6.4

Composition of Sex Groups of the Sample

S. No.	*Respondents Cluster No.*	*Male*	*Female*	*Total No.*	*Percentage*
1.	01 – 50	26	24	50	03.33
2.	51 – 100	25	25	50	03.33
3.	101 – 150	25	25	50	03.33
4.	151 – 200	25	25	50	03.33
5.	201 – 250	25	25	50	03.33
6.	251 – 300	29	21	50	03.33
7.	301 – 350	26	24	50	03.33
8.	351 – 400	25	25	50	03.33
9.	401 – 450	25	25	50	03.33
10.	451 – 500	25	25	50	03.33
11.	501 – 550	25	25	50	03.33
12.	551 – 600	25	25	50	03.33
13.	601 – 650	26	24	50	03.33
14.	651 – 700	28	22	50	03.33
15.	701 – 750	30	20	50	03.33
16.	750 – 800	26	24	50	03.33
17.	801 – 850	25	25	50	03.33
18.	851 – 900	25	25	50	03.33
19.	901 – 950	31	19	50	03.33
20.	951 – 1000	25	25	50	03.33
21.	1001 – 1050	25	25	50	03.33
22.	1051 – 1100	25	25	50	03.33
23.	1101 – 1150	26	24	50	03.33
24.	1151 – 1200	29	21	50	03.33

25.	1201 – 1250	25	25	50	03.33
26.	1251 – 1300	25	25	50	03.33
27.	1301 – 1350	25	25	50	03.33
28.	1351 – 1400	26	24	50	03.33
29.	1401 – 1450	28	22	50	03.33
30.	1451 – 1500	26	24	50	03.33
	TOTAL	782	718	1500	100.00
		52.13	47.80	100.00	

Table 6.5

Marital Status of the Respondents of the Sample

S.No.	*Respondents Cluster no.*	*Married*	*Unmarried*	*Total No.*	*Percentage*
1.	01 – 50	30	20	50	03.33
2.	51 – 100	31	19	50	03.33
3.	101 – 150	26	24	50	03.33
4.	151 – 200	24	26	50	03.33
5.	201 – 250	28	22	50	03.33
6.	251 – 300	32	18	50	03.33
7.	301 – 350	30	20	50	03.33
8.	351 – 400	31	19	50	03,33
9.	401 – 450	31	19	50	03.33
10.	451 – 500	30	20	50	03.33
11.	501 – 550	36	14	50	03.33
12.	551 – 600	34	16	50	03.33
13.	601 – 650	26	24	50	03.33
14.	651 – 700	25	25	50	03.33

15.	701 – 750	26	24	50	03.33
16.	751 – 800	25	25	50	03.33
17.	801 – 850	25	25	50	03.33
18.	851 – 900	26	24	50	03.33
19.	901 – 950	31	19	50	03.33
20.	951 – 1000	27	23	50	03.33
21.	1001 – 1050	28	22	50	03.33
22.	1051 – 1100	32	18	50	03.33
23.	1101 – 1150	28	22	50	03.33
24.	1151 – 1200	27	23	50	03.33
25.	1201 – 1250	26	24	50	03.33
26.	1251 – 1300	33	17	50	03.33
27.	1301 – 1350	30	20	50	03.33
28.	1351 – 1400	31	19	50	03.33
29.	1401 – 1450	27	23	50	03.33
30.	1451 – 1500	19	31	50	03.33
	Total	855	645	1500	100.00
		57.00	43.00	100.00	

Table 6.6

Literacy Status of Respondents of the Sample

S.No.	*Respondents Cluster No.*	*Literate*	*Illiterate*	*Total No.*	*Percentage*
1.	01 – 50	32	18	50	03.33
2.	51 – 100	36	14	50	03.33
3.	101 – 150	32	18	50	03.33
4.	151 – 200	30	20	50	03.33

5.	201 – 250	34	16	50	03.33
6.	251 – 300	34	16	50	03.33
7.	301 – 350	32	18	50	03.33
8.	351 – 400	36	14	50	03.33
9.	401 – 450	36	14	50	03.33
10.	451 – 500	30	20	50	03.33
11.	501 – 550	36	14	50	03.33
12.	551 – 600	30	20	50	03.33
13.	601 – 650	24	26	50	03.33
14.	651 – 700	30	20	50	03.33
15.	701 – 750	29	21	50	03.33
16.	751 – 800	30	20	50	03.33
17.	801 – 850	26	24	50	03.33
18.	851 – 900	24	26	50	03.33
19.	901 – 950	37	13	50	03.33
20.	951 – 1000	41	09	50	03.33
21.	1001 – 1050	34	16	50	03.33
22.	1051 – 1100	41	09	50	03.33
23.	1101 – 1150	34	16	50	03.33
24.	1151 – 1200	44	06	50	03.33
25.	1201 – 1250	35	15	50	03.33
26.	1251 – 1300	25	25	50	03.33
27.	1301 – 1350	25	25	50	03.33
28.	1351 – 1400	30	20	50	03.33
29.	1401 – 1450	26	24	50	03.33
30.	1451 – 1500	20	30	50	03.33
Total		951	549	1500	100.00
		63.40	36.60	100.00	

Table 6.7

Rural/Urban Status of Respondents of the Sample

S.No.	*Respondents Cluster No.*	*Rural Area*	*Urban Area*	*Total No.*	*Percentage*
1.	01 – 50	34	16	50	03.33
2.	51 – 100	44	06	50	03.33
3.	101 – 150	30	20	50	03.33
4.	151 – 200	30	20	50	03.33
5.	201 – 250	14	36	50	03.33
6.	251 – 300	39	11	50	03.33
7.	301 – 350	34	16	50	03.33
8.	351 – 400	44	06	50	03.33
9.	401 – 450	44	06	50	03.33
10.	451 – 500	40	10	50	03.33
11.	501 – 550	43	07	50	03.33
12.	551 – 600	40	10	50	03.33
13.	601 – 650	30	20	50	03.33
14.	651 – 700	15	35	50	03.33
15.	701 – 750	17	33	50	03.33
16.	750 – 800	44	06	50	03.33
17.	801 – 850	35	15	50	03.33
18.	851 – 900	31	19	50	03.33
19.	901 – 950	33	17	50	03.33
20.	951 – 1000	26	24	50	03.33
21.	1001 – 1050	14	36	50	03.33
22.	1051 – 1100	25	25	50	03.33
23.	1101 – 1150	40	10	50	03.33
24.	1151 – 1200	37	13	50	03.33

25.	1201 – 1250	37	13	50	03.33
26.	1251 – 1300	30	20	50	03.33
27.	1301 – 1350	35	15	50	03.33
28.	1351 – 1400	30	20	50	03.33
29.	1401 – 1450	38	12	50	03.33
30.	1451 – 1500	34	16	50	03.33
	Total	987	513	1500	100.00
		65.80	34.20	100.00	

After formulation of the questionnaire, the investigators were trained in detail about filling questionnaires in the field, so that originality and specificity of responses was recorded properly and completely. The trained investigators of this survey were 30 M.A. final students of Department of Sociology of University of Kashmir. In fact, they had opted for this course for which they were guided, supervised, evaluated and graded.

The detailed fieldwork for this survey was carried out for a period of five months from June 2007 to October 2007 as per the 'field action plan'. According to this plan, the entire research for this survey among all 1500 respondents of the sample was carried out in 30 equal clusters of respondents. While each cluster composed of 50 respondents, each investigator surveyed 50 respondents. In totality, 30 investigators carried out scientific investigation among 1500 respondents who belonged to varied sociological categories. As they were trained in advance, researchers selected these particular groups of respondents on the basis of sociological criteria of age, sex, income, literacy, marital status and rural/urban status. In this way, the sample of respondents was made reflective, realistic, relevant and representative.

After statistical data was collected in the field, it was aggregated and tabulated at the cluster average and total average levels. The tables were made on the basis of main themes of the survey. Subsequently, these tables were explained, interpreted and conclusions drawn scientifically and sociologically.

3. FINDINGS OF THE SURVEY

3.1.1. **Average Age/Desirable Age of Marriage:** Every society decides about a particular age at which its young members are supposed to marry. In a way, it may be characterized as 'desirable age of marriage' for men and women. But, to certain factors, marriage of men and women do not take place at desirable age but occurs at a later stage which may be characterized as 'actual age of marriage'. In this context, we enquired from respondents about actual and desirable age of marriage for men as well as women. The response they showed has been included in the following table:

Table 6.8

Actual and Desirable Age of Marriage

S.No.	*Respondents Cluster No.*	*Actual Age of Marriage*		*Desirable Age of Marriage*	
		Males	*Females*	*Males*	*Females*
1.	01 – 50	32	28	22	19
2.	51 – 100	23	21	18	16
3.	101 – 150	33	29	25	23
4.	151 – 200	29	25	23	21
5.	201 – 250	34	31	25	22
6.	251 – 300	32	27	25	21
7.	301 – 350	33	26	24	21
8.	351 – 400	30	28	22	20
9.	401 – 450	23	21	18	16
10.	451 – 500	32	28	25	21
11.	501 – 550	31	29	24	21
12.	551 – 600	33	29	25	23
13.	601 – 650	35	31	25	22
14.	651 – 700	36	30	24	20
15.	701 – 750	39	29	24	21

16.	751 – 800	30	28	22	20
17.	801 – 850	32	28	26	22
18.	851 – 900	37	31	28	24
19.	901 – 950	31	28	23	20
20.	951 – 1000	30	26	24	21
21.	1001 – 1050	34	31	24	21
22.	1051 – 1100	27	25	25	19
23.	1101 – 1150	34	31	24	21
24.	1151 – 1200	31	27	23	20
25.	1201 – 1250	32	28	24	22
26.	1251 – 1300	33	31	22	19
27.	1301 – 1350	35	30	24	22
28.	1351 – 1400	26	24	24	21
29.	1401 – 1450	34	30	23	18
30.	1451 – 1500	30	26	24	21
Total No. of responses		946	835	709	621
Average age of marriage		31.53	27.83	23.63	20.70

The above details clearly show the following 'age of marriage' for males and females on an average:

[i]	Actual age of marriage	Males	31.53 years
		Females	27.83 years
[ii]	Desirable age of marriage	Males	23.63 years
		Females	20.70 years.

3.2 ***Major Causes of Late Marriage:*** The survey revealed that there were five major factors which led to emergence of late marriage in the Kashmir valley. These factors were

[i] Acute poverty	865/1500	[57.66%] respondents
[ii] Increasing unemployment	840/1500	[56.00%] respondents
[iii] Dowry in different shapes	840/1500	[56.00%] respondents

[iv] Attain. Modern education 470/1500 [31.33%] respondents

[v] Present conflict situation 243/1500 [15.60%] respondents

Other minor factors which contributed to the emergence of late marriage in Kashmir included the following factors:

[i]	Illiteracy	98/1500	[06.53%] respondents
[ii]	Modernization impact	98/1500	[06.53%] respondents
[iii]	Health abnormality	71/1500	[04.73%] respondents
[iv]	Customs and traditions	65/1500	[04.33%] respondents
[v]	Caste consideration	64/1500	[04.26%] respondents
[vi]	Search for proper match	55/1500	[03.66%] respondents
[vii]	Irreligious attitudes and behaviour	46/1500	[03.06%] respondents
[viii]	Preference for employed woman	25/1500	[01.66%] respondents
[ix]	Developing professional	24/1500	[01.66%] respondents
[x]	Love affairs/illegal sex relations	23/1500	[01.53%] respondents
[xi]	Huge marriage expenditure	23/1500	[01.53%] respondents
[xii]	Generation gap	22/1500	[01.46%] respondents
[xiii]	Ignorance-innocence	18/1500	[01.20%] respondents
[xiv]	Inflation in the market	15/1500	[01.00%] respondents

3.3. Consequences of Late Marriage: The survey made an investigation about short-term and long-term implications of the late marriage phenomenon on the individuals and society at large. The respondents identified the following impacts:

[i]	Decrease in population	365/1500	[24.33%] respondents
[ii]	Various forms of mental depression	361/1500	[24.06%] respondents
[iii]	Increase in suicide rate	295/1500	[19.66%] respondents
[iv]	Encouragement to immoral activities	182/1500	[12.13%] respondents

[v] Pre-marital sex relations 157/1500 [10.46%] respondents

The respondents also identified the following minor consequences of the emergence of late marriage in Kashmir:

[i] Abnormal child birth 148/1500 [09.86%] respondents

[ii] Lack of child care 143/1500 [09.53%] respondents

[iii] Increase in crimes/ social deviance 137/1500 [09.13%] respondents

[iv] Frustration of the youth 90/1500 [06.00%] respondents

[v] Disturbed social-family life 67/1500 [04.46%] respondents

[vi] Age gap between parents and children 59/1500 [03.93%] respondents

[vii] Sex scandals 47/1500 [03.13%] respondents

[viii] Tension among the youth 44/1500 [02.93%] respondents

[ix] Increase in divorces 41/1500 [02.73%] respondents

[x] Family problems-instability 38/1500 [02.53%] respondents

[xi] Girls remained unmarried 37/1500 [02.46%] respondents

[xii] Imbalanced sex ratio 26/1500 [01.73%] respondents

[xiii] Drug addiction 22/1500 [01.46%] respondents

[xiv] Alienation 18/1500 [01.20%] respondents

3.4. Modern Education and Late Marriage: There is general belief that attainment of modern education especially at higher level and in technical-professional fields takes a long time. So, men and women involved in this process usually experienced late marriage in their lives.This basic proposition was confirmed in this survey as about 85.00% respondents agreed when they were asked to explain this response. They gave responses in following ways:

[i] Modern education is time-taking 875/1500 [58.33%] respondents

[ii]	Educated people wait for proper job	203/1500	[13.53%] respondents
[iii]	Educated people face competition of .jobs	83/1500	[05.53%] respondents
[iv]	Edu. People search for equal edu. Partner	60/1500	[04.00%] respondents
[v]	Edu. People desire for employed spouse	48/1500	[03.20%] respondents
[vi]	Edu. People deviate from tradi. & religi.	27/1500	[01.80%] respondents
[vii]	Rational thinking compels them for l. marr.	25/1500	[01.65%] respondents

However, about 15.00% respondents revealed that attainment of modern education does not contribute directly to emergence of late marriage. Though this seems a correct statement, modern education does not contribute solely to this phenomenon. This response reflects essentially the emphasis on the role of other contributing factors such as poverty, unemployment and other personal problems.

3.5. Poverty and Late Marriage: The general belief in Kashmir is that poverty in all possibilities leads to the emergence of late marriage among poor sections of society. In this survey, about **88.00%** of respondents upheld that when poor people are not in a position to pay for necessary expenses of marriage, it automatically gets delayed. When we asked them to provide the rationale for this argument, the by made the statements which follow:

[i]	Poor girls can never pay dowry	566/1500	[37.73%] respondents
[ii]	Lack of financial resources for marriage	388/1500	[25.86%] respondents
[iii]	Lot of expenditure on marriage ceremony	305/1500	[20.33%] respondents
[iv]	Poor girls are not preferred in marriages at all	155/1500	[10.33%] respondents

[v]	Illiteracy of girls	61/1500	[04.06%] respondents
[vi]	Non-fulfillment of demands by girls family	59/1500	[03.93%] respondents
[vii]	parents arrange money somehow	55/1500	[03.66%] respondents
[viii]	argument that poor girls cannot maintain family	35/1500	[02.33%] respondents
[ix]	simple barrier to a good marriage	32/1500	[02.13 %] respondents

3.6. Conflict Situation and Late Marriage: As the fact stands, conflict situation in Kashmir had certainly contributed to the emergence of late marriage. An overwhelming majority of 88.00% respondents in this survey gave this opinion. When they were asked to provide the rationale for this opinion, they conveyed the following views:

[i]	Youth was involved/killed during conflict situation	274/1500	[14.13 %] respondents
[ii]	Conflict created sex imbalance in marriage market	274/1500	[14.13 %] respondents
[iii]	Death of the sole earning member of the family	200/1500	[13.33 %] respondents
[iv]	Conflict created unemployment and poverty	169/1500	[11.26 %] respondents
[v]	Threat and involvement in militancy	122/1500	[08.13 %] respondents
[vi]	Avoidance of militancy related families	77/1500	[05.13 %] respondents
[vii]	Migration to outside state for several reasons	61/1500	[04.06 %] respondents
[viii]	Conflict created insecurity of life in the valley	48/1500	[03.20 %] respondents
[ix]	Conflict often disturbed family functions	32/1500	[01.40 %] respondents

However, 12.00% respondents in this survey opined that conflict situation was not directly responsible for the phenomenon of delayed marriage in Kashmir. This response essentially conveys two points. First, conflict situation was not the sole determining factor for delayed marriages in the valley. Second, there were other factors equally important in the broader social dynamics which played their respective roles in the emergence of late marriage in the valley.

3.7. Dowry and Late Marriage: As is a known fact, dowry has played certain negative role towards normal marriage in Kashmir. It has created numerous problems for individuals and problems. One such problem created by dowry was late marriage which could not be avoided in a situation in which dowry demands were made by the groom's side. These views were also conveyed by about 92.00% of respondents. When they were asked to explain these views, they made the following points:

[i]	Poor families can never afford to pay dowry	822/1500	[54.80%] respondents
[ii]	Many males refuse to marry without getting dowry	106/1500	[07.06%] respondents
[iii]	Dowry proved a barrier to early marriage	88/1500	[05.86%] respondents
[iv]	Girls feel inferior if they don't get dowry	86/1500	[05.73%] respondents
[v]	Unemployed girls could never pay even little dowry	48/1500	[03.20%] respondents
[vi]	Dowry has made marriage a commercial affair	42/1500	[02.80%] respondents
[vii]	Money-collection for dowry a time-consuming affair	37/1500	[02.46%] respondents
[viii]	Dowry as a customary practice to be followed	36/1500	[02.40%] respondents
[ix]	Non-payment of dowry leads to suicides by girls	28/1500	[01.86%] respondents

[x]	Difficult to find a 'good family' not demanding dowry	26/1500	[01.73%] respondents
[xi]	Harassment of girls in case they don't pay any dowry	25/1500	[01.66%] respondents
[xii]	Non-payment of dowry leads to girls depression	24/1500	[01.65%] respondents
[xiii]	Poor girls wait for long time to get dowry-less marriage	23/1500	[01.53%] respondents
[xiv]	Those who don't pay dowry are often poor and illiterate	10/1500	[00.66%] respondents
[xv]	Non-payment of dowry may lead to divorce	10/1500	[00.66%] respondents

3.8. Unemployment and Late Marriage: It has been generally established that increasing unemployment hassled to the emergence of late marriage in Kashmir. About 91.00% of respondents upheld this kind of opinion. This situation could not be controlled in any way. In this regard, when the respondents were probed further, they presented the following views:

[i]	Unemployed boys and girls were not considered good	408/1500	[27.20%] respondents
[ii]	Unemployed prefer to get jobs and then marry	352/1500	[27.20%] respondents
[iii]	Unemployed cannot take responsibility of the family	141/1500	[09.40%] respondents
[iv]	Unemployed girls cannot pay dowry to boy's family	128/1500	[08.53%] respondents
[v]	Unemployed cannot bear the expenditure of marriage	89/1500	[05.93%] respondents

[vi] Unemployed youth often remain disturbed 45/1500 [03.00%] respondents

[vii] Unemployed maintain poor economic status 40/1500 [02.66%] respondents

[viii] Unemployment creates insecurity among boys & girls 23/1500 [01.53%] respondents

However, 09.00% respondents presented the view that late marriage does not contribute directly to the rise of late marriage. In reality, they wanted to emphasize the role of other important factors responsible for emergence of late marriage.

3.9. ***Pre-marital Sex and Late Marriage:*** The survey revealed an inverse relationship between late marriage and practices of pre-marital and extra-marital relations among the most potent section of society, i. e. youth. In response to our question regarding consequences of late marriage on existing sex relations, 64.46% [976 out of 1500] respondents conveyed that it effected the pre-marital relations in particular. They cited following reasons in order to provide the rationale for their response:

[i] Since sex is a biological need, the youths want to satisfy the sexual needs 768/1500 [51.20%] respondents

[II] The sex control is not possible at all times, since it is at its peak at the younger age. 182.1500 [12.13%] respondents

[iii] There is clear deviation from religious values and there is lack of moral knowledge. 29/1500 [01.93%] respondents.

At the same time, 219/1500 [14.60%] respondents conveyed that the increasing practice of late marriage has led to extra-marital relationship, especially among elder and married sections of society. They quoted more or less same reasons as referred in the preceding case.

3.10. ***Local Culture and Late Marriage:*** Every culture necessarily influences the patterns of marriage. So is the case with Kashmiri society. In response to our question 'whether local culture has influenced late marriage in Kashmir', 840/1500 [56.00%] respondents conveyed 'yes' in their reply. The reasons they put forward were as follows:

[i] People generally imitate the practice of late marriage without considering its consequences. 413/1500 [27.53%] respondents

[ii] The traditional 'wazwan' has becomeunaffordable for many people. 110/1500 [07.33%] respondents

[iii] Unnecessary customs and rituals which discourage early/timely marriage 185/1500 [12/.33%] respondents

[iv] Common demand of dowry by boy's family which necessarily leads to late marriage 168/1500 [11.20%] respondents

[v] Changing culture fails to determine timely marriage 84/1500 [05.60%] respondents

[vi] Rich people encourage late marriage and encourage others to follow this practice. 44/1500 [02.93%] respondents

On the other hand, 326/1500 [21.37%] respondents gave the opinion that local culture has not in any way encouraged late marriage. They gave following reasons for their response:

[i] Our culture demands early-timely marriage, especially of girls. 108/1500 [07.20%] respondents

[ii] Since culture and religion are interrelated, they cannot favour emergence of late marriage. 89/1500 [05.93%] respondents

[iii] Culture has nothing to do with late marriage 44/1500 [02.93%] respondents

[iv] Culture discourages late marriage. 21/1500 [01.40%] respondents

[v] It happens mainly due to false prestige. 14/1500 [00.93%] respondents

3.11. ***Late Marriage and Role of Religion:*** In this empirical survey, the important question about role of religion vis-à-vis iate marriage was asked from the respondents. The dominant response to this question was conveyed that religion has not encouraged late marriage among its followers. It has rather discouraged it for latent and manifest reasons. When we probed among respondents as how religion discouraged late marriage, 1059/1500 [70.60%] respondents said that it [religion] emphasized early marriage in all possibilities and in all situations. Further, 45/1500 [03.00%] respondents opined that religion discouraged late marriage because the early marriage stops individual and society from many social evils. These responses were recorded despite the fact that late marriage has emerged as a significant type of marriage in the present-day Kashmiri society. It follows that religion is not followed strictly in this society. On the other hand, only 53/1500 [03.53%] respondents said that religion encouraged late marriage. But, they had neither theoretical nor practical justification in this regard.

3.12. ***Late Marriage and Marriage Practices:*** It has been observed in this survey that emergence of late marriage in Kashmir has certainly effected the existing patters and practices of marriage. It was recorded that while hyper-gamy was effected in the case of 571/1500 [38.06%] respondents, late marriage had also effected in 132/1500 [08.80%] hypo-gamous cases. Again, 442/1500 [29.46%] respondents reported the influence of late marriage on endogamy and by 137/1500 [09.13%] respondents on the exogamous marriages. While 280/1500 [18.66%] respondents conveyed the influence on polygamous marriages, 129/1500 [08.60%] on monogamous marriages. Lastly, late marriage had influenced considerably the practices related to patri-locality and matri-locality.

3.13. ***Problems of Late Marriage:*** In the social dynamics related to emergence of late marriage, several problems cropped up and created serious difficulties for concerned individuals and families. In the survey, they reported the following problems:

[i] Mental depression and other psychological problems 363/1500 [24.20%] respondents

[ii]	Population decrease and infertility at large	308/1500	[20.53%] respondents
[iii]	Pre-marital sex relations	240/1500	[16.00%] respondents
[iv]	Increase in suicide rate	170/1500	[11.33%] respondents
[v]	Late child birth with associated problems	161/1500	[10.73%] respondents
[vi]	Increase in immoral and vulgar activities	124/1500	[08.26%] respondents
[vii]	Post-marital discard in the family	111/1500	[07.40%] respondents
[viii]	Rise of particular diseases among children and elders	91/1500	[06.60%] respondents
[ix]	Generation gap widened within family	91/1500	[06.60%] respondents
[x]	Increase in crimes and divorces	89/1500	[05.93%] respondents
[xi]	Increase in drug addiction	88/1500	[05.86%] respondents
[xii]	Sex scandals and social disorders	70/1500	[04.66%] respondents
[xiii]	Lesser child care in the parental family	56/1500	[03.73%] respondents
[xiv]	Cronic family tensions	40/1500	[02.66%] respondents
[xv]	Health problems of the couple	24/1500	[01.60%] respondents
[xvi]	Rise in materialistic views	12/1500	[00.80%] respondents

3.14. ***Modernization and Late Marriage:*** The emergence of late marriage had direct relationship with the process of modernization. In fact, there seemed necessary social impact of modernization on marriage practices. So it happened in Kashmiri society too. In our enquiry about late marriage and modernization, we recorded the following responses:

[i]	Modernization emphasized higher education	298/1500	[19.86%] respondents
[ii]	Modernization cautioned		

	about ill effects of late marriage	103/1500	[06.86%] respondents
[iii]	Modernization gave human life the materialistic outlook	97/1500	[06.46%] respondents
[iv]	Modernization changed traditional ideals of marriage	94/1500	[06.26%] respondents
[v]	Modernization encouraged late marriage	73/1500	[04.86%] respondents
[vi]	Modernization followed new fashions of life	71/1500	[04.73%] respondents
[vii]	Modernization Led to deviation from religion	64/1500	[04.26%] respondents
[viii]	Moderrnization Created competitive and complex life	62/1500	[04.13%] respondents
[ix]	Moderrnization Gave career orientation	47/1500	[03.13%] respondents
[x]	Moderrnization Created lust for money	46/1500	[03.06%] respondents
[xi]	It took long time for career-making of the life-mate	43/1500	[02,86%] respondents
[xii]	Usually men want highly qualified wife	26/1500	[01.73%] respondents
[xiii]	Modernization encouraged pre-marital sex relationship	20/1500	[01.33%] respondents
[xiv]	Self-choice marriage goes up and up	11/1500	[00.73%] respondents
[xv]	Media impact encouraged late marriage	10/1500	[00.66%] respondents

3.15. ***Self Choice Marriage and Late Marriage:*** It was observed in the survey that self-choice marriage does and does not lead to late marriage. In the former case, 625/1500 [41.66%] respondents maintained that self-choice marriage necessarily led to late marriage. The reasons they cited included their self-choice to marry at a particular time [31.86%], wait for a suitable match [10.33%] and attainment of education and employment [01.73%] .

On the other hand, 456/1500 [30.40%] respondents conveyed their opinion that self-choice marriage does not necessarily lead to late marriage for the following reasons:

[i]	Lovers choice generally led to early marriage	234/1500	[15.60%] respondents
[ii]	Self-choice marriage stood for a time-bound matter	44/1500	[02.93%] respondents
[iii]	Self-choice mates hardly took care for customs	32/1500	[02.13%] respondents
[iv]	Mates don't faced the problem of dowry	23/1500	[01.53%] respondents

3.16. ***Suggestions about Late Marriage:*** In continuation of the topic of problems of late marriage, the respondents in this survey stressed for the consideration of serious and relevant suggestions. Some of these are noted below:

[i]	There must be legal restrictions or complete ban on dowry	374/1500	[24.93%] respondents
[ii]	Parents must arrange timely marriages of children	275/1500	[18.40%] respondents
[iii]	Children must follow religion seriously and strictly	265/1500	[17.66%] respondents
[iv]	Employment must be provided to marriageable youth	207/1500	[13.80%] respondents
[v]	Marriages must be made less expensive and affordable	94/1500	[06.26%] respondents
[vi]	Awareness campaign against ill effects of late marriage	87/1500	[05.80%] respondents
[vii]	Undesirable customs abolished and guest control introduced	70/1500	[04.66%] respondents
[viii]	Marriages made simple.	65/1500	[04.33%] respondents
[ix]	Religion must be followed in all marriage matters	48/1500	[03.20%] respondents

[x] Education to females even after marriage	40/1500	[02.66%] respondents
[xi] Necessary changes in customs, attitudes and behaviour	38/1500	[02.53%] respondents
[xii] Poverty must be eradicated through all means	33/1500	[02.20%] respondents
[xiii] Population education for the youth	64/1500	[04.26%] respondents

4. **Conclusions:** The following conclusions may be drawn from preceding findings of the survey:

[a] The practice of late marriage has been established in the Kashmiri society. The actual and desirable age of marriage was as follows;

- Actual age of marriage	Males	31.53 years
	Females	27.83 years
- Desirable age of marriage	Males	23.63 years
	Females	20.70 years

[b] The five major causes of late marriage in Kashmir identified by respondents were:

- Acute poverty;
- Increasing unemployment;
- Practice of dowry;
- Attainment of modern education;
- Prevailing conflict situation.

[c] The five major consequences of late marriage were identified as follows:

- Decrease in population at family level;
- Mental depression;
- Increase in suicide rate;
- Encouragement to immoral activities;
- Pre-marital sex relations.

[d] 85% respondents agreed with the proposition that attainment

of modern education has led to the emergence of late marriage among males and females.

[e] 88% respondents conveyed that poverty led to the emergence of late marriage, especially among poor groups and classes.

[f] 88% respondents revealed their opinion that conflict situation in Kashmir had contributed to the rise of late marriage.

[g] 92% respondents upheld that emergence of late marriage could not be avoided in a situation in which dowry demands were made by the groom's family.

[h] 91% respondents revealed that unemployment in all cases contributed to the rise of late marriage in Kashmir.

[i] 65% respondents divulged the inverse relationship between late marriage and practices of pre-marital and extra-marital relations among the youth.

[j] While majority of 56% respondents felt that local culture has influenced late marriage in Kashmir, the rest felt that it had discouraged the practice.

[k] the dominant number of respondents was of the opinion that religion and Islam had not encouraged the late marriage, rather discouraged it for latent and manifest reasons.

[l] The late marriage effected in positive or negative way existing practices of hypergamy-hypogamy, polygamy-monogamy and patri-locality and matri-locality.

[m] Among important problems emerged due to late marriage included the following;

- Mental depression, infertility, pre-marital sex relations, increase in suicide rate, late child birth, increasing immorality and vulgarity, post-marital family discard, diseases among children and elders, generation gap, increase in deviance and crime, drug addiction, social disorders, and lesser child care in family.

[n] The process of modernization effected all practices of marriage, especially late marriage.

[o] The practice of self-choice marriage effected late marriage in 42% cases and not in 31% cases.

[p] Finally, respondents put forth following suggestions for solving problems created by late marriage:

- Complete ban or legal restriction on dowry,
- Parents arrange their children's marriage at proper age,
- Marriageable children follow religion seriously and strictly,
- Employment must be provided to all marriageable youth,
- Marriage must be made simple and affordable,
- Creating awareness about ill effects of late marriage,
- Undesirable customs must be rejected and abolished,
- Education to women even after marriage,
- Change in attitudes and behaviour,
- Poverty eradicated through all means and
- Population education for youth.

[II] PHENOMENON OF 'NEVER MARRIED' IN KASHIR

1. It has been observed sociologically that nature, pattern, practice and other features of marriage in the human society have been shaped by various socio-economic and other factors, in addition to natural and biological factors. At the same time, sociological studies have revealed that all marriage practices and patterns have undergone a significant degree of change as a result of implications of processes off change and development. Like other human societies in the world, the preceding propositions can be applied equally to the Kashmiri society. Thus, in an important study about marriages in the Kashmir valley, carried out by the author in 2008,[1] it revealed that 'late marriage' has emerged as a significant trend. According to this study, the average actual/desirable age of marriage for men and women was revealed as mentioned below:

[i]	Actual age of marriage	Males	31.53 years
		Females	27.87 years
[ii]	Desirable age of marriage	Males	23.63 years
		Females	20.70 years[2]

The survey identified the following major causes of late marriage:

[i]	Acute poverty	57.66%
[ii]	Increasing unemployment	56.00%
[iii]	Dowry in different forms	56.50%
[iv]	Attainment of higher education	31.33%
[v]	prevailing conflict situation	15.60%[3]

The survey also showed following major consequences of late marriage:

[i]	Decrease in household popu.	24.33%
[ii]	Mental depression	24.06%
[iii]	Increase in suicide rate	19.66%
[iv]	Emerging immoral activities	12.36%
[v]	Pre-marital sex relations	10.46%[4]

2. In the same way, in another survey about "Changing Marriage Practices in Kashmir" [report of the survey not published so far], it was revealed that following practices of marriage are in vogue in the Valley at present:

[i]	Monogamous marriage	89.10%
[ii]	Polygamous marriage	10.10%
	Pattern of Polygamy	
	- II wife	85.56%
	- III Wife	07.57%
	- IV Wife	05.96%
[iii]	Endogamy	45.35%
	Exogamy	54.80%
[iv]	Hyper-gamy	23.76%
	Hypo-gamy	16.11%
[v]	Patri-local	64.21%
	Matri-local	07.31%
	Neo-local	28.53%[5]

3. Similarly, the practice of "Never Married" represents a social

phenomenon which in all human societies, less in primitive societies and more in modern societies. In the demographic sense, it has a population dimension, i.e. it refers to a particular population group entitled as "Never Married"[6]. The composition of this group had definite implications for general population dynamics, fertility-mortality rates and marriage rates [which refers to a number of married persons in the total population].[7] It has been observed that this composition affects marriage-rates in some particular groups and areas. Accordingly, while migrants have generally lower marriage-rate due to their extreme degree of mobility, the low rate also figures in areas of conflict. Thus, this category of "never married" has certain set causes and consequences.[8] The perpetual armed conflict situation plays a negative role vis-à-vis marriages, i.e. it generally lowers the marriage –rate and, consequently, increases the number of "never married" persons. That has happened at different times, especially during war times, and in different places such as Bosnia and is now happening in the Indian state of Jammu and Kashmir. Though in these situations, normal demographic factors affect the composition of married people in total population, but the Constant conflict and migration has proved a determining factor in this regard.

4. Though actual figures about latest situation in J&K are not available, Census statistics of 2001 is Available which tells us about this situation in the preceding decade, i.e. 1990s.[9] According to this census, total number of "never married" and "married" persons in the state in 2001 was as follows:

Table 6.9

Number of Never-Married and Married Persons in J&K, 2001

S.No. Sex	*Never-Married*		*Married*	
	No.	*% of total pop.*	*No.*	*% of total pop.*
1. Persons	5,649,235	55.69	4,187,479	41.21

2. Male	3.099,875	54.87	2,161,741	51.62
3. Female	2,549,360	45.12	2,025,738	48.51

The distribution of these never-married and married persons in terms of age and sex was as reveals in the following table:

Table 6.10

Number of Never-Married and Married Persons in Terms of and Sex and Sex in J&K, 2001

S.No.	*Age Groups*	*Never-Married*		*Married*	
		Number	*% of total pop.*	*Number*	*% of total pop.*
1.	00-09	2,256,366	39.94	000	00.00
2.	10-14	1,332,333	23.58	26,642	00.60
3.	15-19	1,061,859	18.79	83,313	01.98
4.	20-24	581,596	10.29	304,317	07.26
5.	25-29	243,983	04.31	538,353	12.85
6.	30-34	71,710	01.26	615,882	14.70
7.	35-39	23,089	00.40	653,636	15.60
8.	40-44	11,163	00.20	511,090	12.20
9.	45-49	6,447	00.11	432,335	10.32
10.	50-54	4,951	00.08	308,157	07.35
11.	55-59	3,153	00.05	227,027	05.42
12.	60-64	5,091	00.09	191,673	04.56
13.	65-69	3,532	00.08	119,080	02.84
14.	70-74	5,219	00.09	84,120	02.00
15.	75-79	3,204	00.05	37,084	00.88
16.	80 +	4,022	00.07	41,597	00.91

The above tables clearly reveal that there existed a huge number of 'never-married' persons in J&K, i.e. 5,649,235 in 2001. This also reveals in all age groups, especially younger and elder age groups. It seems important to note here that these figures deal with the situation in the decade of 1990s and reported in 2001. Concerned experts feel that number and proportion of never-married persons must have increased significantly in unstable and conflict-ridden valley of Kashmir. Even the number and proportion of 'never-married' persons in 2001 in J&K was higher than the national average, which can be seen in the following table:

Table 6.11

Number of 'Never-Married' Persons in 2001, India and J&K

S.No.	*Census Unit*		*Persons*		*Male*	*Female*
	No.	*%*	*No.*	*%*	*No.*	*%*
1. India	512,667,639	49.84	289,619,359	54.42	223,048,280	44.92
2. J&K	5,649,235	55.69	3,099,875	54.87	2,549,360	45.22

The preceding table shows clearly that difference between the proportions of 'never-married' persons at the national and state levels. While it is higher in the case of J&K, i.e. 55.69%, it stands lower at the national level, i.e. 49.34%. In both cases of male and female proportions, it stands higher in the state than at the national level.

5. All three tables and following population developments reveal that proportion of 'never-married' persons has increased significantly in last two decades which has dangerous implications for overall balanced growth of population in J&K, especially the Kashmir province. While the normal demographic dynamics has led to this undesirable situation, it was equally contributed by conflict situation factor. In addition to moral, ethical, cultural and social implications, this increasing phenomenon has posed potential demographic threat to the local community. In this context, the local intelligentsia must respond to this alarming situation and must initiate the relevant efforts to restore credibility, applicability and respectability to the practice of marriage at the household and societal levels.

[III] RISE OF DISABILITY IN J&K

AN ANALYSIS OF DISABILITY IN J&K

[1] *Disability:* The term "disability" generally refers to "the people with a permanent illness or injury that makes it difficult for them to move part of their body completely or easily." These people are also known as "handicapped". [see *New Oxford Advanced Learners Dictionary, 2009, Oxford*] In other words, it essentially implies loss or lack of functioning, either physical or mental, such as blindness, paralysis or mental abnormality-which unlike illness, is usually permanent. It has been observed that "disability" is generally 'stigmatizing' and thus need personal, social and financial support from the society. The "disability" has a population dimension too. It follows that a group of population becomes 'defunct functionally' and effect social and population growth in the society. Moreover, it needs specific and focused programmes and schemes and liberal financial allocations to fulfill basic needs of these people.

[2] *Total Number of Disabled Persons:* Like other developing countries, the society in J&K state too face the situation of disability. According to *Census of India, 2001,* the state had following number of disabled persons:

Table 6.12

Total Number of Disabled Persons in J&K, 2001 [Male-female and rural-urban]

S.No.	*Sex*	*Total*	*Rural*	*Urban*
1.	Persons	302,670	229,718	72,952
2.	Males	171,816	129,443	42,373
3.	Females	130,853	100,275	30,579

Source: Census of India, 2001.

It may be mentioned here that there must have been the experience of significant increase in disabilities in J&K even in normal conditions in the last decade. The added dynamic factor to this situation in the state was the militancy conditions which, in all possibilities, gave rise to a huge number of such cases. In the context of these normal and abnormal conditions, unofficial and informal sources reveal that the number of disabled in J&K during last one decade has doubled. The details in this regard are given in the following table:

Table 6.13

Total Number of Disabled Persons in J&K, 2009

S.No.	*Sex*	*Total*	*Rural*	*Urban*
1.	Total	605,340	459,436	145,904
2.	Males	343,632	258,886	84,746
3.	Females	261,708	200,550	61,158

Source: Calculated estimates based on Census of India, 2001.

[3] *Types of Disability:* According to the *Census of India, 2001*, the following types of disability prevailed in the state in that year:

Table 6.14

Types of Disability in J&K, 2001

S.No.	*Type*	*Total*	*Males*	*Females*
1.	Total Disabled	302,670	171,816	130,854
2.	Dis. In seeing	208,713	116,034	92,679
3.	Dis. In speech	16,956	9,748	7,208
4.	Dis. In hearing	14,157	7,693	6,464
5.	Dis. In movement	37,965	23,312	14,653
6.	Mental Disability	24,879	15,029	9,850

Source: Census of India, 2001.

Though these figures [in columns 1-4] cannot be challenged for the decade ending 2001, the figures about movement and mental disability seem underscored. This is more correct about the figures which may come up about the decade following 2001. It is solely because of prevalence of armed conflict in the Kashmir region and its physical and psychological implications in the last decade.

It was in this background that while general hospitals received exceptionally higher number of 'movement disabilities', the sole psychiatric hospital in Kashmir experienced unusual rush of mental health patients.

The local experts in the field revealed in the recent years that one out of every 6-7 Kashmiris face one or the other psychological problem/s seriously.

[4] *Disability and Literacy Status:* As per the figures of 2001 census, the literacy status of disabled in J&K was as shown in the following table:

Table 6.15

Number of Disabled Persons and their Literacy Status in J&K, 2001

S.No.	*Type of disability*	*Literate*	*Illiterate*
1.	Total disabled persons	121,162	181,508
2.	Dis. in seeing	93,228	115,485
3.	Dis. in speech	3,825	13,131
4.	Dis. in hearing	2,959	11,198
5.	Dis. in movement	13,362	24,206
6.	Mental Disability	7,788	17,091

Source: Census of India, 2001.

[5] *Disability and Economic Status:* The economic status [in terms of income and economic activity] of the disabled differ considerably. The state of J&K had handicapped persons with economic activities in 2001 as mentioned in the following table:

Table 6.16

Number of Disabled Persons with Economic Status in J&K, 2001

	Total	*C.L.*	*A.L.*	*H.H.I.*	*Others*	
1. Persons	103,716	45,606	7,718	6,567	43,825	198,954
2. Seeing	76,425	31,922	5,559	4,822	34,125	132,285
3. Speech	5,622	2,960	521	361	1,780	71,334
4. Hearing	5,103	3,008	410	314	1,371	9,054
5. Movement	9,564	4,577	561	613	3,813	28,401
6. Mental	6,999	3,139	667	457	2,736	17,680

Source: Census of India, 2001.

In both preceding tables, the upward trend of disabled persons in the state must have been experienced in the decade following 2001, while the literacy rate, especially in rural areas and among lower-female groups did not increase significantly, more and more people faced downward trend in their income. Both these trends among the disabled in J&K in the last decade have been observed by many experts.

[6] *Disability: Comparison with Other States:* It seems highly realistic and purposeful to analyse this statistics in tables 6.16 in the comparative framework, i.e. comparison with the situation at national level and other states level. This will reveal the real nature of existing reality in this regard. The number and distribution of disabled at the country level and state level is mentioned in the following table for comparison:

Table 6.17

Number and Distribution of Disabled at National and State-JK Levels, 2001

S.No.	*Disabled popula*	*India*		*J&K*	
		Number	*Percentage of the total*	*Number*	*Percentage of the total*
1	Total	21,906,769	2.12	302,670	3.00

2 Males	12,605,635	2.36	171,816	3.24
3 Females	9,301,134	1.87	130,854	2.74

Source: Calculated figures based on Census of India, 2001.

At the same time, it seems realistic to compare the disability scene in J&K with other relevant states of India, i.e. Panjab [which also face the militancy situation in 1980s], Himachal Pradesh [which shares the hilly and demographic character with J&K], and Chandigarh [a relatively stable and peaceful area]. This comparison reflects in the following table:

Table 6.18

Disability Situation in J&K, Punjab, Himachal Pradesh and Chandigarh

S.No.	*Population*	*J&K [No. &%]*	*PUNJAB [No. & %]*	*H.P. [No. & %]*	*Chandigarh [No. & %]*
1.	Total	302,673 [3.00]	424,523 [1.74]	155,950 [2.56]	15,538 [1.72]
2.	Males	171,816 [3.24]	252,856 [1.95]	90,444 [2.93]	9,538 [1.87]
3.	Females	130,854 [2.74]	171,647 [1.52]	65,506 [2.19]	6,000 [1.53]

Source: Calculated figures based on Census of India, 2001.

The table 6.18 clearly reveals the lowest percentage of disabled at the national level, i.e. 2.12% and highest in the case of J&K, i.e. 3.00%. In the case of males-females too, the percentage was higher in J&K [i.e. 3.24% and 2.74%] in comparison to national average, i.e. 2.36% and 1.87%. These features of disabled in J&K can be explained in terms of population dynamics and intrinsic traits in the state. But, at the same time, the situation of armed conflict and its physical implications has also contributed to this highest degree of disability.

The table 6.18 also reveals highest percentage of disability in J&K and lower/lowest percentage in other states/union territories in India. While Panjab [which also faced militancy situation during 1980s] had 1.74% disabled population, Himachal Pradesh [which shares the hilly and other demographic characteristics with J&K] had 2.56% in

2001. At the same time, the union territory of Chandigarh [which had comparatively lesser impact of armed conflict] had only 1.72% of such population. Same is the case with disability in both sexes in these states. These levels of disability can be explained in terms of contributing factors which include dietary inputs, health profile, hereditary reasons and so on. But, the highest levels of disability in J&K can be explained in terms of militancy situation, especially in the increasing cases of movement disability and mental disability.

[7] *Districtwise Comparison of Disability:* It will prove beneficial and realistic if we study disability situation in the inter-district context. This situation is portrayed in the following table:

Table 6.19

District-wise Disability Situation in J&K, 2001

S.No.	*District*	*Total*	*Rural Persons*	*Urban*	*Percentage of total*
1.	Kupwara	20,809	19,821	988	3.25
2	Baramulla	45,152	37,013	8,139	3.86
3.	Srinagar	34,844	7,255	27,589	2.81
4.	Badgam	15,316	13,574	1,742	2.58
5.	Pulwama	16,003	14,375	1,628	2.53
6.	Anantnag	30,781	26,813	3,968	2.63
7.	Leh	2,717	2,228	489	2.31
8.	Kargil	2,892	2,577	315	2.51
9.	Doda	22,743	21,527	1,216	3.29
10.	Udhampur	22,183	19,137	3,046	3.00
11.	Poonch	14,130	13,118	1,012	3.80
12.	Rajouri	15,119	14,409	710	3.15
13.	Jammu	47,514	29,969	20,545	3.02
14.	Kathua	12,467	10,902	1,565	2.30

Source: Census of India, 2001.

This comprehensive table reveals the following relevant points:

[i] The border districts in J&K state face extreme form of disability. Thus, Baramulls and Poonch districts had 3.87% and 3.80% cases. Other districts which followed this trend included Doda [3.29%], Kupwara [3.25%], Rajouri [3.15%] and Jammu [3.02%]. Other districts in the state experienced below 3.00% disability.

[ii] During the last one decade, the state faced extreme form of violence in Kashmir and Jammu provinces. So, there is every possibility of heavy increase in the injured persons. Consequently, this had led to highest level of disabled persons. This will certainly reflect in the next census to be carried out in 2011.

[iii] Males have generally higher proportion in disabled proportion than their counterparts in the state. But, in the case of J&K, males have highest proportion among disabled. This can also be related to the violence in J&K.

[iv] Rural areas have generally higher percentage of disabled persons than the urban areas. This was also correct about J&K. But, this situation got radically different mainly due to the situation of violence. Thus, in J&K, the rural areas have got more or less equal proportion or more than the urban areas.

[8] *Social Causation:* The social causation of disability in J&K can be explained at two levels. At the individual level, several factors contributed to this situation which include hereditary factor, medical-pathological factor, and diet and other deficiency factors. Most of these factors apply primarily to economically lower classes, rural and female groups. One more important contributory factor which applies to all classes and groups is directly related the violence in the state during last two decades. The rationale lies in the fact when increasing number of injured could not get full or relevant treatment either due to non-availability of experts/expertise or due to absence of financial resources to go outside for treatment led to huge number of handicapped who still remain unattended.

[9] *Social Implications:* At the individual-personality level, while the short-term implications of disability reflects in making the individual defunct in which even the free movement and action is not possible. In the long-term, the personality proves 'dysfunctional' and all roles and functions related to it get lost. At the societal level, disability gives rise to a particular group of all sexes, ages, areas and so on. So, it hardly contributes to social, economic, demographic, educational, cultural, religious and psychological developments in society, thus, becomes 'social disability'. Special mention may be made about younger age and male groups. The former stands as most important and most active group of population, this social function gets restricted and even stopped due to disability. The latter usually stands as heads or elder members of their families and also sole bread earners of their families. But, disability creates economic baselessness and grave crisis in their life. At the societal level, this situation gets alarming when its proportion to the total population crosses the maximum limit. That is what has happened in J&K where disability proportion exists between 3% and 4%.

[10] *Central Government Response:* Taking into consideration serious implications of disability, several macro and micro level initiatives are needed to be carried out by the central and state governments in public, private and NGO sectors. In order to raise the wider consciousness about disability among people at large, the United Nations General Assembly adopted a 'World Programme of Action' in 1982. Following this global programme, the govt. of India recently responded by allocating/providing increased funds for disabled in India. As per the reports, the Union Ministry of Justice [which deals with disability in India at the country-level] annual budget has been increased from Rs. 25,000 crores to Rs. 45,000 crores. The Deendayal Disabled Rehabilitation Scheme will have Rs. 120 crores for annual budget. An amount of 70 crores had been sanctioned for seven National Institutes of Disability and 100 crores for schemes under Persons with Disability Act. [See *Times of India*, New Delhi, 12 February, 2010]

[11] *State Government Response:* The state government has not responded to the problem of disability in a proper and desirable way. In fact, it has not started any specific programme or scheme for disabled in the state, though their proportion has reached to the alarming level. Only some central govt. schemes and programmes are implemented but not with commitment and sincerity. Its role nay realistically be characterized as 'apathetic' as basic needs of these suffering people have not been fulfilled. In this context, it seems highly desirable that, on the pattern of central government, the state govt. makes higher financial allocations and start specific programmes-schemes for all disabled in the state. The important step to deal with disability in J&K in a realistic and effective may be taken by adopting [i] a formal comprehensive policy concerning the militancy as well as non-militancy related disability in the state; and [ii] various relevant and focused programmes and schemes for short-term as well as long-term relief and rehabilitation of all disabled in the state. This needs to be done on priority basis. Last but not the least, the role of national and international NGOs stands very crucial, especially in the fields of movement disability and mental disability. The actual role of the Organization known as "Doctors without Borders" in Kashmir stands as an ideal in this regard.

[IV] DOMESTIC VIOLENCE AGAINST WOMEN

Domestic Violence against Women [DVAW] refers to a social phenomenon which reveals violent and non-violent behaviour of male members of society towards female members in and around domestic framework, especially after the marital life of women starts. It includes all types of attitudes and behaviour related to the personal and social interests of women in post-marital life. It involved all verbal and physical acts which abuse, hurt, and offend women in general by men related through marriage. In actuality, this phenomenon stood not only as inter-sex affair but an intra-sex affair too. In the operational sense, DVAW represents the "force whether overt or covert used to wrest from an individual [a woman] something she does not want to give of her own free will and which causes her physical injury or emotional trauma or both."

It is believed that traditional Kashmiri society about 70 years back was considered a non-violent society. The attitude and behaviour of people was oriented towards peace, harmony and consensus, while social ethos was totally non-violent. It was observed/reported that people at large were neither involved in nor heard about violent acts. This social ethos provided the rationale for characterization of Kashmiri society as "completely non-violent". Even in the case of women, violent acts were never practiced.

However, this situation changed radically due to various developments in last one century, especially in last two decades. The century-spread developments included processes of change and development, especially modernization, urbanization, industrialization, migration, and materialistic outlook which transformed the entire life-style in Kashmir qualitatively as well as quantitatively. In this social dynamics, women at large were exposed to the positives and negatives of modern life.

Thus, the Kashmiri society joined the mainstream developing societies which also gave rise to many problems for them. Subsequently, in the recent decades, social environment created by the forces of militancy and militarization increased the phenomenon of DVAW, especially of the criminal nature. This new trend has exposed the entire womenfolk to extreme forms of violence and cruelty within and outside the domestic framework. In reality, this inhuman trend has crossed all limits of civilization and hundreds of women were raped, murdered, tortured and molested.

DVAW in Kashmir was introduced through two 'gateway processes'. The first series of processes was related to broader social transformation due to change in this background. The attainment of modern education, and adoption of regular-remunerative employment by women in large numbers gave rise to dual role of women, one at home and other at office, created a situation of 'role conflict' for them. This gave rise to many social problems for them at both places. While women in Kashmir faced one set of problems in traditional situation such as dependency, denial of rights, discrimination, dependence, torture and offending, they now encountered a new set of problems such as post-marital discard, harassment and eve-teasing.

The second series of processes was related to the entry of women in post-marital life situation. Though women became increasingly educated and economically independent, social attitude and behaviour towards this new role of women could not be changed proportionately. A situation of 'change and continuity' emerged. It can be explained in a way that though women's economic independence was achieved, it could not be availed fully due to snatching of income by in-laws family in considerable number of cases. In this changing situation, the post-marital life brought further problems for women which included mental-physical torture, harassment, post-marital disharmony, dowry demand and dowry death. This behaviour against women also included many violent acts of wife-beating, physical torture and so on. In that situation, even religious injunctions and moral codes were violated. Islamic orders regarding separation, divorce, maintenance, inheritance rights, payment of mahr and so on were not followed seriously. It was essentially in that social context that a law about domestic violence against women was implemented in Pakistan in 2008.

STUDY OF DVAW IN KASHMIR

Methodology: A sociological study about DVAW was carried out in 2003-2004. The universe of study was the Kashmir province which composed of six administrative districts of Srinagar, Baramulla, Budgam, Kupwara, Pulwama and Anantnag. The sample of this study composed of 200 women respondents selected on the basis of sociological criteria of age, literacy, income, rural-urban and marital status, family structure and working status. The necessary data-information was collected by trained research investigators through questionnaire and interview techniques. The participant observation method was also used. After collecting required information, it was aggregated, tabulated and explained rationally.

Major Findings: The first important finding was that systematic discrimination against women was going-on in the social life of Kashmir. The following response reveals its clearly:

While majority of respondents, 63.00%, felt that the practice of discrimination against women in family existed at large, minority of them, 37%, felt otherwise.

Though these responses can be explained in relation to different variables, in general it was observed that women got discriminated

Table 6.20

Discrimination Against Women within Families

S.No.	*Response*	*A*	*B1*	*B2*	*K*	*P*	*S*	*Total*
1.	Yes	63.33	60.00	60.00	56.66	66.66	68.00	63.00
2.	No	36.33	40.00	40.00	48.33	33.33	32.00	37.00

A = Anantnag B1 = Baramulla B2 = Budgam
K = Kupwara P = Pulwama S = Srinagar.

usually. But, it was also observed that a dominant trend of change was expanding fast.

The areas in which the above-mentioned women were discriminated were as follows:

[i]	Education	16.00%
[ii]	Gifts	23.00%
[iii]	Clothes	11.00%
[iv]	Diet/food	24.00%
[v]	Ownership	13.00%
[vi]	Decision making	35.00%
[vii]	Property	54.00%
[viii]	Social treatment	30.00%
[ix]	Employment	18.00%

Women's Working Role: In the post-marital life, women got different kinds of treatment from in-laws family which may be characterized as positive or negative. In this regard, the respondents gave the response noted in the following table:

Table 6.21

Treatment of In-Laws Families

S.No.	*Response*	*A*	*B1*	*B2*	*K*	*P*	*S*	*TOTAL*
1.	Positive	17.64	14.70	14.70	11.76	14.70	26.47	39.08
2.	Negative	14.81	14.81	11.11	14.81	18.51	25.92	31.03
3.	Both	19.23	15.38	11.53	19.23	15.38	23.07	29.88

The table reveals that 39.08% women got appreciation, while 31.03% got condemnation. At the same time, 29.88% got both kinds of responses on the part of their respective in-laws families. It follows that a significant number of women didn't get appreciation which spoiled the normal post-marital life. This undesirable response reflected in jeolesey, teasing, harassment, mental and physical torture, discrimination, dowry demand and so on.

Separation between the Couple: The continuous post-marital strain and discard often led to separation between husband and wife, which continued for years and decades. In this study, we got the following number of separation cases:

- Srinagar district	05
- Baramulla district	05
- Budgam district	06
- Anantnag district	05
- Pulwama district	03
- Kupwara district	04
Total	28 / 200

The particular reasons for separation were given by the women as follows:

- Undesirable behaviour/torture by in-laws family members 07
- Misunderstanding between husband and wife 04

- Husband's suspicion about his wife's extra marital relations	05
- Government job of women and its impact	01
- Love affair of the husband with other girl	01
- Physical assault on wife	02
- Initiative for establishing new family unit	02
- Husband was forced to marry the present wife	02
- Economic problems	02
- Husband's ill treatment	02
Total	28 / 200

Practice of Wife-beating: This study revealed that a significant number of women got regular beating by their husbands. It stands clear from the following table:

Table 6.22

Practice of Wife-beating by their Husbands

S.No.	*Response*	*A*	*B1*	*B2*	*K*	*P*	*S*	*Total*
1.	Yes	22.00	18.00	16.00	16.00	14.00	14.00	31.83
2.	No	19.62	17.75	18.69	14.95	14.95	14.01	68.15

The table shows that 32% of women got regular beating by their husbands after their marriage, more in rural than in urban areas, while 68% women were not experiencing this inhuman practice. It was observed that in some cases not only husbands but other family members too involved in this practice. Regarding the recurrence of this practice, it was found that 18% respondents were beaten twice, thrice or four times, while 7% were beaten more than these times. 75% respondents revealed their beating once in life-time. The apparent cases for wife-beating were identified as follows:

- Efforts to establish new family unit	20.00%
- Suspicion of husband about his wife's relations	20.00%

- Bad food preparation	05.00%
- Talking with neighbours about marital disharmony	05.00%
- Husband to marry another girl	10.00%
- Improper handling of household items	10.00%
- Exchange of heated arguments	10.00%
- Husbands were short tempered	10.00%
- Husbands feeling of 'superiority'	10.00%

Torture and Harassment: This study observed that about 40% respondents faced torture and harassment in their post-marital life on the part of in-laws family members, both men and women. These practices were organized and their examples were as follows:

- Creating conditions for mental disturbance;
- Hurting, abusing and offending without any reason;
- Providing basis of tension and anxiety within families;
- Physical beating;
- Showing no satisfaction on the work done by daughter-in-law;
- Never treated them well and equal;
- Unnecessary interference in their personal affairs;
- Getting all household work done by them showing arrogance abd superiority;
- Asking them to handover personal things;
- Grabbing the amount of salary;
- Attempts to humiliate on important occasions;
- Imposing all decisions on us;
- Always finding faults;
- Giving us the feeling that we are worth nothing.

It was observed that 14% women approached their parents and relatives regarding this matter, while 28% tolerated all this silently. Only 14% respondents reacted sharply and showed strong, open and continuous opposition. According to respondents, the ways and methods through which these practices could be stopped were as mentioned below:

- Mass education to all 32.00%
- Separation from parental household and estab. of nuc. family 34.00%
- Developing mutual understanding 09.00%
- Overall social transformation 04.00%
- To raise consciousness among women 11.00%
- Very difficult to stop these practices 10.00%

Demand of Dowry: Usually problems for women in the post-marital life started with the demand of dowry by in-laws family. While in some cases, this demand was met, in other cases, could not be met leading to cruel acts against daughter-in-law. In this study, 9% women were demanded dowry by in-laws families who included husbands. It also divulged that 25% respondents gave various items to in-laws family, while 75% refused categorically.

Threat to Divorce: This study revealed that 22% of respondents were given the threat to divorce. But, at the same time, while 5% men practised it, 95% didn't practice it. It follows that this problem existed in Kashmir but its intensity was not deep and it was considered 'undesirable'.

Molestation: The findings of this study were that 33% respondents faced/observed/heard/read about cases of molestation of women, while 42% didn't face/observe/heard/read about such cases within and outside domestic framework. The acts of molestation were performed by

- Near relatives 09 / 30
- Distant relatives 07 / 30
- Neighbours 14 / 30
- Office colleagues 10 / 26
- Young unknown persons 02 / 26
- Armed forces 07 / 30

These acts of molestation were committed at

- Residential houses 26/66

  Public places/roads 12/66

- Offices/places of work 10/66
- Agricultural fields 09/66
- Public parks 09/66

The apparent reasons for committing molestation were reported as:

- Raids by armed forces 16/66
- Over-crowd in the public transport 11/66
- Love related matters 08/66
- Enemy of working women 06/66
- Sexual lust 07/66
- Indecent dress of women 04/66
- Physical beauty of women 09/66
- Acts of juvenile delinquency 06/66
- Impact of Hindi films 06/66

Role of Female Sex: The study divulged that it was not men only but women too imposed cruelty against women in the domestic framework. The respondents conveyed the following views in this regard:

- Women tortured them more 32.00%
- Women played major role in violence against them 55.00%
- Violent behaviour in in-laws family was based on wishes of all women 20.00%
- Women were initiators and perpetrators of domestic violence against us 44.00%
- Women were more responsible for domestic violence 30.00%

Thus, this study and its findings convey a clear message for the entire society that there stands an absolute need for a desirable social legislation against DVAW in order to restore safety, security, dignity and basic gender rights to women.

[V] INCREASING SUICIDES IN THE VALLEY

1. *Introduction:* Suicide in general terms means 'killing oneself

intentionally'. Sociologically, it refers to "an act on the part of individual which is essentially subject to social forces." [*Oxford Dictionary of Sociology*] The tendency to commit suicide depends less on individual psychology or the physical environment and more on individual's relations to the broader society. [Ibid.] Thus, it follows that suicide primarily represents 'an individual action which necessarily reveals the failure of social solidarity and is indicative of the ineffectiveness of social bonds.' [*A Dictionary of Sociology by G. Duncan Michell*]. One of the founding fathers of modern Sociology, Emile Durkhiem [who has produced the trend-setting sociological study on suicides in modern times] has developed following types of suicides:

[i] *Altruistic suicide:* In this type of suicide, the individual is too strongly integrated in to society – a society which encourages or even requires the individual to sacrifice his or her own life.

[ii] *Egoistic Suicide:* In this type of suicide, the individual is insufficiently integrated into society and so is not subject to the collective forces that prevent suicide and experiences an isolation and detachment conducive to it.

[iii] *Anomic Suicide:* This type of suicide depends on the social regulation of the individual's desires and ambitions. Where anomie [normlessness] is heightened in society, the individual's passions, ambitions and appetites are increased to a level where they cannot find satisfaction, opts for suicide.

Moreover, sociologists have emphasized that one must assess the impact of social and cultural factors on the construction of suicide statistics as well as the tendency to commit suicide. A range of studies have provided some empirical support for the evidence of the impact of social factors on levels of suicide.

2. *Suicides in Kashmir:* The number of suicides in present-day Kashmiri society has experienced a phenomenal growth in recent decades. In fact, the pattern of committing suicide has emerged as a significant trend in Kashmir. It was partly because of sudden rise of suicides and partly because of

peaceful social situation in the traditional Kashmiri society in which suicides were either totally absent or very insignificant. Thus, we may argue that a significant trend of suicides has emerged in Kashmir.

The phenomenon of suicide in the valley needs to be observed in the above-mentioned sociological framework. The global-oriented sociological propositions need to be utilized in order to explain causes, consequences, nature, solution and other important features of the on-going trend of suicide.

This may prove a serious academic exercise. But, there are some serious limitations which make this work difficult, even impossible. These limitations include non-availability of relevant data from any source, including the government sources, and absence of any academic study on suicides in Kashmir. In this context, this micro-level study stands highly relevant and badly-needed. It is an attempt to identify and explain major sociological features of the acts of suicide in Kashmir during the period of last one year.

3. *Methodology:* As mentioned in the preceding section, no academic study was carried out about suicides in Kashmir. It was partly because of academic apathy towards scientific study of this problem and partly because of non-availability of information/data and other source material on this problem. In that situation, the only source which provided some raw, but basic, information was the local press in Kashmir. The local newspapers, both in English and Urdu languages, published daily reports about suicides and gave details about sex, age, area, cause, method, police investigation, medical treatment, religion, literacy and marital status. The study of these relevant contents and details stood a credible method for scientific investigation about increasing suicides in Kashmir. Though having certain inherent limitations, this method proved meaningful in our case.

In this content study, the investigation of daily news-reports was carried out for the period of one year, i.e. September 1999 to August 2000. The total cases of suicide reported in the local press during this period was 185. The local daily newspapers which were studied for this purpose were as follows:

[i] *Greater Kashmir* [English daily], Srinagar;

[ii] *Srinagar Times* [Urdu daily], Srinagar

[iii] *Aftab* [Urdu daily], Srinagar.

Keeping in view broader sociological propositions about suicide, this content study dealt with suicide cases in the Kashmir province which was considered the unit of analysis. At the initial stage, news items about suicides reported in these newspapers were collected for a year. Subsequently, the data was aggregated and tabulated which enabled to provide sociological explanation of suicides in the valley.

4. Findings of the Study

4.1. *Number and Occurrence of Suicides:* The phenomenon of suicide was near-absent in the traditional Kashmiri society. But, at present, it has emerged as a significant social phenomenon. Though this act on the part of an individual has attained crucial importance, it has not been given due academic treatment. Consequently, there is hardly any authentic information/data available on the topic. There are two basic methods for getting relevant data.

These are [i] the empirical investigation and [ii] study of reports about suicides published in the local press. We opted for the second method. This method has certain limitations mainly because all cases of suicide were not reported in the local press. But, such a limitation is associated with every relevant source. According to an unofficial estimate, about 40% cases of suicide were reported in the local press.

However, taking into consideration broader coverage such incidents, it seems that about 50% cases were reported. On the basis of study of suicide reports in the local press during the period September 1999 – August 2000, we assume that about 15 suicides in a month on an average were committed in Kashmir.

More or less, the same estimate [30 suicides in 2 months] was made by a local English daily newspaper in July 2000. The month-wise details about suicides in our study are as follows:

Table 6.23

Number of Suicides in Kashmir, 1999-2000

S.No.	*Period*	*Number of Suicides*
1.	September 1999	17
2.	October 1999	20
3.	November 1999	18
4.	December 1999	11
5.	January 2000	13
6.	February 2000	13
7.	March 2000	14
8.	April 2000	15
9.	May 2000	12
10.	June 2000	19
11.	July 2000	17
12.	August 2000	16
Total	12 months	185
Total	01 month	15.41 [average]

It follows that about 2,000 persons committed suicide in Kashmir during last one decade starting from 1990. This study also revealed that about 23.00% persons were saved by their family members and in different health centres and hospitals.As the local press reported, suicides were spread throughout the valley. The occurrance-pattern, especially rise and fall, of suicides was determined by various factors. It may not be out of place to mention here that this content study was primarily sociological in nature. All major propositions were fully supported by relevant statistics. However, the statistics must be taken primarily as indicative, directional and revealing trends and patterns.

4.2. *Male-female Ratio:* The cases of suicide reported in the local press were 77.41% females and 22.58% males. It also revealed that 70.00% females were house-wives, while 30.00% were working women. This huge number of women in comparison to men was attributed to their [women's] lesser patience, lesser care inside and outside families, lesser exposure to unprecedented violent situation, discrimination and harassment.

4.3. *Rural-Urban Ratio:* The content study divulged that among all reported cases of suicide, while 85.71% were committed in rural areas, 14.28% were committed in urban areas. Primarily, this unequal proportion of suicides can be related to the demographic factor of unequal proportion in the population of these two different areas, which, according to census, was 74% rural and 26% urban.

This may go against the conventional view that suicide rate is generally higher in urban than in rural areas. But, different pattern of suicides in Kashmir can be explained in terms of impact of armed conflict on population dynamics in general and on particular groups in particular.

4.4. *Religious Affiliation:* This study showed that dominant majority of 95.23% of those who committed suicide in Kashmir were local Muslims belonging to both major sects of *Sunnis and Shias*.

One other case of suicide was reported and he was a *Bihari* labourer working in the valley for many years. All others who committed suicide and were reported in the press were Hindus of local or outside origin.

Their proportion was about 4%. All of them were working in armed forces and central government offices.

4.5 *Age Groups Ratio:* Our study reflected the participation of different age groups in committing suicides as follows:

Table 6.24

Age Group Composition of Suicide-Makers

S.No.	*Age Groups*	*Participation Rate [%age]*
1.	06 – 15 years	03.07
2.	16 – 25 years	76.92

3.	26 – 40 years	20.00
4.	41 + years	00.00

The most active age group in committing suicide belonged to 16–25 years. This group of youngsters belonged to all demographic, economic, educational, marital, social-cultural, occupational and other groups. They also have affiliation with all communities and castes. The second active group belonged to 26 – 40 years whose members were generally senior, mature and were settled in life. This group had more independence than the former group. The third group which had minor participation in suicides belonged to teenagers. They were very young and mostly students in colleges. Some of them became even the suicide-bombers against the army in Kashmir.

4.6. *Married-unmarried Ratio:* The study showed that there was significant degree of difference between married and unmarried people who committed suicide. While the proportion of married was 40.32%, the proportion of unmarried was 59.67%. The higher proportion of unmarried in committing suicide can apparently be related to younger age-groups, lesser experience of complex problems, and extensive as well as intensive impact of the militancy situation. Moreover, in the psychological framework, unmarried people have sown more tendency to commit suicide in comparison to their married counterparts.

4.7. *Literate-Illiterate Proportion:* The news reports in the press didn't provide in all cases the literacy status of the person who committed suicide in the valley. However, other information indirectly hints towards this aspect. Thus, our inference conveys while about 60% people who committed suicide were literate, about 40% of them were illiterate. There is general feeling that literate were more attached to social, economic, political and ideological factors, while illiterates were found more attached to marital, domestic and other related problems. So, the suicides were committed on the pattern related to these diverse factors. It was also found that literates attempted suicide that led to sure death in most cases, while this was not the case with illiterates.

4.8. *Occupational Composition:* The suicide reports in the local press did not mention occupation of all of those who committed suicide. On the basis of part information and other available information, we may put forward the proposition that most of the people who committed suicide, even up to 65% were house wives in rural and urban areas. The other group involved was composed of the employees in government and non-government offices working on lower/ petty positions. The third group belonged to petty occupations and small business, especially in urban areas.

4.9. *Ratio of other Social Categories:* In addition to above-mentioned groups and sub-groups of suicide-makers, other social categories composed of 27.41% of the total people.

[i] The first distinctive group was of the students studying at pre-college and college levels and their involvement was 72,17%. They, both boys and girls, were very young, belonged to early and middle teens and showed desperation and frustration. Many of them committed suicide because they could not pass the exam. And could not get good position or job in future. Some of them were ideologically so committed that became 'suicide squads' and finished their lives for their 'cause'. Some of them finished their lives simply because they had a dispute with their parents and other family members.

[ii] The second important group in this series was composed of 'pregnant women' whose percentage was 11.96. Their compelling factors for taking this extreme step included marital disputes, economic compulsions and discrimination and harassment.

[iii] Another group, having the proportion of 05.88%, composed of the personnel of security forces. They belong to other parts of the country and have come here for their official duty. It was observed that their living and service conditions were worse and they were often not allowed to proceed on leave. They always lived in fear and threat. In that situation, they became frustrated and trapped and some among them committed suicide to get rid of all these problems.

[iv] Another group having 05.88% proportion was of 'Bihari Labourrs' who came here for work in the recent years. This outside labour force, less skilled and more unskilled, lived in isolation but earned sufficient amount of money. Since they have come here with certain expectations which are not fulfilled in the prevailing conditions here, they prefer the to follow the 'escape route', i.e. suicide.

[v] Another group which was actively involved in suicides in Kashmir was that of prisoners in jails in the state. Since living conditions in all jails were worst and any protest meant dangerous consequences for inmates, the jailed prisoners preferred death through suicide.

4.10 *Suicide Cases Registered by Police:* Though the suicide rate was increasing fast, there had been no formal major and organized protest against this practice. The percentages referred in this report were not 'more' or 'higher' in comparison with the related situation prevailing in metropolitan areas. But, even the present percentage stood 'higher', even alarming, when considered in the context of the traditional society in Kashmir. However, people 'feel' for this increasing practice that reflected in their minor protests/condemnations at individual and social level. This was followed by registration of cases in police stations against the persons who were considered responsible for compulsion for committing suicide. Among all cases of suicide, about 31.00% cases were registered in local police stations against the following categories of people:

- In-laws of the suicide-maker	22.58%
- Husband of the suicide maker	12.90%
- Family members and relatives	09.67%
- Others and unknown persons	54.83%

It was observed that though the above-mentioned cases were registered, neither relatives of the suicide-maker nor the police were serious in pursuing these cases till their end. Moreover, the police delay and relatives apathy made the situation more tragic. The analysis of the press reports revealed that police had taken some action under relatives and other pressures in only 13.62% cases.

4.11 *Methods of committing Suicide:* This study showed that suicides were committed in Kashmir by adopting the following methods:

[i]	Consuming poison	83.87%
[ii]	Jumping into the river	06.45%
[iii]	Self-immolation	04.83%
[iv]	Hanging from ceiling fans	03.22%
[v]	Shooting self with gun	01.61%

4.12. *Apparent Reasons for Committing Suicide:* The reports in the press conveyed the following apparent reasons for committing suicide:

[i]	Heated arguments with parents on various personal issues	30.64%
[ii]	Strained marital relations with the husband, disturbed marital life in the family, and wrong expectations about post-marital life	20.96%
[iii]	Extreme poverty, difficult economic conditions and unemployment	11.29%
[iv]	Ill-treatment, discrimination and harassment by in-laws family	08.06%
[v]	Father's or guardian's death	06.45%
[vi]	Psychological depression and social pathology	06.45%
[vii]	Compulsion for marriage with exclusive parents' choice	06.45%
[viii]	To avoid rape/molestation by security forces and other armed groups	04.83%
[ix]	Social-status factors	03.22%
[x]	Harassment and eve-teasing of girls outside their homes	01.61%

4.13. *Suicides among the Armed/Security Forces:* Like the phenomenon of suicide among the local civilians, it also existed among all sections of armed/security forces who all are outsiders and have been transferred here for a specific period.

Though no exact figures about suicides among the security forces were available, the local press has reported several cases of suicide among them on regular basis in last few years. During the period of this study, many cases of suicide among security forces were reported in the local press. They belonged to upper-cadre and lower-cadre posts and reasons for their suicides included constant threat and fear of death, alienation, worst life conditions, no social-cultural life and refusal to grant them leave. All such suicides were committed by shooting themselves by their service rifles. In some cases, they killed themselves and their colleagues and seniors.

5. Concluding Points

The preceding details about cases of suicide prove that a high rate was experienced in the Kashmir valley in the previous one decade. So, it has emerged significantly qualitatively as well as quantitatively. It may be necessary to mention here that there was no information available about suicides in Kashmir in the past. In that situation, it was really difficult to draw the correct picture. Only inferences and estimates may help in this regard.

In the above-mentioned situation, we may argue about co-relation between the acts of suicide and various socio-economic factors. It follows that incidence of suicides in the Valley may be explained in terms of varying degrees of social, psychological, educational, political, economic and other relevant factors. These acts may also been explained partly in terms of implications of the on-going militancy in the Valley. Thus militancy has added certain other features to the acts of suicide such as their peculiarities which include fast increase in the number of suicides, more suicides committed by females than males, more suicides committed in rural than urban areas, no formal and organized protest against increasing suicides, extreme ups and downs in suicide trends, and no official, formal and complete record of suicides.

Though seemed absolutely desirable and functionally necessary that the incidence of suicide in Kashmir must be totally stopped and finally eliminated, but the total elimination of this phenomenon seemed difficult, if not impossible. In actuality, this process seemed irreversible in the broader social dynamics. However, it may be controlled to the maximum extent by existing social forces/factors. In order to make this control more realistic and effective, serious and long-term efforts need to be carried out at the psychological, family and societal level. In this regard, reference may be made to the social environment created during the month of *Ramdan* which recorded the least number of suicides (i.e. 11 in a month) during the period of study.

Last but not the least, it may be noted that there emerges an urgent and basic need to record all cases of suicide formally by the government and non-government agencies and organizations and make detailed studies of these cases by professionals, academicians and other experts. This will certainly help in the formulation and implementation of relevant policy and programmes to control and eliminate suicides in Kashmir.

[VI] RISING GRAPH OF SUICIDES IN KASHMIR

In general, suicide means 'killing oneself intentionally'. Sociologically, it refers to an 'act which is essentially subject to social forces.' In this perspective, the tendency to commit suicide depends less on individual psychology and more on individual's relation to the broader society. In other words, suicide primarily represents an individual action which necessarily reveals the failure of social solidarity and is indicative of the ineffectiveness of social bonds.

The phenomenon of committing suicide has emerged strongly in the Kashmir valley. In fact, the problem of committing suicide in Kashmir was considered by experts as "a significant social trend". This has happened in the situational background of the armed conflict between militants and security forces from 1989 in the erstwhile non-violent society of Kashmir. The long-term and short-term implications of the conflict situation such as net human and material loss, economic devastation, educational backwardness, physical-mental health deterioration, mass migration, extreme psychological depression, social disorder-disorganization, molestation-harasssment-discrimination of women and children, deviance and delinquency and crime and drug abuse created an 'anomic' situation for the people in general and youth in particular. In this context, the degree of social solidarity and cohesion reached to its lowest possible limit. It was primarily in this background that huge number of suicides was reported in Kashmir in the local press from 1990 onwards. Though this number was not huge in the initial years, it got increased heavily in the following years, especially from mid-1990s. The number/rate in suicides in Kashmir emerged significantly in the context in which there was hardly any such case reported 20-30 years.

Though the number of suicides increased fast, no factual and comprehensive study was carried out so far by any expert or agency or organization. On the basis of reports which came from diverse sources like local press, hospitals, police stations and personal communication, we may formulate certain estimates about number and other features of suicides in Kashmir. Here, we present figures of suicides revealed in two sources: first, the author's study based on press reports of the local press in 2000 and, second, an estimate made by a largest local newspaper:

Table 6.25

Number of Suicides in Kashmir, 2000 and 2008

S.No.	*`Year*	*Number of Suicides*	
		Author's Study	*Newspaper Estimate*
1.	1990	40	57
2.	1991	65	105
3.	1992	77	155
4.	1993	95	195
5.	1994	110	210
6.	1995	125	300
7.	1996	145	360
8.	1997	155	380
9.	1998	170	390
10.	1999	175	400
11.	2000	185	450
12.	2001	195	500
13.	2002	205	520
14.	2003	240	560
15.	2004	260	600

16.	2005	325	650
17.	2006	410	665
18.	2007	495	700
19.	2008	575	750
	Total	5,000 [minimum]	8,000 [maximum]

Thus, total number of suicides committed in Kashmir during last 19 years may be calculated as follows:

1. Suicides committed and reported in press	5,000(mini.)	8,000(maxi.)
2. Suicides committed but not reported in press	2,500	4,000
3. Suicides registered in different hospitals	3,500	4,500
4. Suicides registered in police stations	1,500	2,000
Total	12,500	18,500

It follows that 12,500 to 18,500 suicides were committed in the 19 years period of militancy, 658 to 974 suicides were committed each year and 55 to 81 suicides were committed each month.

The main sociological features of these suicides were as follows:

While 85.71% suicides were committed in rural areas, 14.84% suicides were committed in urban areas. This has happened mainly because of demographic factor, i.e. more population in rural than urban areas.

The most active age groups of those who committed suicide were 16-25 years [76.92%] and 26-40 years [20.00%]. Rest belonged to other age groups.

In terms of marital status, while 40.33% were married, 59.67% were unmarried. In the field of literacy, 60.00% were literate [some of them even of high qualification], 40.00% were illiterate. 65.00% of women who committed suicide were housewives and others were government-private sector employees. 11.96% of women were pregnant when they committed suicide.

The methods used for committing suicides included consuming poison 83.87%, jumping in to the river [06.45%], self-immolation [04.83%], hanging from the ceiling fan [03.22%], and shooting with gun [01.61%].

The apparent reasons for committing suicides, as was reported in the press, were as mentioned below:

[i]	Extreme poverty and unemployment	11.29%
[ii]	Strained marital relations, post-marital discards	20.96%
[iii]	Heated argument with parents or family members on personal issues	30.64%
[iv]	Ill treatment, harassment, and torture of women husband and in-laws	08.96%
[v]	Parent's or guardian's death	06.95%
[vi]	Psychological depression and social pathology	06.45%
[vii]	Eve-teasing and molestation	03.22%
[viii]	Threats and actions of security forces and police	04.83%

It is interesting to note that near-total number of suicides (i.e. 98.00%) was committed by local Muslims. But, a significant number of non-local military and para-military forces such as B.S.F, C.R.P.F., and R.R. have also fallen prey to this disaster. As a result, hundreds, even thousands, during the entire period of conflict, of security personnel posted in Kashmir for official duty in militancy conditions have committed suicide mainly by shooting themselves within their security camps. Taking into consideration the negative implications of this phenomenon among securitry forces, the concerned authorities have taken some necessary measures such as granting leave to soldiers for more time, making soldiers' interaction with their families more often, and introducing tension-reducing therapy and mechanism.

[VII] EMERGING JUVENILE DELINQUENCY IN KASHMIR

[i] Juvenile Delinquency (J.D.) refer to under-age criminals or juveniles who engage in offences that constitute 'crimes'

when committed by adults and are between the age of 7 – 16/18 years, as prescribed by the law.

The maximum age today for JD, as per Juvenile Justice Act of 1986, is 16 years for boys and 18 years for girls.[10] In the sociological framework, JD embrace a broad range of social behavior from offensive to values and norms to petty and severe crime.[11]

[ii] The JD has been classified by concerned experts according to the offences committed by them. The details follow:

- Incorrigibility [disobedience];
- Truancy [staying away from schools];
- Lareemy [petty theft to armed robbery];
- Destruction of property;
- Violence against individual and community using weapons;
- Sex offences – homosexuality to rape.[12]

[iii] *The Indian Context:* In the context of broader Indian society, the phenomenon of JD has following prominent features:

- The deviance rates are much higher among boys than among girls.
- The deviance rates tend to be highest during early adolescence age of 12 - 16 years.
- JD is more an urban than a rural phenomenon. Thus, metropolitan areas like cities of Delhi and Kalkotta produce more JD in comparison to small cities and towns.
- Children living with parents are found to be more involved in juvenile offence.
- Low educational background stands primary attitude for JD.
- Poor economic background also figure as important characteristic feature of JD.
- Huge majority of about 80% of JD are first offenders and only a tiny minority of about 10% was offenders.
- There is not an organized group related to JD but some of them have the support of organized groups.[13]

The sociological studies in Indian society have revealed that there prevail four major types of JD and these are:

- Individual type delinquency;
- Group-supported type delinquency;
- Organized type delinquency;
- Situational delinquency[14].

Sociological studies have also identified three major factors in the causation of JD in Indian society. These factors are family, neighbourhood and mass media.[15]

1. JAMMU AND KASHMIR SITUATION

[i] A general sociological observation is that the rate of JK is much lower in comparison to other states in India and the national average. The rate is also lower in the city of Srinagar and there are more boys than girls involved.

However, the militancy situation has encouraged and intensified JD in the state. Though normal situational factors contributed to the rise of JD, militancy and militarization increased-intensified this phenomenon. The actuality of JD in JK reveals in the following table:

Table 6.26

Major Aspects of J.D. in JK, 2003-2007

S.No.	*Crime*	*2003*	*2004*	*2005*	*2006*	*2007*	*Total*
1.	Murder	00	00	00	01	00	01
2.	Abt. Murder	02	00	00	00	01	03
3.	Can. Murder	00	01	00	00	00	01
4.	Rape	01	00	00	00	01	02
5.	Theft	01	01	01	03	01	07
6.	Riots	00	01	00	00	00	01
7.	Arson	00	00	00	00	00	01
8.	Hurt	00	00	01	00	00	01

9.	Molestation	00	00	01	00	00	01
10.	Other IPC crimes	00	02	02	00	04	08
11.	Total crimes IPC	09	09	05	08	10	41

Source: Crime in India, 2003-2007, Ministry of Home Affairs, New Delhi, 2008-09.

The following table supports the preceding trends in crime in JK and gives details about age and sex of juvenile offenders in the state:

Table 6.27

J. D. by Age and Sex in JK, 2003-2007

S.No.	*year*	*4 -12 years*		*12-16 years*		*16-18 years*		*Total[all groups]*		
		Boys	*Girls*	*Boys*	*Girls*	*Boys*	*Girls*	*Total*	*Boys*	*Girls*
1.	2003	02	04	17	00	00	00	18	18	00
2.	2004	01	00	11	00	00	00	11	18	00
3.	2005	00	00	06	00	00	00	06	06	00
4.	2006	00	00	06	00	01	00	07	07	00
5.	2007	01	04	00	00	00	00	15	11	04

Source: ibid.

It is important to note the figures in above tables do not include the militancy-related incidents, offences and crimes. These tables clearly show lesser number of juvenile offences during the period of 2003-2007, while 7 and 8 cases of theft and other IPC crimes, 2 cases of rape, 1 case of murder and 3 cases of abetment to murder were registered. The table-6.27 clearly shows that boys were more active in the crime scene from that of girls. The proportion was 11 and 4 in the toal of 15 incidents. It also revealed that 12-16 years age group was most active in the offences.

[ii] The judicial response to JD cases reveals from the table which follows:

Table 6.28

Disposal of Juveniles Arrested and Sent to Courts, 2003-2007

S.No.	*Year*	*arrested and sent to court*	*sent to home after advice and admo*	*released on probation and placed Under care of parents and Institu.*	
1.	2003	18	04	05	06
2.	2004	11	00	01	00
3.	2005	07	00	00	00
4.	2006	08	00	00	00
5.	2007	15	00	00	00

Source: Ibid.

The above table reveals that, in 2003, out of 18 arrested juveniles sent to court, 4 were sent to home after advice. 5 and 6 juveniles were released on probation under parents and institutional care. No child was sent to 'Children's Home' as there is none in Kashmir. In 2007 again, 15 juveniles were arrested but not sent to home care or released on probation. Thus, the passive role of police and courts can be noted.

[iii] The table below gives details about economic offences committed by juveniles in terms of their value:

Table 6.29

Classification of Juveniles Arrested by Economic Offences, 2003-2007

S.No.	*Year*	*up to 25,000*	*25,001 50,000*	*50,001 1,00,000*	*1,00,001 2,00,000*	*2,00,000 3,00,000*	*3,00,000+*	*Total*
1.	2003	15	02	01	00	00	00	18
2.	2004	09	01	00	00	00	01	11

3.	2005	07	05	00	05	00	00	17
4.	2006	00	00	02	02	03	01	08
5.	2007	05	05	05	00	00	00	15

Source: Ibid.

The above table shows that most juveniles commit economic offences up to the value of Rs. 25,000/- [i.e. 15 in 2003, 9 in 2004, 7 in 2005 and 5 in 2007]. On the other hand, offences of the value of 1,00,000 – 3,00,000 was 7 only [i.e. 1 in 2004, and 6 in 2006]. Rest of the offences fell in the range of 25,000 – 1,00,000.

2. J. D. AND JUVENILE JUSTICE – CONDITIONS IN KASHMIR

[i] The general feeling in Kashmir is that the problems of J. D. prevail at its lowest level. Though this seems correct, the entire reality is not so simple. In fact, no real assessment and actual study on this on-going phenomenon has been carried out. The reality stands with lot of evidence that JD has emerged as a phenomenon in the present-day Kashmiri society through normal factors. At the same time, the implications of militancy and militarization have intensified it. More important is the fact that the direction of this process is towards rising, expanding and increasing trend. Various studies of this author have confirmed this repeatedly. In a recent report, it was mentioned that "the unlawful activities perpetrated by juvenile are increasing at an immense pace and persistently juveniles are facing trials in the courts."[16]

Though JD has become a fact of life, no relevant law has been enforced in the state so far. In fact, there is a law called "Juvenile Justice [Care and Protection] Act, 1997" [on the pattern of Union Juvenile Justice Act of 1986] but it has not been implemented in the state.[17] In this situation, juveniles in JK are "tried in the normal courts, kept in normal jails, and produced before routine magistrates who don't have any lore of child psychology."[18]

When juveniles are kept in common jails, the tendency to deviate aggravates their problems and they may even commit major crimes. It was essentially in this context that the National Commission for

Protection of Child Rights [NCPCR], after visiting the state in 2009 and observing the conditions of juveniles, expressed concern over non-functioning of 'Juvenile Justice System' in JK.[19] The Commission had clearly pointed out:

"In view of non-functional Juvenile Justice system in the state, the existing juvenile justice legislation for JK needs to be reexamined and institutions like reservation needs established."[20]

3. THE SOCIOLOGICAL STUDY OF J.D. IN KASHMIR

A micro sociological study of JD in the city of Srinagar was carried in 2009. The main features of this study were as follows:

[i] During the period 2001-2008, 19 cases of juvenile offences were reported which included:

- 06 cases of offences against persons;
- 06 cases of offences against property;
- 02 cases of offences of criminal breach of trust;
- 02 cases of rash driving.[21]

[ii] During the period 2001-2006, the following offences were committed by juveniles:

-	Theft - auto	03
	Car	01
	Bike	01
	Stealing	03
	Stealing-sh 01 Total	09
-	Offences against persons - hurt	02
	Fighting	03
	Rash driving	01
	Forgery	02[22]

[iii] Disposal of juvenile cases, 2001-2008 - Total cases 19:

-	Sent to homes	00
-	Released on bail	00
-	Fine	00

- Release on bail 05
- Acquitted 03
- Pending cases 11[23]

[iv] 19 juveniles belonged to the following age groups:

Age group	Boys	Girls
07 – 12 years	07	00
12 – 16 years	09	00
16 + years	03	00[24]

6. ANOTHER MICRO SOCIOLOGICAL STUDY

In another related micro sociological study about JD in the Kashmir valley, conducted through informal interviews with Juveniles in Srinagar city in 2009,[25] the following features were observed:

[i] While all 36 juveniles were Muslims, they had 29-06 male-female ratio. All of them belonged to the city of Srinagar. 29 juveniles were illiterate while 7 were literate with matriculation and above-matriculation qualifications.[26]

[ii] These 36 juveniles belonged to the following in income [per month] groups:

- Rs. 500/- and less 04
- 501 – 1,000 11
- 1,000 – 1,500 00
- 1,500 – 2,000 00
- 2,001 – 2,500 08
- 2,501 – 3,000 09
- 3,000 and above 04[27]

[iv] The family occupation of these juvenile respondents was as mentioned below:

- Beggary	18	Student	10
- Rag picking	02	Retail goods	02
- Stay at home	03	Labour	01[28]

[v] The size of families of juveniles was explained as under:

-	02 - 03 members	00	04 – 05 members	09
-	06 - 07 members	10	08-09 members	03
-	10 - 11 members	10	12 and above	04[29]

[vi] The charges of offence leveled against these juveniles were as follows:

-	Theft	10	Fighting	03
-	Drug addiction	03	Eve-teasing	02
-	Gambling	02	other offences	16[30]

[vii] According to the investigation, the role of parents, which is responsible partly for delinquency, was explained in following terms:

- Lack of understanding	11	compelling social trends	08
- Parents' role in opting	08	parents alcoholic	03
- Mothers intervention	06[31]		

[viii] While 20 out of 36 considered drug addiction and gambling as main factors for committing offences, 24 out of 36 regarded mass media as the major factor for crimes.[32]

[ix] The friendship pattern of these juveniles was as mentioned below:

- Labourers	04	Rag pickers	02
- Beggers	18	School going	03
- Petty jobs	03	Doing nothing	04[33]

[x] The major factor responsible for increasing JD in Kashmir were identified as follows:

- Broken homes,	bad company	bad locality,
- Mass media,	social disorganization,	poverty and dependency,
- Unemployment	maladjustment,	nature of schooling,
- Psychological problems,	slums,	deviant behavior,
- Depression & tension,	drug addiction,	gambling,

- Alcoholism,	educational drop-out,	mobility and transformation,
- Defective,	entertainment,	programmes.[34]

7. NEED FOR STUDY AND INTEGRATED APPROACH

[i] The above-referred studies have proved sufficiently that the process of JD has started in Kashmir and its direction is towards expansion and intensity. All local groups, classes and communities have been involved in this process and all types of delinquency exists here. The normal factors of family, school, neighbourhood, community and mass media have been identified as major factors for causing this situation. At the same time, conflict situation has also proved the potential factor for increasing and intensifying the practices related to delinquency.

[ii] But, the response of the local government has proved insufficient, lukewarm and improper. There is no relevant law implemented in the state to tackle the problems created by and to control JD. There are no juvenile courts, juvenile homes and so on. So, the legislative and administrative actions on the part of state are highly needed for establishing 'Juvenile Justice system'.

[iii] Equally apathetic is the attitude and behaviour of society at large towards emerging phenomenon of JD in Kashmir. In actuality, there is lack of awareness about dimensions and implications of JD. So, there are no serious, sincere and organized efforts to control and to debase JD. Even the local, national and international NGOs and other concerned groups have not started working in this field.

[iv] In this dangerous situation, there is the basic need of studying the JD in scientific framework in order to arrive at its rational and realistic understanding. This must be followed by an integrated approach towards problems created by JD. The family, school, neighbourhood and mass media must in unity and in an integrated way work for the objective of controlling and debasing the JD in Kashmiri society. This needs to be

done immediately, otherwise more sections and sectors of society will face the disastrous impact of JD.

[VIII] KASHMIR: FROM CRIME-FREE TO CRIME-FULL SITUATION

It is generally believed that the traditional Kashmiri society of 70 + years back was completely a crime-free society. It follows that crimes were neither committed in an organized way in that society nor were reported by people at large. The dominant majority of people in that situation lived a peaceful non-violent life in which they witnessed or heard about any major crime. In actuality, there existed a non-violent social ethos in the extreme form and any kind of violent or criminal act was considered undesirable and condemnable.

But, this situation has changed radically. As a result of this basic change, crimes have emerged as prominent feature of the present-day Kashmiri society. Consequently, various trends of crime have developed and engulfed entire life in the Kashmir valley. The following over-view of daily reports about various crimes in Kashmir in the local print and electronic media and issued by local Police Control Room reflects these trends glaringly:

- The father was killed/murdered/stabbed by his son/nearest relative/friend;
- A person was butchered/beheaded/massacred by unknown gun-holders;
- A woman/girl was molested/raped/murdered by security forces and other unknown gun holders;
- Hundreds of theft, cheating, burglaries, fraud, pick-pocketing, threat, robbery, force cases take place daily in the valley;
- About 750 cases of suicide cases were attempted among men and women of all age groups, in rural and urban areas in last 4 months;
- Police caught many gangs of drug producers, drug growers, drug suppliers and drug users, both male and female of younger age group;
- A college girl was followed, teased, hit and murdered by his college mates;

- A boys of 15 years was killed by another boy of same age and his body was thrown in the graveyard;
- Nudity, moral degradation, erosion of ethics, and violation of traditional values were spreading fast in Kashmir;
- The parents feel disturbed about the involvement of their children of teen-age groups in deviant-delinquent tendencies and behaviour;
- Violence against women has reached to its climax in the murders of Romana, a school girl, and, Farzana, a married women and finally in the cases of Assiya and Neelofar in Shopian;
- Domestic violence against women in Kashmir reflects continuously in their harassment, dowry-demand, bride-burning, wife beating, separation, threat to divorce and other undesirable practices; and
- Cyber crime has also started invading the valley.

The above statements reported or quoted by local media do not stand for abstract theoretical propositions but essentially portray the actual situation of crime in present-day Kashmir. They also reflect a transition in the Kashmiri society from a crime-free to a crimefull situation.

Sociologically, the emergence of crime in Kashmir can be explained in terms of factors which are used in other cases. The environment of inequality, competition and conflict created through the processes of modernization, urbanization, industrialization, material development and so on contributed to this change. In this particular social dynamics, sociological-pathological factors of social disorder, disorganization, lesser socialization, least family-school control could not be avoided and were considered as 'co-relates' of this grand transformation. Again, the features of deviance and delinquency could also not be avoided. The added factors to the emergence of criminal trends were media exposure and IT revolution. In actuality, these processes proved the accelerating factors. All this situation led to emergence of crime as a social trend which attracted the younger elements in society and was solely aimed to get maximum material gains. This has happened in other societies in the developing world and this has also happened in the Kashmiri society.

But, the different feature of crime in Kashmir is its relationship with the armed conflict between militants and security forces for last 20 years. In fact, this conflict and its implications proved accelerative-intenseficatory factor for crime. It follows that conflict increased and intensified the criminal trends and provided much needed social-institutional support and organized form. Though the introduction of gun was not socially legitimized, it provided the motivation for its use for personal ends and group interests. The contribution of the gun to the crime also dehumanized the entire social ethos particularly agencies and organizations of crime control.

The political factor made the situation complex. Some parties, especially media at the global level, characterized Kashmir as a "global spot of crime and terrorism". These factors led to a cumulative effect of 'criminalization' of Kashmiri society according to which every section of society has got associated with this phenomenon. In this background, all in-family and out-family activities have been effected and the individual lives under the threat to his life, dignity, property and status.

It has been reported that thousands of men and women were killed, injured and disabled during the conflict period of 20 years. Though murder is considered an inhuman act in all civilized societies, these murderous killings were carried out in most dehumanized forms, like torture, blasting, butchering and so on.

The second major type of crime committed was molestation and rape of local women especially of younger age. The fact stands with sufficient evidence that this crime was introduced in Kashmir by the security forces. The famous incidents of mass rape in Kunan Poshpora and other places in the valley are still remembered by the people. Subsequently, the crime was committed by many outsiders as well as by insiders. In the recent past, this new trend of molestation, rape and murder has been established in the valley.

The minor crimes committed in Kashmir include thefts, cheating, burglary, snatching, looting, pick-pocketing, fake currency involvement, eve-teasing, harassment, suicide, drug abuse, nudity, immorality, sexual permissiveness, financial embazelment, fraud, bribe, and corruption. This list is added by acts of violence against women, especially torture-harassment-molestation, wife-beating, separation, threat to divorce and so on. Domestic violence and problems emerging from dual role of working women also figure in this list. It was observed that these crimes showed continuously upward trend during last two decades of conflict. This proposition was confirmed by daily crime reports issued by State Police Control Room and news broadcast-telecast by local media. This dangerous trend of crime in Kashmir crudely reflects in the following statistics about nature and number of crimes committed during the year 2008 [issued by the State Police Department]:

Nature and Number of Crimes in Kashmir, 2008

Suicide	28	Rioting	203
Arson	20	Murder	14
Attempt murder	69	Molestation	190
Rape	22	Women kidnap	44
Eve-teasing	111	Cruelty of husbands	30
Burglary	263	Robbery	19
Dacoity	19	Car theft	178

Though these figures are scanty, partial and for a brief period of one year, these necessarily reveal dangerous trend of various crimes which have engulfed the entire society in Kashmir. In this context, there seems a dire need to formally document all crimes so that these can be studied and treated properly.

In the background of increasing use of IT in the Kashmir valley, the cyber crime has also started invading the locals. Some local internet and mobile users have become the victims in past few years. The first type of cyber crime was committed through fake-fraud lottery and prizes. The second type of cyber crime was related to the misuse of confidential and personal information. The third type of cyber crime was related to cyber cafes which used it for immoral acts and legally prohibited sex behaviour.

The community leaders, social notables-activists, senior-eminent citizens and various groups and organizations have consistently protested against the rising trend of major and minor crimes and warned whole society about is disastrous implications. But, at the same time, it was observed that these crimes were not controlled. Instead, these acts got increased and intensified. In this context, it seemed necessary to activate the role of crime control agencies and organizations, so that a broad-based and organized social movement is established.

[IX] LIFE CONDITIONS OF CHILD LABOURERS IN KASHMIR

Introduction: Like in other parts of the country, the child labour in its acute form exists in JK State, particularly in the Kashmir valley partly because of historical reasons and partly because of occupational reasons. Historically, it was considered 'conventional occupation' in the extreme poverty situation in rural as well as urban areas in Kashmir. In the rural areas, children of early age used to be employed in the child labour works against petty sums or little amount of rice or grain. They were also engaged for cattle-rearing and domestic services against petty sums of money. On the other hand, in urban areas, most of the children belonging to poorer section of society used to work in various handicraft sectors for petty wages. A significant number of children were engaged in handicraft sectors [and on other fields too] at an age when they should have been in homes or schools. In this situation, the life conditions of child labourers [CL] were pathetic and got worse day by day. As per an unofficial estimate, more than 50% CLs work in the handicraft sector in organized-unorganized sectors in Kashmir. The existing life conditions of CLs revealed that they suffer in all fields of life, especially education, health, income, diet, hygiene, environment and so on. Though they work about 10-14 hours a day and six days a week in the handicraft centres [HC], they got very meager wages which didn't fulfill even their dietary needs. Even the girl children working in this sector were exploited and harassed. During the last 18 years of militancy in the Valley, the exploitation of these CLs at the hands of proprietors and wholesalers has certainly not reduced but increased. Not surprisingly, militarization stood as one of the vibrant causes (among other social causes) of child labour.

It was in the preceding situational context that a study was carried out in last two years by a team of sociologists. This study was based completely on detailed investigation of 372 respondents, who included 240 CLs, 60 parents [P], 36 employees [E], 12 government officials

[GO] and 24 social workers [SW]. The entire focus of this study was on knowing the reality related to life conditions of CLs in an area which has not been studied so far in various studies of child labour in Kashmir.

Methodology

Theoretical Approach: This study stands for an empirical study in totality. It is based exclusively on broader and deeper empirical investigation in its universe. No theoretical or ideological framework was followed in order to avoid pre-conceived notions, value-based propositions and distortion of existing reality. In actuality, all statements in the study are exclusively based on large-scale field investigation in all units and sub-units of the concerned item. All propositions and conclusions were drawn after following an extensive methodology in the broader sociological perspective. However, some theoretical propositions were followed keeping in view the generalizations about the prevailing situation.

Universe of the Study: The universe of study was the present-day Kashmir valley which composed of six administrative districts of Anantnag, Baramulla, Budgam, Pulwama, Kupwara and Srinagar. The Kashmiri-speaking people living outside the valley have not been covered in this study.

Areas of Handicraft Work: There are several areas of the handicraft work in the Kashmir valley. Among all these fields, we have selected

Table 6.30

Fields of Handicraft Work in Kashmir

S.No. Field	*A*	*B1*	*B2*	*K*	*P*	*S*	*Total*
1. *Paper Machie*	00	00	00	00	00	02	02
2. Woolen work	05	03	03	05	00	00	16
3. Wood carving	01	00	00	00	00	01	02
4. *Shawl-bafi*	00	03	03	01	06	03	16
Total	06	06	06	06	06	06	36

A = Anantnag B 1= Barammulla B2 = Budgam
K = kupwara P = Pulwama S = Srinagar.

4 core fields of work for sociological study. The details of these fields follow:

Sample of the Study: The total sample of this study represented 5 main categories of respondents which were CLs, Ps, Es, GOs and SWs. The details follow:

Table 6.31
Total Sample of Respondents

S.No.	*District*	*CLs*	*Ps*	*Es*	*GOs*	*SWs*	*Total*
1.	Anantnag	40	10	06	02	04	62
2.	Baramulla	40	10	06	02	04	62
3.	Budgam	40	10	06	02	04	62
4.	Kupwara	40	10	06	02	04	62
5.	Pulwama	40	10	06	02	04	62
6.	Srinnagar	40	10	06	02	04	62
	Total	240	60	36	12	24	372

Sociological Features: Several sociological features were taken into consideration while considering the composition of the sample of respondents. These factors included age, residence, marital status, sex and family status.

Methods and Techniques: The questionnaire method was extensively used to gather the information about respondents. In fact, three separate sets of questionnaires were prepared for CLs, Ps and Es which were structured and all questions had open-ended options on various themes of the study. All these questionnaires were approved by ICSSR, New Delhi experts. The relevant information was collected through these questionnaires which were either filled by respondents or responses were recorded by research investigators. At the same time, GOs and SWs were interviewed, guided by the 'interview guide'.

Field Work: After preparing questionnaires for CLs, Ps, and Es and interview guide for GOs and SWs, highly intensive as well as extensive fieldwork was carried out in all districts. Attempts were made to record real and correct responses by the research investigators and research officer who were appointed for this purpose. All groups and sub-groups in concerned areas were covered in the study. After completing fieldwork in all districts, the total information was aggregated and tabulated according to pre-fixed themes of study. Subsequently, this work led us to the finalization of 'draft report' of the study.

Findings of the Study

On the basis of detailed empirical and sociological study, we have observed a number of existing realities related to life conditions of child labourers in crucial sector of our economy. These observations include the following:

[i] This research revealed that 36 handicraft centres [HC] were established by private employers during the period 1970 – 2005 in all districts of the Kashmir valley. The number of children, boys and girls, working in these centres in 2006 was 352 [40.74% males and 57.26 % females]. The motivating agencies for joining the HCs were Ps in 41.25% cases, friends in 10.41% cases, relatives in 04,16% cases, poverty conditions in 12.92% cases and self-motivated in 31.25% cases.

[ii] It was divulged that while 147 [61.25%] CLs had 3 - 6 years experience in HCs, 46 [19.16%] CLs had 7 -10 years experience. 47 [19.20%] CLs had worked for the period of 11 - 14 years. Though there were many HCs functional in the valley, 4 main areas/fields of handicraft work, i.e. *Shawl-bafi, Kaleen bafi, Doon-hutche kaem* [wood-work] and *paper-machie,* were dominant and common activities in this regard. While majority of CLs [51.25%] considered it 'desirable', minority of them [48.75%] considered it 'undesirable'. However, these responses have to be viewed in the situational context.

[iii] It was found in the study the following basic facilities of life were not provided to the CLs in HCs:

[A] Toilet-Urinal facility 209 [87.08%] respondents

[B] Water facility 238 [99.16%] respondents

[C] Electricity facility 235 [97.91%] respondents

[D] First-aid facility 06 [02.50%] respondents

[E] Cleanliness 49 [20.41%] respondents

[F] Heating arrangement during winter 65 [27.08 %] respondents

[G] Good environment in HC 133 [55.41 %] respondents

[H] Lunch facility 95 [39.58 %] respondents

[I] Entertainment facility 169 [70.40 %] respondents

[J] Sufficient space 114 [47.50 %] respondents

[K] Modern instruments/ technology 01.00 [00.41] respondents

[iv] The responses of Ps and Es match the responses of CLs as the former confirmed the responses of the latter. All these responses revealed clearly that CLs were working in a situation in which even minimum basic human facilities were not provided at the HCs, as a result of which they suffered physically and mentally.

It was observed that the work schedule of all CLs in HCs was very tight. In this regard, relevant details showed that CLs worked 05.86 days in a week on an average, 24.82 days in a month and 07.98 hours in a day. At the same time, research revealed that they availed 01.08 days holidays in a week and 04.85 days in a month. In a year, they avail holidays only on religious festivals, important national occasions, marriage ceremonies and so on.

[v] This research confirmed the feeling about wage conditions of CLs and their exploitation at the hands of Es who own the private HCs. It was mainly because the wages in actuality were determined by Es only. The CLs [71.00%] and Ps [65.00%] upheld the point that, after determining Sages solely by Es, it was the quantity or production of work which determined the amount of wages. Since there were no rules or laws or directions in this regard on the part of government, Es took over maximum benefit and paid least wages to CLs.

[vi] Though huge majority of CLs, Ps and Es believed that the government had to play its role in regard to the fixation of wages on different handicraft items and of different forms/ types, it has not done so. It has led to a situation open for Es to exploit the wage labourers. Though these meager wages were paid regularly in the case of 72.91% CLs, these wages were not considered 'satisfactory' by 90.83% CLs as these did not fulfill even basic family needs.

[vii] The dominant response of CLs [83.75%] and Ps [90.00%] conveyed the feeling that the former were exploited to the maximum extent. Moreover, their wages were not increased even after decades time. This research revealed following details about monthly income of CLs on regular and *theka* basis:

Table 6.32

Monthly Income of CLs through Regular Work

S.No.	*Amount/Month Rs.*	*No. of Respondents No.*	*Percentage*
1.	500 and below	53	27.89
2.	501 – 1000	112	58.94
3.	1001 – 2000	23	12.10
4.	2001 – 3000	02	01.05

Table 6.33

Monthly Income of CLs through *theka*

S.No.	*Amount/Month*	*No. of Respondents No.*	*Percentage*
1.	500 and blow	00	00.00
2.	501 – 1000	35	72.91
3.	1001 – 2000	13	27.08
4.	2001 – 3000	00	00.00

This research upheld that 90.00% of wages of CLs were handed over to their Ps which was spent spend on personal and family purposes. Other items of expenditure included saving for CLs marriage [16.66%], and medical requirements of the family [33.33%]. On the other hand, their parents spend for children and family.

[viii] This research showed that CLs and their Ps were provided advances by the Es.

The details follow:

Table 6.34

Amount of Advances Provided to CLs and Ps

S. No.	*Amount (Rs.)*	*No. of Respondents*	
		No.	*Percentage*
1.	4000 and below	23	62.16
2.	4001 – 8000	11	29.72
3.	8001 – 12000	03	08.10

It was observed that the Es by providing this amount of loan or advance trapped CLs for ever in their exploitative framework and also got back more amount than they paid to them.

[ix] The life-long work of CLs in HCs has given rise to some dangerous and cronic diseases and disability among them. The following diseases were identified by CLs which have emerged solely because of continuous work in HCs:

Table 6.35

Diseases Among CLs Due to Continuous Work in HCs

S. No.	*Name of Disease*	*Total*	
		Number	*Percentage*
1.	Weak Eye sight/irritation in Eye-sight	25	10.41
2.	Headache	35	14.58

3.	Aching - shoulders, back, body	30	12.50
4.	Weakness	40	16.66
5.	Tiredness	01	00.41
6.	Mental Stress	03	01.25

Despite the fact that a significant number of CLs were suffering from many diseases because of their work in HCs, the Es have not provided even minimum health facilities.

[x] This research divulged that 173/240 [72.09%] CLs had dropped from schools up to 8th class for working in HCs. At the same time, this rate was increasing heavily. The reasons responsible for this situation were conflict situation, poverty, no motivation by Ps, and health problems. However, 98/240 [40.83%] CLs showed positive response towards education. This applied to both, male and female, children.

[xi] An inquiry was made about the situation which will emerge if CLs stop working in HCs. The responses received was as follows:

[a] Increase in food insecurity 11/60 [18.33%] respondents

[b] Mental/physical health problems 03/60 [05.00%] respondents

[c] Lack of marriage expenditure 02/60 [03.33%] respondents

[d] Abject poverty 12/60 [20.00%] respondents

[e] Survival difficulty 32/60 [53.33%] respondents

[xii] In our research related to government and non-government organizations, 81.66% CLs said that government don't play the required role. In fact, they have no expectation from the government for betterment in their wages. On the other hand, Es were very conscious about government role in the development of HCs. They expect the govt. to provide good financial help to them, good market facilities, technological support, health-care facilities, basic amenities, raw material at minimum price and welfare programmes.

[xiii] In regard to the societal views about handicraft work, while 33.00% CLs characterized as 'good', 66.25% considered it 'bad' and 'harmful'. At the same time, 65.00% of Ps

characterized child labour as 'bad' but 18.33% of them viewed it as 'normal'. In a situation if they get an opportunity to send CLs to schools, 52.50% said 'yes' and 47.57% said 'no'. In order to know views of CLs about different occupations which they may adopt in case of opportunity, they gave the names of following occupational positions for adaptation in future:

[a] Teacher 08/240 [03.33%] respondents

[b] Businessman 16/240 [06.66%] respondents

[c] Social Worker 08/240 [03.33%] respondents

[d] Sincere and honest child 42/240 [17.50%] respondents

[e] Good citizen 26/240 [10.83%] respondents

[f] Economically sound person 65/240 [27.08%] respondents

[g] Government employee 15/240 [06.25%] respondents

[h] Earning hand of the family 08/240 [03.33%] respondents

[i] Socially respectable person 14/240 [05.83%] respondents

[j] Highly educated person 08/240 [03.33%] respondents

[k] A politician 02/240 [00.83%] respondents

[l] A cricketer 01/240 [00.40%] respondent.

[xiv] Regarding abolition of child labour, there were different views of CLs, Ps and Es. While 96.00% CLs favoured its abolition, 04.00% among didn't favour it. About 82.00% of Ps favoured its abolition, while 06.00 % remained silent. Finally, 25.00% Es liked its abolition while 70.00% didn't like it. 5.00% among them remained silent.

1. *Suggestions*

I the light of observations made during this study, e submit a set of suggestions which may be considered government and non-governmental organizations in the long process of eradication of child labour in Kashmir. These suggestions are mentioned below:

[i] It was found in the field that there stands a need for vocational

education among CLs working in HCs. In fact, the entire group of CLs was illiterate. So, the government must establish HCs where part of the functioning must be related to literacy. Thus, arrangements must be made in all HCs for morning/ evening literacy classes. These centres must be characterized as handicraft-cum-literacy centres in the locality. Help from ICDS centres may also be sought. The financial incentive must also be provided for losing the part of handicraft work.

[ii] In the present situation, there seemed no particular criteria or basis for wages of different items of handicrafts. So Here is basic need for the determination of wages for all items of handicrafts. This will certainly the CLs because of increase in their income.

[iii] It was observed that girl CLs were not paid equal wages. This difference and discrimination must be legally banned and practically done away with.

[iv] Both government and non-government organizations must work for safeguarding the rights, interests and wages of CLs according to the market standard. The latter may also work for its awareness and formulation of relevant policy.

[v] All basic facilities and amenities of life must be necessarily provided to CLs working in HCs. This seemed must for their quality and safe work. These amenities/facilities refer to heating, water, toilet, electricity, ventilation, environment, hygienic conditions, space, standard wages and their regular and full payment.

[vi] All processes of awareness and action must start among the CLs and their Ps about short-term and long-term implications, governmental policies and programmes and benefits of abolition of child labour.

[vii] Since significant proportion of CLs composed of orphans in Kashmir, they must be preferred in terms of payment of wages and other benefits.

[viii] While the CLs need regular counseling and guidance for mental and physical health betterment, they also require proper guidelines for mobility-oriented career-making. They must

also be helped in the adoption of alternative occupations.

[ix] A strong socio-political movement was needed to focus on positive public opinion for CLs and against Child labour practices in order to make positive initiatives on the part of government and NGOs.

[x] The health problems of CLs must get first priority in the process of responding the problem of child labour in Kashmir. All necessary arrangements and facilities must be provided for this purpose.

[xi] Parents must go for life insurance policy, so that in case of their sudden death, their families do not suffer extremely. The government must take initiative in this regard.

[xii] A number of co-operatives must be established which will work for overall welfare of CLs.

[X] SOCIAL PATHOLOGY IN KASHMIR

[i] *Meaning and Implications:* The term 'pathology' has been borrowed from biological science and refers to social problems or deviant behavior like diseases.[35] In sociology, it stands analogous to 'deviance' and studies the basis of "disordered functions".[36] It specifically focuses on behavioural deviation from moral state of social life.[37] In this context, it deals with pathologies as parts of social life, i.e. crime, delinquency, deviance, alcohal, drug addiction, vagrancy and illegitimacy.[38]

As is clear from the preceding sections and chapters, the situation of conflict contributed seriously and significantly to the wider process of social pathology in the Kashmiri society. Consequently, it led to the rise of sick behavior, social diseases and disordered social life. In this way, the entire social ethos in Kashmir got disturbed, dislocated, perturbed, and disorganized. At the same time, all basic roles, institutions, processes and inter-relationships got pathological character. This situation in totality gave whole society a pathological form in which everything desirable got in to the background and everything undesirable came to the fore. In this paper, we will explain the ongoing social pathology in Kashmir with special focus on social deviance, social dis-organization, social disorder and social delinquency.

[ii] *Social Apathy:* The most important aspect of 'social pathology' in the Kashmiri society reflects in large scale 'social apathy' among large, influential and important sections of society which can mostly be characterized as the outcome of continuous conflict situation for 20 years. This stands for a 'paralyzed behaviour' on the part of members of society. It gives rise to a situation of 'functional paralysis'.[39] In this situation in Kashmir, while the individual sought refuge within family institution, at the social level, he proved disinclined, dis-associative and deviationist. They showed no consistent and regular response to all social developments which affect them and their families too. While avoiding all social functions and engagements, home engagement and home entertainment were prepared. It was in that situation that one used to enjoy 3 to 4 movies in a day. There was no concern shown on social, economic, educational, and other fields' upheaval outside family. This behaviour reflected the "hartal mentality" which implies 'lotus eater' behaviour and wasting time without any purpose.[40]

In this situation of 'social apathy', no concern was shown in an organized way to the social environment and its issues and problems. Individuals behaved in a way that were not component part of the whole system and were not participating even in elementary form of social life. This erased the 'social courtesy' and 'social reciprocity' from the Kashmiri mind. They hardly took interesting, regional, national and international issues and problems. Moreover, levels of social relationship in terms of relatives' closeness, neighbours' friendship and colleagues' comradeship diminished considerably. Most of the people forgot 'we' and 'me'. They only remembered 'I' and 'me'. However, the concept of 'they' was always strong because of its political connotation.

[iii] *Sexual Proximity:* In this situation of mass violation of values and norms, there emerged a strong trend of undesirable sex behavior which may be characterized as "sexual promiscuity". It refers to the sex behaviour of youngsters of both sexes before and after their marriage. They do involve in these sexual activities mostly outside their families and mostly without informing their family members. These immoral

scenes can be observed more in urban than in rural areas and educated as well as uneducated youths are involved in this vagrancy. They belong to all economic classes and occupations. In the Kashmir valley, these scenes can be observed in famous tourist spots-resorts, in Dal Lake *shikaras*, public parks, private vehicles on roadsides and even on open sites and roads.[41] An observer commented about this situation in the following words:

"Visiting a garden or a tourist place with family and children becomes really embarrassing. Young couples behind a bush in lewd if not obscene acts in routine.[42]

As Kashmiri society used to be a conservative and traditional society, there was a strong negative reaction to this emergence of undesirable sex behaviour involving the local youth. Two related points may be mentioned in this regard. First, this reaction was shown mainly by the conservatives represented by religious preachers and leaders. They delivered fiery speeches and warned against these irreligious practices. They even threatened the youth with dire consequences, so that they abandon these activities.[43] But, it proved counter-productive. The local youth didn't accept these moral dictates of religious preachers and law enforcing police, especially when militancy was over. Thus the youth got involved more in sexual activities and crossed even decent limits. Second, the local police didn't respond to this youth behavior effectively partly because it was extremely busy with anti-militancy operations and partly because less interest in controlling and curbing these undesirable activities.[44] Other details about these sexual activities have been discussed earlier on Though prostitution as an established and organized institution has not developed in Kashmir, some prostitution-like activities have increased mainly due to militancy and militarization. The 2007 sex scandal in Kashmir revealed the nature of prostitution network in JK, and involvement of top bureaucrats, politicians, businessmen, police officials, hoteliers and contractors.[45]

[v] *Moral Waywardness:* The prolonged conflict over two decades in Kashmir created a situation characterized by two opposite directions. On the one hand, there emerged a situation of commitment and sincerity on the part of militants and their local supporters at the earlier stage of the movement. But, on

the other hand, there emerged a situation of 'degeneration' among all local groups, classes and communities. While the former was a minor trend, the latter proved major, dominant and determining trend which led to distortion of moral-ethical standards. It was observed among all aged, economic, social, and linguistic groups. Thus the public—social life became a 'casualty' in this environment in which systematic violation of values and norms [especially of religious-oriented] took place. Again, continued deviation from moral standards became a 'usual practice' which seemed like 'de-legitimization' of ideal roles and institutions. What followed from this rot was the moral quos. An analyst made the following observation in this regard:

"While first generation is distressingly moving away from time tested and centuries evolved moral and ethical standards, young ones seem to be quite oblivious of any moral system. It is a well established fact, Kashmir of today is mired in a moral morass."[46]

He further comments that

"Do we demonstrate from our own moral conduct that sexual waywardness is recipe for disaster? ... If home, school and society have all failed, wherefrom the children will learn the values? ... Youth of today is faced with a deep moral vacuum."[47]

[vi] *Social Apathy and Social Crisis:* It was observed that widespread social disorder in Kashmir created an environment of social apathy and social crisis at individual and collective levels. The former convey the notion of disordered situation of social disturbance – social deviance, social problems and so on.[48] It was observed by experts in Kashmir that social apathy at the individual level effected attitudes and behaviour. The general apathetic attitude was individualistic, self-oriented and showed no social-community concern. The individual considered himself as 'whole' and world revolving around this whole. In this attitude, the individual remained confined to his family and hardly bothered about out-family situation. If seen in totality, this attitude towards life leads to such kind of collective behaviour. In other words, it gave rise to 'social apathy' which reflected in whole society. It contributed to

'social abnormality' and 'abnormal social input' which led to 'abnormal social output'. Consequently, the processes of socialization got disturbed and misdirected. In turn, it created a lot of social problems, especially among children, youth and women. An objective observer commented on this situation in the way which follows:

"... concerned citizens too have become insensitive and indifferent not only to all kinds of violations of rights but to the misdeeds and moral depravity of the populace [because of abysmal official apathy to all cries for justice]. The death of accountability and some responsibility in society has opened a Pandora's box of all kinds of nefarious activities and profilgacies."[49]

She further observes that "the civil society, on the whole, has become apathetic to all deviations from approved and agreed upon norm of public and personal morality so much so that people in general have started kicking loose on the earth or kicking the very moral loss of the earth to pieces. Civil society has become indifferent and insensitive to what is happening around."[50]

[vi] *Social Crisis:* As has been explained above, the impact of conflict on the roles, institutions and inter-relationships led to broader social disorder which crudely reflected in erosion of values-norms, negative social ideas and views, antagonism and conflict. The associated social dynamics gave birth to deep crisis in social ideas and social ideology. In this situation, one does not know how to react these potential problems, how to approach and study these problems and how to arrive at solutions. When social problems are not studied rationally and satisfactorily, they develop intensity and complexity and resist resolution.

These problems are further accentuated by implications of the processes of change and development. In this social crisis, other crucial problems follow which include deviance, delinquency, antagonism, conflict, inequality, crime, drug addiction, social insecurity, social antipathy, loss of sense of social wellbeing, social distress, depression, unjust social-economic mobility, generation gap, value erosion, loss of role model, marriage problems, abnormal kinship ties, immorality and vices, sexual anarchy and no positive worldview.

[vii] *Dehumanization, Corruption And Misgover-nance:* One of the important features of social pathology is the process of 'dehumanization'. Strictly speaking, it refers to killing the basic human sentiment. In the sociological framework, it applies to a situation in which a human being's behaaviour is devoid of any human feeling while dealing or interacting with others. It involves attitudes as well as behaviour. At the level of former, it involves a series of attitudes at ideational level, and at the level of later, it includes whole social behaviour involving all social activities in which there is hardly any human feeling or consideration. In the Kashmir context, it is essentially related to the relationship between conflict implications and the process of dehumanization. In fact, this process has been introduced, spread and intensified by the continuous conflict situation and effected all fields, dimensions and at all levels the social life. In actuality, it has effected some crucial areas where human consideration has been negated consciously and made the concerned social ethos as 'dehumanized', though there should have been maximum human consideration. The expanding conflict gave the expansion to this process also.

The process of 'dehumanization' has engulfed the whole society. However, one of its prominent reflections comes from a particular attitude and behaviour of police force in JK. It has been generally observed that police in Kashmir behaves in a way which can only be characterized as 'dehumanized'. While this behavior starts with offensive-abusive language and humiliated-uncivilized welcome, it culminates in inhuman treatment and brutal torture of civilians or common people. These may not be considered as individual acts of the policemen on duty, but have developed in to a culture which they follow consciously and transfer to junior/new generations very proudly. How they treat, dominate, discriminate, harass, torture and kill in the police stations and jails stand as glaring examples of 'dehumanization'. Even outside police stations, the vulgarity exhibited by them know no limits. The way they 'lathi-charge' and injured blind and disabled persons during their demonstration are telling cases of their dehumanized behaviour. The conflict situation gave a boost and license to this police behaviour in Kashmir. From the humanitarian, democratic and liberal point of view, this behaviour stands highly undesirable, objectionable and against civilized norms. Though the police department has recruited some young and new faces to change its entire image. But, that process has started recently and its impact has to be assessed later on. At present, the dehumanized culture stands in practice.

[viii] *Corruption:* As conflict started in Kashmir, corruption too started simultaneously at mass level, in all fields, in all groups and classes. It seems that there is inverse relationship between conflict and corruption. In many cases, this proved correct. All political parties, groups, organizations, political leaders and activists and various intelligence agencies were involved in all matters related to corruption. So, it seems a realistic proposition that politics stands as the root cause of corruption in Kashmir. In a way, the practice/s was legalized and legitimized by the state. The political developments often compelled the governments to "encourage" corrupt practices of bureaucrats, administrators, businessmen, contractors, media persons, police officials, professionals and technocrats.[51]

On the other hand, civil society too got corrupt in Kashmir. It seems that every individual is involved in the corrupt mileau. Even if one opts out of this situation, he continues to suffer. In a way, it has emerged as a "way of life"[52] and there seems no hesitation by individuals to follow it. This situation started from 1947 and it was increased and intensified with the expansion of militancy in the valley. Thus both, state as well as society, were equally involved in the operation of corruption. It led to extreme deterioration and degeneration in social life and exploitation of those masses who already suffer in life conditions.[53] It was primarily in this pathetic and widespread background of corruption that 'Transparency International' rated the JK state in whole of India as the "most corrupt state in India" after the state of Bihar. This 'award' was given to the JK sate after assessing the performance of some government departments in the state.[54]

Despite this grave nature of the problem, the state has not been able to counter and to counter this phenomenon. There seems no will and lower level of action in this regard on the part of the government. Though several cells have been established in most of the departments, their functioning has remained unchanged. No effective and realistic performance has been shown in this connection. Even State Vigilance

Organization [SVO] and its units seem defunct. Finally, the vacancy of Chairman, State Accountability Commission [SAC] for last so many years reveals the actual reality related to state's fight against corruption.

[ix] *Misgovernance:* In the whole pathological situation, how the government could have avoided or resisted corruption in its offices, agencies and organizations, especially during the conflict situation. But, the actual situation in Kashmir reveals that the government with any ruling political party proved the "root cause of corruption and mis-governance".[55] It was involved in all kinds of misdeeds under political powers, especially from Delhi. The Delhi-dominated politics has been seen as the most crucial factor for institutional corruption and mis-governance in JK. In this situation, most of the government claims were manipulated, sponsored and exploited. With this situation, how could state government have behaved rationally, reasonably and scientifically. The natural result was "mis-governance". This inefficiency was matched by societal passiveness. In this development of mis-governance, while the masses suffered absolutely, the political elites-families got benefited. Taking note of this situation, the Supreme Court of India observed that governments in JK have been using conflict as an "excuse" not to perform.[56] In connection with this situation, an observer commented in a local newspaper that in the context of a study carried out by Supreme Court of India regarding food and livelihood] the state government must be held far more accountable than it is at present to secure the rights of people to food, healthcare, education, livelihood, and security. So, it is the kind of governance which has been held responsible for mission of the people of the state."[57]

He further commented that "governance has always remained hostage to the basic conflict and in such situations one cannot expect good governance in future too."[58]

NOTES AND REFERENCES

1. Report on *Emergence of Late Marriage in Kashmir [2008,* Department of Sociology and Social Work, University of Kashmir, Srinagar]
2. *Ibid.*
3. *Ibid.*

4. *Ibid.*
5. Survey on *Changing Marriage Practices in Kashmir Valley [2009, Department of Sociology and Social Work, University of* Kashmir, Srinagar], unpublished.
6. See Census of India, 2001.
7. Peter R. Cox, *Demography* [New Delhi, 1972, United Book Store].
8. *Ibid.*
9. See Census of India, 2001.
10. Ram Ahuja, *Social Problems in India* [New Delhi, 1997, Rawat].
11. *Idid.*
12. *Ibid.*
13. *Ibid.*
14. *Ibid.*
15. *Ibid.*
16. The Times of India, New Delhi, 6th June 2010.
17. *Ibid.*
18. *Ibid.*
19. See 8th Report of NCPCH, New Delhi, December 2009.
20. *Ibid.*, and *Greater Kashmir,* Srinagar.
21. This micro-level study was carried out by Shimayel Wani under the guidance of the author in connection with her M. Phil. Programme.
22. *Ibid.*
23. *Ibid.*
24. *Ibid.*
25. See micro-level study, op. cit., no.12.
26. *Ibid.*
27. *Ibid.*
28. *Ibid.*
29. *Ibid.*

30. *Ibid.*
31. *Ibid.*
32. *Ibid.*
33. *Ibid.*
34. *Ibid.*
35. Gordan Marshall, ed., *Oxford Dictionary of Sociology* [New York, 1994, Oxford Univ. Press, p. 383.
36. *Ibid.*
37. G. Duncan Michell, ed., *A Dictionary of Sociology* [London, 1987, R & K], pp. 173-74.
38. *Ibid.*
39. See *Oxford Dictionary, no.* 1.
40. See relevant comments in the local print media by local observers and analysts during all these years.
41. B.A. Dabla, "Worrying Trend", *Greater Kashmir,* Srinagar, 5th June 2008.
42. Firdous Baba, "The Poison of Waywardness", *Greater Kashmir,* Srinagar, 13th March 2010.
43. See contents of their speeches in local Urdu Newspapers, especially *Srinagar Times* and *Aftab*, Srinagar.
44. This behaviour has been repeatedly shown by the local police in Srinagar and other towns in the valley.
45. See B.A. Dabla, report entitled "Tourism and Sex Practices in Kashmir" [Srinagar, 2008].
46. Baba, *op.cit.,* no. 8.
47. *Ibid.*
48. See *A Dictionary of Sociology, op. cit.*
49. Hameeda Nayeem, "End this Culture of Impunity", *Greater Kashmir,* Srinagar, 18th April, 2010.
50. See Khursheed Wani, "Official Criminalization", *Kashmir Life,* Srinagar, 7th June 2010.
51. See Ph.D. proposal of Humera Yaqoob on the topic

"A Sociological Study of Bureaucracy in Kashmir" submitted to Department of Sociology, University of Kashmir, Srinagar.

52. See *Greater Kashmir,* Srinagar, 11th March, 2010 and 11th April 2010.

53. *Ibid.*

54. For details of this negative award can be seen in the original report of Sweden-based NGO, Transparency International in 2009.

55. Sajjad Bazaz, "Governance and Conflict", *Greater Kashmir,* Srinagar, 9th May, 2010.

56. *Ibid.*

57. *Ibid.*

58. *Ibid.*

CHAPTER 7

PRIME VICTIMS OF VIOLENCE IN KASHMIR

[I] WOMEN AND CHLDREN

[A] ORPHANS OF THE ORPHANED VALLEY

1. *Impact of Militancy:* The impact of militancy in Kashmir has proved widespread and deeply-felt. In actuality, every family in the valley has suffered in terms of death of a person [who usually was head of the household and sole bread-earner], injury to a person, missing of a person, disability of a person, humiliation/torture of some or all members. All groups and communities had to face unprecedented torturous situation at the hands of security forces.

   The orphans represent one such group which has suffered in extreme sense of the word. This clearly reflects in their tragic situation which emerged immediately after death of fathers, especially the militants, who were heads of their families in most cases.

2. *Findings of the Study:* In this situational context, a macro-level sociological study was carried out in the Kashmir valley in 1999-2000 and its report was released in late 2000. It was carried out among the representative sample of 300 orphans spread in all districts of the valley and belonging to all age, economic, demographic, social, educational and other relevant groups. The total information about orphans was collected through questionnaire/interviews and was analysed scientifically. The study focused on three aspects of the situation related to orphans. These were :

[i] Situation of orphans which prevailed just at the time of death of their fathers;

[ii] Situation of orphans which emerged with the death of their fathers; and

[iii] An assessment of multi-dimensional future needs of the orphans.

Some of the major findings of this study on orphans were as follows:

First, in the series of problems, the first problem of orphans [and their mothers, now widows] was related to their house accommodation. In the situation in which fathers belonged to 20-35 years age group [with no or one/two children] and father's fathers were alive, the orphans [and widows] were denied the share in their parental property. This didn't happen in all cases, but a significant number of orphans had to face this situation. At this stage, the matri-kins of their mothers, i.e. mother's parents, brothers and sisters, came to their rescue and took them to their houses. But, here also, the orphans [and their mothers] could not live peacefully. Finally, they had to live in rented accommodation or had to construct their own house. The fact stands that all orphans in the valley didn't face this situation. But, a significant number of them faced this acute situation.

Second, other crucial problem faced by the orphans was discontinuity/stopping of the practice of school-going in rural as well urban areas. It follows that, after death of their fathers, a large number of orphans had to stop going to schools, especially at primary and middle levels. This drop-out rate had gone up to 35 to 40% mainly because they were not in a position to bear even the minimum expenses on education.

Third, after the death of their fathers who were often sole bread-earner of the family, the orphans and their mothers had to go out of their homes to work and earn for their families. The huge majority of these children [up to 57%] worked in the handicraft sector, others worked in the fields of domestic service [7%], automobile workshops [8%], shops [9%] and hotels-dhabas [4%]. In this situation, while nearly all child labourers were exploited, they were harassed too.

Fourth, nearly all orphans faced 'social downfall' and 'downward mobility'. The normal processes of socialization and internalization could not be carried out in the situation of conflict, which effected negatively children in the family in terms of transformation of culture from one generation to other generation. This gave rise to the questions of relevance of traditional values-norms and ends-means. This situation also reflected in the minor or major threat posed to the traditional patriarchal authority maintained by the eldest male member of the family/clan. This situation also revealed in the emerging trends in 'marriage market'. The orphans, especially the girl orphans, were thrown to the lowest social status. While they were not treated as 'untouchables', they were treated neither 'preferable' nor equal partners in marriage. In actuality, they were cleverly avoided and ignored. The net result was that the orphans got socially discriminated by their own near and dear ones. Finally, when orphans faced 'dehumanized' social environment within and outside their families, they too developed 'dehumanized' traits in their personality.

Fifth, the orphans faced certain 'psychological depression' in the conflict situation. When they could not be socialized properly and traditional values and norms could not be maintained by them, they developed a certain degree of deviance within and outside their families. This also reflected in the rise of petty criminal tendency among some orphan children. The violent situation all around them gave rise to 'violent worldview' and 'violence-oriented hobbies' among them.

Sixth, the orphans had to pay in terms of health. The most important point in this regard was related to 'immunization of children'. In actuality, the entire system of immunization crumbled during the last decade. In that situation, neither all children could be given all necessary dozes nor regularity in these dozes could be maintained, particularly in rural areas. Moreover, children in general and orphans in particular could not get proper medical treatment to their health problems. Consequently, these children will have to face certain disabilities in their future life. On the other hand, the perpetual tension situation gave rise among orphans several dangerous diseases including neurological and heart diseases.

Seventh, dominant majority of orphans faced the worst financial problem, which had devastating effect on their entire life. It may be correct that near and distant relatives, neighbours and others, including NGOs and government agencies, helped financially these unfortunate children after death of their fathers for months and years. But, in totality, this help could not continue for long. This help also didn't prove regular, systematic and fulfill all basic needs of the orphans. In that situation, they felt compelled to work to earn.

Eight, the enquiry revealed that the orphans faced following problems prority-wise:

- Economic hardships;
- Educational discontinuity;
- Undesirable lower social status;
- Psychological setback;
- Denial of love and affection;
- Apathy by relatives, neighbours and near-dear friends;
- Stopping of the help by NGOs and government agencies after some time.

2. *Existing Help Framework: It* may be realistic to say that there was no significant, widespread and systematic effort to provide the required help to the orphans in the earlier years of militancy here. However, in many rural and urban areas, the local *Mohalla-Masjid* committees provided the help to orphans [whose number was very less at that time] to fulfill their basic needs. The government's help at that time was very limited. Though this non-government help didn't prove durable, it fulfilled the short-term needs of orphans and their families.

In the following period, i.e. mid-1990s, several NGOs established various programmes of help to orphans with the local, national and international financial support. It is believed that significant amount of money was at the disposal of the NGOs, it didn't prove sufficient partly because of increasing number of orphans in the valley and partly because of mismanagement. It was argued that all this happened because there was no transparency of all necessary dealings. At the same time, government agencies and organizations at the state and central level started helping orphans and their families, though not at the large scale. However, there were allegations of corruption and discrimination against these agencies too.

After the mid-1990s, the help of national and international NGOs [and also government agencies and organizations] came in a big way in the Valley. Whether this helped orphans and their families in Kashmir stood as a big question. An inquiry in this regard revealed that the following NGOs were active in different programmes related to orphans in the valley:

- J & K Yateem Trust;
- J & K Yateem Foundation;
- J & K Yateem Khana;
- *Shehjaar* – J & K Help Foundation;
- Rajiv Gandhi Foundation;
- Save the Children;
- Action Aid International.

It seems important to note here that no international agency or organization was allowed to work in Kashmir for the welfare of local children. The United Nations organizations were no exception in this regard. The UNICEF had taken interest in welfare programmes of local children in general and orphans in particular and that also in collaboration with the state government. Though the UN agencies prefer to work with NGOs elsewhere, but here, they had to work with government agencies and organizations. The UICEF chief, during his last visit to Kashmir, gave two reasons for this. First, the tradition of NGO work here stands very poor. Second, the 'charity approach' of local individuals and organizations does not prove helpful. In that situation, even International Red Cross Committee could not work in the valley even in its traditional framework. Now, International Red Cross and Indian Red Cross Society have started some work in this regard. We may argue that, at present, three categories of agencies and organizations were active in welfare activities of orphans in the Valley. These were :

- Local and national NGOs;
- Government agencies and organizations;
- International and U.N. agencies and organizations.

It has been observed that these agencies and organizations were carrying out welfare activities according to their financial resources and policy-objective preferences. While some organizations have concentrated on some adopted children or/and their families, others were providing general help in the traditional framework. Again, some organizations were providing cash assistance to orphans, others focused on providing the daily necessities. However, it was observed that their functioning was more hidden than open. Even an agency or organization had no knowledge about functioning of others agencies and organizations. Though all NGOs pursued the same sacred cause related orphans life [and their dependent families], they had hardly any coordination and collaboration between their organizations. No serious study of this situation has been made so far. Moreover, from the orphans' viewpoint, the functioning of these NGOs was not well-organized, systematic and transparent, especially in financial matters. While their help didn't prove durable, it could not fulfill all their basic needs.

On the other hand, the government agencies and organizations provided help to orphans in an open framework and in a planned way. Cash compensation and government job to the orphans were two important aspects of this help framework. Moreover, international agencies, including U.N. agencies, provided their help through the government agencies. However, the government's help could reach to lesser number of orphans. Even in this type of help, there were allegations of corruption, favourtism, nepotism and exploitation.

4. *Need for Help Network:* In the context of above critique, there arises the need for 'Help Network' in order to benefit the orphans in totality and effective way. Some crucial points in this regard are mentioned below.

- The help to the orphans must be organized scientifically in order to fulfill their short-term and long-term needs. It must be systematic, continuous, transparent and institutionalized.
- The 'help network' must cover all orphans belonging to all cities, towns and villages irrespective of their father's political and other differences.
- Theoretical and practical work must be carried out by the managers of 'help network' to avoid duplication of efforts in the same area. If the need of education was taken care of by one NGO, others must work in the fields of health, nutrition, and other need-based areas. This can be done well if

specialization and coordination between NGOs matures. While the former emphasizes to work seriously in a particular area such as health, the latter will necessarily keep the NGOs in close contact. Thus, both these features will make their efforts more meaningful and more productive.

- The role of government and non-government organizations must be seen in complementary rather than contradictory terms while dealing with orphans. While the government had lot of infrastructure, expertise, experienced personnel and large net-work of institutional facilities, the NGOs had dedicated, specialized, trained and sincere persons. The cooperation between the two will make the efforts for welfare of orphans more realistic, intensive and extensive. However, these joint efforts must be jointly controlled and monitored.
- There must be full appreciation of national and international efforts to help the orphans in Kashmir. But, at the same time, proper planning and strategy must be developed to utilize that money. The local NGOs must also develop dedication and reputation, so that international NGOs get enough basis to trust them and their work.
- All efforts towards the betterment of orphans must be community-oriented. It follows that there must be largest possible community participation in orphans' welfare programmes which must seem as 'community affair' rather than the individual or agency affair.
- Keeping in view the political situation in J&K, only short-term plans and programmes must be framed for short-term objectives.
- As far as possible, help in terms of payment of huge amount in cash to orphans or their families must be discouraged because it has proved completely' unproductive' for orphans.
- All efforts must be carried out to negate all aspects of gender discrimination. This was more important in the fields of education, health, financial support and so on.
- The attainment of education, especially at the elementary stage, on the part of orphans must be made compulsory.

At the same time, all related facilities and services required for this purpose must be made available.

- The most competent and more meritorious students among orphans must be taken in the professional and technical courses necessarily.
- The government must provide to the orphans a regular income through a part-time/full-time government job according to her/his competence and qualification or through any other arrangement. This will ensure the orphans economic stability and social mobility.
- The child labour on the part of orphans must be stopped or discouraged through government and non-government actions. If it stands impossible in practice, the extreme exploitation of orphans must be stopped formally to the maximum possible extent. This may be done by fixation of standard wages and monitoring its payment regularly and strictly.
- Large-scale societal efforts need to be initiated to give the impression to the orphans, both boys and girls, that they were normal but suffering societal members with equal rights. Their suffering must be projected as imposed on them. The taboos developed in this connection must be exposed and discredited. In this process, the social acceptability and social security of orphans must be projected as natural, desirable and highly needed in the process of emancipation and development.
- The marriage chances of female orphans in the 'marriage market' must be increased tremendously through formal action on the part of government, civil society and all individuals. But, at the same time, marriage of these females must be formalized only after they develop certain career/ profession.
- The home environment must be developed in such a way that orphans' physical and mental growth becomes a normal functional process. This will ensure the growth of 'positive personality' and effective control over their behaviour.

[B] WIDOWS AND ORPHANS IN KASHMIR

1. Impact of the Armed Conflict

The militancy in Kashmir affected all sections and sectors of society. Lakhs of innocent and common people were killed, injured, tortured and made disabled-handicapped. Most of the local elders were abused and dishonoured repeatedly, all local youth brutally treated, all local children harassed and tortured, and most of the women teased, molested and raped. Thousands of residential houses and business establishments were burnt or destroyed. In brief, the militancy brought a devastating and catastrophic effect in totality in the entire Kashmiri society, especially in the fields related to large scale economic destruction, widespread social disorder and disorganization, educational backwardness, mass psychological depression. Physical and mental health deterioration, mass humiliation and extreme helplessness, degenerated cultural aggression, political deception and domination, cronic social problems such as deviance, suicides, drug abuse and crime, which were experienced by majority of Kashmiris.

In addition to the human and material loss, the Kashmiri society experienced a new group of "widows and orphans" in very large numbers whose existence was ignorable in pre-militancy times. At the initiation of the armed conflict in Kashmir between pro-freedom militants and Indian security forces in 1989, their emergence and presence was not felt seriously by all. But, with increasing intensity in the conflict, their number increased fast and their presence was felt seriously by all observers. When the first report of a study about widows and orphans in Kashmir, prepared by the author in 1999, was released in April 2000, this proved a shock to many people in the valley as they never expected such a large number of widows and orphans. Thus, these unfortunate people emerged as a significant group primarily because of the direct effect of armed conflict and immediate implication of the militancy. In actuality, every death in the conflict situation make 3 – 4 members addition to this newly-created 'suffering group'. In reality, they clearly stand for 'human suffering' and 'human tragedy' in present-day Kashmir.

2. Composition of Widows and Orphans

The widows and orphans in Kashmir compose of four main sub-groups. They are (i) wives and children of civilians/common people killed by the security forces or by militants or were killed in armed encounters between militants and security forces; (ii) wives and children of ex-local militants; (iii) wives and children of ex-officials-personnel of Indian security forces which include regular army, B.S.F., C..R.P.F., R.R. and I.T.B.P.; and (iv) wives and children of ex-officials-personnel of J.K.A.P. and S.T.F.

3. Number of Widows and Orphans

The fact stands that no comprehensive and factual survey about the number of widows and orphans in present-day Kashmir has been carried out so far. There are different estimates made by different sources which reveal extreme difference in their total number. While the pro-freedom political sources give one extreme figure, governments and intelligence agencies give other extreme figure. Some human rights groups, NGOs and civil societies present comparatively realistic figures. Taking in to consideration all these estimates and official population data given in Census of India-2001, we present the calculated estimated number of widows and orphans in the following table:

Table 7.1

Estimated Number of Widows and Orphans in Kashmir, 2008

S.No.	*Group of People Killed*	*Total Number ofDeaths*	*Married Persons*	*Widows*	*Orphans*	*Total*
1.	Military Personnel	3,000	1,800	1,800	5,400	7,200
2.	Para. Mili. Security forces	6,000	3,600	3,600	10,800	14,400
3.	JKAP-STF	7,000	4,200	4,200	12,600	16,800
4.	Militants & Civilians	54,000	32,400	32,400	97,200	1,29,600 [@ 3]
			32,400	1,29,600	2,26,800 [@ 4]	
Total		70,000[1]	42,000 [2]	42,000[3]	1,26,000[4]	1,68,000 [5]

[1] This estimate is based on the calculated average estimates given by these sources by their official representatives and published in the local media.

[2] This proportion represents the 60% married lot among the deceased. The Census of INDIA-2001 shows that there were 45% ever married persons in the country. 15% more has been added to it keeping inn view the heavy concentration of married population among the armed forces.

[3] This number represents widows @ one widow per person.

[4] This figure gives the total number of orphans @ 3 and 4 orphans per widow. While the Census of India-2001 shows 3 children per household at the national level, the state has the higher number of children per household.

[5] This figure gives the total estimated number of widows and orphans @ 3 children per widow.

The preceding table reveals that there are 1,29,600 – 2,26,800 widows and orphans living in Kashmir who belong to ex-militants and civilians killed in the armed conflict. It follows that an estimated number of 8,842 per year and 737 per month [widows and orphans] were added to the total during the last 19 years from 1990 to 2008. The following Table 7.1 shows the increasing number of widows and orphans in Kashmir during the period of 1990-2008.

4. Multi-dimensional Problems

The living conditions of widows and orphans of army, security and police personnel are not worst mainly because their concerned agencies and organizations have taken sufficient care of their needs, especially in the fields of education and employment to family members. But, their counter-parts belonging to ex-militants and civilians are living in miserable and pathetic conditions. Economically, they have been debased and no stable source of income is available to them. Some of them face even starvation. Many among them were compelled to come out of their homes to work in the handicraft, child labour, domestic work and automobile sectors where they were exploited and harassed and were not paid due wages regularly. Educationally, they have become backward permanently. While some of them [even up to 40%] had to drop-out from primary-middle schools, others can never dream of quality, professional, technical and higher education. At the initial stage after the death of their husbands/fathers, the in-laws families provided them shelter. But, after some time, most of them were thrown out due to social compulsions.

Majority of these widows and orphans faced mass depression and other psychological problems. These mental health patients suffered more in the absence of treatment facilities in the valley. Very few among them could go outside the state for ideal treatment. These unfortunate families faced social disorganization in terms of loss of traditional patriarchal authority, loosening of social control, erosion of values and norms, and undesirable socialization. In this situation, late marriage and sexual promiscuity could not be avoided. Traditional kinship ties got disturbed which created a feeling of 'helplessness' and 'insecurity' among widows and orphans. The presence of security forces and other elements increased this feeling.

Consequently, a large number of widows and orphans developed several health problems. It can be generally observed that they developed abnormal health scenario in which they could neither fulfill basic health needs nor could stop emergence of most dreaded diseases like cardiological, neurological and psychological diseases. The total dependence of widows and orphans on others outside their own families has made them totally and socially handicapped in the patriarchal society of Kashmir. It has been observed that these families are more worried about the future careers of their children. Lastly, lack of parental/proper authority, socialization and social control has given rise the trends of deviance, delinquency, drug abuse and crime among some of the orphans. The living conditions of those widows and orphans who belong to ex-pro-government militants stands more worse, as helping them is still considered a 'taboo'.

5. The Societal Response

The earliest response to the problems of Widows and orphans came from family and kin group members who provided financial and non-financial help, in addition to accommodation, education, security, diet and so on. But, this type of help, which was not regular, stable and organized, could not last long. In many cases, the in-laws families proved more cruel to these widows and orphans and these suffering people had to search themselves for some income. At this time, some *Mohalla-Masjid* committees informally came to help these widows and orphans, but this type of help too didn't prove last long and some of its units got complaints of fraud and embezzlement. In this situation, came the response of the NGOs of the local, national and international level. At the local level, the local NGOs, generally composed of local area committees, collected money and material in all localities/colonies and distributed regularly among the needy widows and orphans. This meager help helped them to purchase essential daily-items. In this context, some local NGOs were formed here with the sole objective to serve the cause of widows and orphans. Some of these prominent NGOs included JK Yateem Trust, JK Yateem Foundation, Yateem Khana JK, JK Help Foundation, JK Chinar Foundation and Sakhawat Trust. These organizations have 100% transparency in their functioning. They collect money from different sources and distribute among the needy widows and orphans in an organized and systematic way. They also maintain the ideals of sincerity, honesty, commitment, discipline and management in their activities. These organizations maintain their accounts properly and get them audited and published regularly.

It is important to note here that there was mushroom growth of local NGOs in Kashmir from mid-1990s. Within a brief period of a few years, many such NGOs, even up to thousands in number, cropped up. Most of these organizations were fake and fraud and existed on paper only, but grabbed the whole money collected on the name and cause of widows and orphans. In fact, some of these organizations were sponsored by outside agencies and were also used in counter-insurgency measures.

In the meantime, several national and international organizations/ agencies arrived here to serve the cause of widows and orphans. Some of these prominent NGOs were as follows:

- Save the Children;
- Action Aid International;
- Doctors Without Borders;
- Rajiv Gandhi Foundation;
- Agha Khan Foundation;

- Village India;
- WISCOM;
- Child Care and You.

These NGOs specifically focused their efforts on the victims of violence, especially women and children, in the areas of personality development, social-psychological empowerment, educational improvement, mental-physiological health, psychological disorders, peace environment, conflict resolution and overall mobility of widows and orphans. Though these organizations organized many seminars and workshops in the Kashmir valley on some important topics but could not develop much-needed institutional infrastructure, except the mental health centre by M.S.F. in Srinagar, which would have served long-term interests of widows and orphans in Kashmir.

6. The Government Response

At the initial stage, the JK government showed no response to the existing problems of widows and orphans. But, when these problems increased and intensified, the state government adopted the policy of providing a job and an ex-gratia payment of Rs. 50,000/- [later raised to 1,00,000/- and now to 4,00,000/-] to the next of kin of the deceased was adopted. This policy would have certainly helped some widows and orphans but it was manipulated in the process of its implementation in order to ensure these benefits to ruling party members/activists. In this process, no person killed by security forces or local police was able to get this financial assistance. At the same time, no serious concern was shown by the state government about deteriorating living conditions of widows and orphans. Though the JK govt. established 'Rehabilitation Council' a decade back, it could not prove functional. It could not even carry out a comprehensive survey about total number of widows and orphans in the state. In reality, the JK govt. lacks the social policy perspective regarding rehabilitation of large number of widows and orphans in the state.

7. Role of Orphanages

As the role of orphanages stands crucial in the lives of orphans, several such institutions were established in Kashmir during last two decades. With increase in the number of orphans, the number of orphanages also increased. Most of these institutions were established in Srinagar and their functioning remained limited to this district. As mentioned above, while some orphanages have developed reputation for their functioning for the cause of orphans, many such institutions were established by fraud entities whose sole aim was to grab and loot money accumulated on the orphans name. The latter didn't perform well, so proved discredited. These institutions never maintained proper account of dealings, never recorded their activities, never practiced transparency and never got their accounts audited and published. But, on the other hand, some orphanages in Kashmir have developed clean reputation in taking proper care of orphans and their mothers. These institutions have provided the orphans schools, hostels, scholarships, financial aids, all basic facilities such as health, diet, clothing, entertainment, sports, career-building, outings, interaction sessions, family meetings, religious gatherings, participation in radio-television programmes and counseling services. These orphanages are completely transparent in their functioning and prepare accounts properly, get them audited and published in the press regularly. These institutions have developed a real 'help network' for orphans in Kashmir. These institutions prominently include JK Yateem Trust, JK Help Foundation, JK Yateem Khana, JK Baitul Hilal, Chinar Hostel, Koshish, Chotey Tarey, govt. orphanages and Muskaan.

It is pertinent to mention here about the role of Awkaf which is not fulfilling its social obligations towards orphans and widows in Kashmir, especially those who are victims of militancy. Though the JK Wakf Board has enough financial strength and administrative network for helping all orphans and widows in rural as well as urban areas, its attitude seems apathetic towards this unfortunate lot.

[C] HALF-WIDOWS AND HALF-ORPHANS

Half Widows in Kashmir: Since Kashmir experienced armed conflict between Kashmiri militants and Indian security forces from 1989, many uninvolved civilians were lifted, arrested and taken into custody of armed forces and never came back to their homes, neither their relatives could see them again. Their parents, wives and children generally believe that they were tortured and killed in custody of armed forces and their bodies were disposed in any way. But, they have no legal proof to support this statement. In the broader society, the half-widows faced the argument that their husbands might be alive somewhere else. Security officials held that these persons might have crossed the LOC. But, this is not correct because, in that case, they would have conveyed this to their family members in any way. In fact, the government wanted to hide the reality because of its necessary implications. It follows that if it agreed on these disappearances, their direct or indirect involvement will be established and it has to pay damages and compensation. As the locals' perception go, all these men disappeared during their custody with security forces.

Number of Half-widows: The exact number of half widows in Kashmir was not known because no census or survey was carried out in this regard. While the state government admitted in state assembly in August 2009 the number of 3,500 during last 20 years in this connection. [See *Srinagar Times*, Srinagar, 27th August 2009], the unofficial sources claim much more than this number. According to a well-known local NGO, APDP, about 10,000 persons disappeared during last 20 years [See its Report prepared in late 1990s-2007] and most of these cases have been well documented. The spouses of these persons can be seen in regular demonstrations of the disappeared in Srinagar.

Legal Status: The most basic problem for half-widows was related to their legal status in society. They are not in a position to claim what they are? No specific law safeguards them. In reality, there was no specific law which dealt with them in particular. In general, courts have waited for 6 or 7 years for locating their husbands, after which their status was decided. As per the Islamic law, half-widows have to wait for 4 years, after which the decision about remarriage of the concerned woman can be taken. In this situation, the local Islamic scholars felt the need of 'innovation' in the Islamic law for the betterment of these suffering women. Thus in this unusual legal situation, the half-widows suffer more than widows and their life-conditions were also much worse than widows.

Social Conditions: The social conditions of half-widows and their children stood extremely pathetic. It was observed that a significant number of them were continuously tortured, harassed and exploited by some relatives, neighbours, employers, police, family friends and so on. Since their family life faced disorganization, their children faced numerous problems, especially abnormal socialization. The absence of patriarchal authority in family created an environment for violation of traditional vales and norms and negation of expected attitudes and behaviour. The social control mechanism over children of upper age group could not be implemented effectively. In that situation, emergence of socially undesirable trends of deviance, delinquency, drug abuse and crime was the natural result. In all such in-family and out-family situations, offensive, aggressive, criminal and asocial tendencies among the local youth could not be controlled. Frustration, negative worldview and violent behavior behaviour followed in the social ethos. The taboos attached to the marriage of children of half-widows on the part of broader society led to its serious implications particularly related to pre-marital and extra-marital sex relations. The 'social ostracism' imposed on half-widows was also supported by allegations on their chastity, purity and dignity. This often led to emotional breakdown among them. It was reported that these women have not celebrated any occasion for years together. Further, half-widows total dependence on others in the patriarchal society of Kashmir robbed them of any initiative, change or programme for their overall safety, security and welfare. In addition, they were constantly exposed to threats from security forces. All these social problems led to 'social pathology' among them.

Deterioration in Mental Health: It was observed that due to situation they were caught in, half-widows proved a 'psychological wreck'. They faced many psychological/psychiatric problems related to tension, stress, strain, anxiety, emotional breakdown and so on. Many of them suffered from PTSD. In actuality, they could not avoid the psychological breakdown in the situation in which their husbands disappeared and their whereabouts could not be known for long. A significant portion of these women visited the lone psychiatric hospital in the valley where they found shortage of experts and technology. With these problems, depression was found common among half-widows and their family members. In this context, rise of suicidal tendencies among half-widows could not be avoided. One of the author's studies revealed the total number of suicides in 20 years as 18,000. Half-widows composed about 30-35% among those who committed suicide. In this situation, development of their own and their children's personalities got 'off the track' and adopted undesirable traits in attitudes and behaviour. It was also observed in several studies that these children developed aggressive and violent and delinquent behaviour inside as well as outside their families. This was explained in terms of their faulty socialization and absence of patriarchal authority and collapse of social control mechanism.

Economic Downfall: After disappearance of their husbands, half-widows experienced extreme economic downfall. While the entire basis of their income was debased, they could not stand new and parallel economic activities. In that situation, they were compelled to come out of their homes and work for their families. Several studies revealed that these women, who usually worked in handicraft sector and their children in child labour sector, were often discriminated, abused, harassed and exploited. If their disappeared husbands were government or private employees, their respective offices neither considered their claim on husband's salary nor approved pension benefits to these women as the officers were not sure about life status of their ex-employees. If their disappeared husbands were small or large businessmen, half-widows and their children lost entire share in business as other partners denied then the husband's share. Similarly, they could not claim property rights of their husbands' property. If their husbands were artisans skilled/unskilled workers, half-widows could not get any amount of money left by their husbands with their employers, handicraft centres and others. This created a situation of extreme poverty for half-widows and they were not in a position to start alternative business activities. The uncertainty about death of their husbands became the main stumbling block in their business initiative.

Educational Backwardness: The direct and immediate implication of disappearance of husbands led to a situation which can be characterized as 'educational backwardness'. It was because while children of all age groups had to drop out of schools at all levels and, consequently, enrolment at the primary level dropped completely. It happened absolutely when half-widows had no money for educational expenditure. As per an unofficial survey, this drop-out rate in late 1990s had gone up to 35% and 40% in case of females.

Breakdown of Health Standards: There was complete breakdown of physical heath of half-widows and their children. It was observed that continuous tension and depression had given rise to suicidal tendencies and other cronic diseases among them. Studies have also revealed the occurrence of neurological, cardiac and other tension-based diseases among third group of women. On the other hand, neither relevant-required medical expertise nor the professionally-desired facilities were available in the valley. But, huge majority of half-widows was not so affluent and could not go outside state for treatment. Thus, their health problems increased and intensified.

Problems of Half-widows and Half-orphans: After studying psycho-social aspects of the life of half-widows and half-orphans, the following multi-dimensional problems were identified:

- Non-determination of their legal status;
- Physical insecurity and threats;
- Downward trend in literacy;
- Poverty and economic baselessness;
- Harassment, torture and exploitation;
- Mental depression;
- Perpetual tension;
- Suicidal and deviant tendencies;
- Loosening of family control over children of upper age group;
- Uncertain future of them and their children;
- Deterioration in mental and physical health standards;
- Total social dependency in the absence of patriarchal authority;
- No economic initiative and planning;
- Apathy of the government;
- Abnormal socialization of children;
- Deviant, delinquent, criminal and drug behavior of children;
- Social criticism and ostracism.

Government and Societal Response: The government response towards the problems of half-widows and their children can realistically be characterized as "apathetic" because of getting involved in 'violation of human rights problem'. It behaved in a way that it was not concerned with this grave and dangerous problem. It had also not helped them in any way. On the other hand, the societal response towards the problem of half-widows was not on desirable lines.

Primarily, individuals, groups. *Mohalla-masjid* committees and local organizations provided some financial and non-financial help for some time. But, this help was not organized, systematic and durable. In that situation, life conditions of half-widows turned miserable and worst even than widows.

In the context of entire assessment, we may mention about two immediate and preferable needs of half-widows and half-orphans.

First, to carry out a detailed, comprehensive and credible survey of half-widows and their children in Kashmir for last 20 years; and

Second, to initiate and help in the investigation aimed at to know whereabouts of disappeared persons [husbands and fathers] during last 20 years.

[II] SUFFERING CHILDREN

Due to conflict situation for two decades, Kashmir has produced a generation of children who suffer in one way or the other. The conflict-exposed children suffer directly or indirectly and pay for living in Kashmir. Two points may be explained in relation to these children, which are disturbing and reflect the increasing trends in this group of population. First, in the situation of not getting proper response from the broader society, the existing problems of these conflict-effected children have increased tremendously in the recent past and intensified with highly dangerous consequences for the entire society. Second, no academic/professional study of large number of these children has been carried out so far. In order to develop a realistic understanding of these children and their problems, a scientific and empirical study seems necessary.

[a] *Orphans:* The first group of militancy related suffering children compose of orphans in the Kashmir valley whose estimated number is 98,000 in 2009.[13] A detailed analysis has been done in chapter no. 7 [i].

[b] *Half-orphans:* The second suffering group of children belongs to the category of those whose fathers have disappeared in the conflict situation. People in general feel that these persons have disappeared due to the deadly actions of security forces. Their number, problems and living conditions have been discussed in chapter no. 7 [ii].

[c] *Disabled Children:* There are thousands of disabled children

in Kashmir. Their disability has been given in terms of vision, sight, listening, body movement and mental disturbance. These children with cronic problems emerged during last 2 decades. They and their sociological features have been explained in chapter no. 6 [iii].

[d] *Mentally-physically Diseased Children:* There are thousands of children in Kashmir who face mental and physical diseases. Though their number and problems are increasing fast, there are neither sufficient expertise/experts nor health facilities in Kashmir. They and their families face lot many problems. The sociological assessment of their life and problems has been done in chapter no. 4 [v].

[e] *Children of Ex-militants:* These are the children of ex-militants, dead or alive. Their number goes in thousands, some estimate about 35,000. They face dual-natured life-long problems: discrimination and harassment by the government and its agencies; and ostricization-alienation by the society at large. Their life and their problems have been identified in chapter no. 7 [iii].

[f] *Conflict-exposed Children:* These are the local children exposed to the vagaries of armed conflict and suffered mentally and bodily. In other words, they are direct or indirect victims of situation created by armed conflict. They include children involved in child labour, domestic sector, handicrafts, automobile workshops, hotels, dhabas, shops and so on. They are often exploited, suppressed and harassed and paid very less wages and that also irregularly. Their basic rights are violated systematically and in an organized way. Their life conditions have been discussed in chapter no. 6 [viii].

[g] *Child Rights Commission:* Following a visit to many districts of Kashmir to assess the condition of children's homes, orphanages, child labour, access to education and healthcare, early childhood care, children in conflict with law, National Commission for Protection of Child Rights [NCPCR] suggested the state government to draft a "Child Policy" and set up' State Commission for PCR' .[1] It was reported that the Commission's Report emphasized the need of introducing different schemes for children including ICDS and ICPS. It

also suggested formulation of district level policies for ensuring protection of child rights.[2]

[III] RAPED WOMEN

One of the most-sufferers of the militancy among the women is a tiny group of those women who have been gang-raped or raped by security forces or their supported gunmen. Their suffering is very deep and their feelings tragic. They feel that they were innocent but were treated in most inhuman way by sub-human uniformed men. Their sufferings have four major dimensions. First, as a result of dastard act on the part of forces, local or outsider, they suffered physically and emotionally.

Most of them experienced emotional trauma, stress and depression. Second, though they were not responsible in any way for this horrible act on them, they became the victims of negative social reaction. In fact, many of them have been socially ostracized or discriminated. The relevant example in this regard can be denial of matrimonial relations with children of these women and no consideration of significant help to them and their families. It has been reported that they have been discriminated even in the schools. Thus they live a full pathological life.

Third, due to the downfall of social image and status, they always feel psychologically disturbed. They remain depressed, stressed and tensionful. Consequently, they became victim of many mental and physical health diseases. Fourth, as a result of influence and resultant situation, they and their families, especially their husbands and parents, lost economic resources and earnings which they had before the tragedy fall upon them.

Though the government and security agencies deny the charge of mass rape and rape of women in Kashmir, there are many incidents of these heinous crimes in which forces have been involved directly. These incidents have been recorded and documented by the concerned individuals, organizations and agencies. Here, we refer to some of these incidents and documents. The mass rape of Kashmiri women in Kunan Poshpora and Trehgam [both villages in Kupwara district] and Natipora colony [in the sub-urban Srinagar], several villages in the valley, especially in frontier districts of Baramulla and Kupwara, are clear cases of this crime.[3] Moreover, mass rape of some brides, even on the night of their marriage, in different districts have been reported.[4] According to local reports, there are several cases of mass rape and rape of Kashmiri women which took place during crackdowns and search operations, during which men were often taken out of their houses and women left alone. These cases have not been reported because of the fear of its negative implications on themselves and their children in addition to social ostracism and discrimination.[5]

On the other hand, the documents which support these cases include periodical reports of international organizations like Amnesty International and Asia Watch, of human rights-civil rights groups like PUDR and PUCL, and of civil societies and NGOs. There are also credible reports made in the local Urdu and English press from time to time, especially during 1990s and afterwards.[6]

There are two credible and quality books which have recorded many cases of rape of Kashmiri women by security forces and the life conditions in which they survive.[7] Seema Qazi has clearly established the point that rape of Kashmiri women by Indian security forces was used for political purpose, i.e. to teach the lesson to KMs for their revolt against the Indian state.[8]

The exact number of these women is not known. In the case of official denial, one can depend on unofficial credible sources like primary-source and research based documents. From the incidents and cases referred in the preceding para, we may put the estimate to hundreds, if not thousands.

In the context of the above, there emerges the need for systematic efforts at two levels. At the governmental level, necessary economic and other rehabilitation measures for these suffering women and their families must be initiated at the earliest possible time. At the societal level, social initiatives must be carried out to integrate these women in the mainstream and to negate their ostracism and discrimination.

[IV] YOUTHS – A GENERATION LOST

As the fact stands, militancy and subsequent militarization effected all groups and classes in Kashmiri society. Among the suffering groups, the youths too stand at the top qualitatively as well as quantitatively. This group experienced wider and deeper impact of developments and suffered more than other groups in their life, career and future. They lost everything they had. In actuality, many among them were massacred, killed, tortured, injured, harassed, handicapped and raped. This can be seen in the stories of Basharat Peer[9] and poetry of Agha Shahid Ali.[10] It is believed here that the whole generation of youths in the age group of 15-35 years were 'eliminated' in the frontier districts of Baramulla and Kupwara.[11]

[i] Youths continue to suffer even after militancy was reduced to a considerable level. They were caught in a situation in which many youths abandoned militant activities voluntarily or under social pressure. There were others who consciously opted for the role of government forces sponsored militants under their security and protection. Though many youths dropped militancy, they had no productive and purposeful economic activity to perform and to earn for their family members. Most of them were wasting time and roaming on the roads. There is an argument presented by analysts and experts that if these youths are not provided an economic role and honourable living, there is a possibility of their return to militancy.[12] In the present situation, they are exploited by all political parties, including separatist political parties. On the other hand, the government has not shown credible response to their problems, neither the civil society and NGOs have started any social movement and other efforts. This governmental and non-governmental apathy has contributed to their added problems.

[ii] *Unemployed Youth:* As mentioned in the preceding section, the crucial and complex situation of unemployment of youth in JK. This has two main reasons. First, accumulation of huge number of vacancies during last two decades. Even normal, regular and essentially-required staff was not recruited on permanent basis. Second, the official blanket ban on new recruitments in government offices during last two decades. The government revealed recently in the state assembly that about one lakh vacancies are there to be filled.[13] In this way, the government itself created this grave problem which was further accentuated by addition of thousands of graduates, post-graduates and other professional-technical and highly qualified youth from different educational institutions within and outside the state. As a result of this situation, the total

number of unemployed youth in JK has accumulated to 5,67,358. This was confirmed by an official casmpaign to register the number and names of unemployed educated youth in JK in December 2009.[14] Among these unemployed, while 2,95,286 belonged to Jammu report and 2,72,072 to the Kashmir region.[15] These registered unemployed are skilled, semi-skilled, professional, technical, and highly qualified in different fields. When this problem was not solved by the government, it led to its grave implications for whole society not only of economic nature but of social, psychological and educational nature. While it led to perpetual tension, depression among the youth, it also created an environment for major and minor crimes.

On the other hand, the response of the state government towards this grave problem has not been realistic and suitable. In fact, the political instability and political uncertainty in the state in last 6 decades has not enabled state governments to formulate relevant policy-planning and programmes in this regard. The private-corporate sector in India also could not help the state. The state governments adopted the policy of recruiting youths on contractual, ad-hoc, and temporary basis. In reality, this policy was adopted to appoint their-own-men without facing any test or interviews. The state government always emphasized the youth to adopt self-employment schemes. But, the local youth was not attracted to this scheme because there were neither resources nor markets in Kashmir for this type of economic activities. In order to resolve the problem of unemployment on long-term basis in JK , the state government recently introduced 'Sheri Kashmir Employment and Welfare programme for Unemployed youth in December 2009.[16] But, it also seems to be a failure due to its hard conditions such as eligibility for a limited age group, the income limit of Rs. 50,000/- per month, non-eligibility of persons engaged in any studies, and property ownership of 10/20 kanals of agricultural/horticultural land.[17] It was in this context that the Chief Minister had to intervene by saying that "provisions of the scheme need to be reviewed" and asked the concerned department to deliberate upon "it and suggest measures for making it more viable and easy for the youth to adopt it."[18]

[iii] *Compromised-surrendered Militant Youth*: After militancy started in Kashmir in 1989, thousands of Kashmiri youth

crossed LOC and went to PAK for arms training. Many of them came back after short periods and joined armed struggled against the Indian state. The earlier impression of these youths was that the goal of *Azaadi* was nearby. But, that didn't come true. That proved to be a distant dream. Several factors worked for this. First, strong offensive and counter-insurgency operations created insecurity among the youths and some of them abandoned militancy. Second, When the armed struggle was used by some elements for personal/ family interests, many militant youth felt disheartened and left these activities in order to live a peaceful life. Some of them were compelled to surrender before security forces.

Third, in this depressing environment, some militants were persuaded or compelled to surrender and to work for security forces in their fight to militants. These government-sponsored ex-militants were known as renegades, *Ikhwanis*, *Mukhbir*[19], agent, traitor and so on. These ex-militants were barberious in their treatment of the militants and their unarmed supporters-sympathizers. They killed, raped, injured, tortured, kidnapped, disappeared hundreds of youths under cover from army-security forces. Their terror-tactics proved decisive in the security forces' fight against local militants. But, when the militant movement was nearly eliminated, these armed youths were left alone on their own fate by the state government and security forces. While some of them were recruited for some time for carrying out anti-militancy operations, others were not provided any job as was promised to them earlier. Many of them still fight for jobs.[20] On the other hand, since they had worked against the local population, they had invited social wrath and were socially isolated, alienated and boycotted. The social opposition to them was so intense that it was considered a taboo to talk, to interact and to help them. In this way, these youths and their families, particularly children and women, emerged as the suffering group.

All these ex-militants and their families face acute poverty and other related grave problems in the present-day situation, which if not taken care of, may turn them more offenders and criminals. The first group of militant youth had some kind of economic activity which enabled them and their families some livelihood. After they joined and subsequently left militancy, they became jobless and aimless and their families face worst conditions. They and their children need to be involved in to purposeful and long-term economic engagement and overall rehabilitation. Their children need not be discriminated in any field of engagement and employment. It was in that context that the N.C. MPs appealed to the government that these children must not be discriminated. "They need extra care and the government should extend all benefits to them so that they consider themselves as a part of society"[21] They also emphasized on chalking out programmes and schemes for these children.[22] The second group of ex-militants and their families face more or less same problems. They too face systematic and official harassment and discrimination.[23] The number of these two groups is not known, but unofficial estimates vary from 5,000 to 8,000 families.[24] They need to be treated humanly and rehabilitated properly, so that they can live an honourable life with minimum descent standard.

The third group of ex-militants, *Ikhwanis,* and their families are worst suffers. Their number vary from 3,000 to 5,000 families. In addition to their acute economic problems, they face social, cultural, psychological and all other problems. They still face worst kind of 'social boycott' and social taboos, which has degenerated their life-living conditions. From the humanitarian viewpoint, these families need to be taken out of this hell-like inferno. Both, state as well as society, have to contribute in this direction. The govt. must initiate their and their children' rehabilitation and it must get social support.

[iv] *Imprisoned Youth:* With the on-going militancy in JK, many youths were arrested and lodged in different jails inside and outside the state. They compose mostly of political-militant leaders and activists and innocent civilians. They have been jailed under various laws, including the draconian law of "Public Safety Act". Some of these jailed youths have not been charged with any formal offence.[25] Huge majority of this group belongs to the age group of 15-40 years. Even children of 14-16 and 16-18 years have been detained here.[26] According to a report, a youth of 15 years age involved in stone-pelting was put in to jail in Srinagar.[27] According to the records of Association of Parents of Imprisoned Persons [APIP] and Hurriet [G] sources, there are 1500-2000 Kashmiri prisoners languishing in different prisons.[28]

The number of these prisoners was so large that even Central Jail, Srinagar accommodates 488 prisoners, while it was meant only for 300 prisoners maximum.[29] Many of these prisoners have not been presented in the courts and if presented but not regularly. Some of them have not been issued even the charge-sheets. All these prisoners and their families live a pathetic life, mostly in the absence of regular income. The SHRC took a strong note of this and asked the government to stop these practices.[30]

Moreover, there prevails a unique practice in JK according to which if a political prisoner is released under court orders, he is arrested again immediately after the release under new charges framed at that time. This negates the very essence and purpose of justice. The SHRC criticized this behaviour of jail authorities and directed to stop this practice.[31]

It has also been observed that majority of these young prisoners are political activists and not involved in any serious offence or crime. In this situation and the declined militancy, these youths need to be released in order to live a peaceful life, though with full political participation. This young, creative and active segment of youngsters deserve their involvement in purposeful and productive economic activity and overall rehabilitation.

[v] *Loc Youth:* As mentioned earlier, the Kashmiri youth in large numbers crossed LOC for arms training in PAK. While many of them came back, some of them stayed there for different reasons. As per unofficial estimates, thousands of these youths were trapped there and they want to return back to their homes. The improving conditions in JK has emboldened them to return. According to the reports, some youths have returned Kashmir from the Nepal route.[31] In this political environment, the regional and national political parties favoured their return to their homes and live a peaceful normal life. On the other hand, while militants rejected this 'India-made trap' plan, the rightist political parties, especially BJP, characterized as 'anti-national'.[32] However, the state government presented it as the 'rehabilitation programme' and 'home coming strategy' for the local youth which, according to it, was misled in 1990s.[33]

NOTES AND REFERENCES

1. See the 8th Report of NCPCR, New Delhi released in 2009.
2. See *Greater Kashmir,* Srinagar, 2nd June 2010.
3. These incidents of mass rape of Kashmiri women by security forces were their first such experience in history. So, they remember these incidents strongly.
4. See Basharat Peer, *Curfewed Nights* [New Delhi, 2007, Routledge].
5. Local men and women are highly conscious about these disastrous implications of mass rape. So they hardly report these incidents to anybody.
6. See reports in the local urdu and English newspapers.
7. B. Peer, *op. cit.*
8. Seema Kazi, *Between Democracy and Nationhood: Militarization and Gender in Kashmir* [New Delhi, 2009, Women unlimited].
9. B. Peer, *op. cit.*
10. See Agha Shahid Ali, Country without post-office [U.S., 1994].
11. As was reported in the local press.
12. It reveals in their interviews with "*Honour*", Srinagar, April 2010.
13. See *Greater Kashmir,* Srinagar, August-September, 2009.
14. *Greater Kashmir,* Srinagar, 4th June 2010.
15. *Ibid.*
16. *Ibid.*
17. See the text of the SKEWPCY introduced by the government in December 2009.
18. *Greater Kashmir,* Srinagar, 4th June 12010.
19. *See "Honour", Srinagar,* March 2010.
20. *See Greater Kashmir,* Srinagar, 20th March 2010.
21. *Ibid,* 16th and 18th Feburary 2010.
22. *Ibid.*

23. *Ibid. and 20th March 2010.*
24. Zulfikar Majid, *"Released Militants Seek Rehabilitation"*, *Greater Kashmir*, 20th November 2009.
25. *See Greater Kashmir*, Srinagar, 19th March 2010 and 3rd May 2010.
26. *Ibid*
27. *Ibid.*
28. *Ibid.*, 10th June 2010.
29. *Ibid.*, 2nd May 2010.
30. *Ibid.*, 19th March 2010 and 3rd May 2010.
31. *Ibid.*, 24th March 2010.
32. *Ibid.*, 12th Feburary 2010 and 13th Feburary 2010.
33. *Ibid.*

CHAPTER 8

NEED FOR SOCIAL POLICY IN J & K

In modern times, every state has adopted certain specific social policies in order to fulfill predetermine social objectives. In actuality, these policies reflect the nature and enormity of problems which hurt general societal interests of individuals and groups. In this regard, the states in developed as well as developing countries have formulated, adopted and implemented the social policies to resolve general and specific problems related to health, education, housing, deviance, crime, delinquency, drug abuse, corruption, unemployment, moral degeneration and so on. These policies have also focused specifically on most suffering social groups such as women and children and on most crucial social institutions such as family, school and religion.

Like many societies in the Asian and African context, the Kashmiri society at large has developed some crucial problems mainly due to the processes change and development, especially modernization, urbanization, secularization, educational expansion, demographic transformation, materialistic worldview, social mobility and so on. At the same time, short-term and long-term implications of the perpetual conflict situation have exposed this society to the phenomena such as violence, crime, deviance-delinquency, social disorder and disorganization. These and other social problems have accumulated to the maximum extent during the last two decades. Several studies of these problems have revealed their emerging and alarming nature. Some brief details in this regard are mentioned below:

Violence: Though the Kashmiri society was peaceful completely till a few decades back, it is emerging fast as the violence-prone society, not only at the regional level but at the global level too. It has been observed in the present-day Kashmiri society that while violence [and its necessary implications] is fast emerging as an inseparable component in the social ethos, it is effecting fast all 'in-family' and 'out-family' situations. In a way, it may be characterized as the 'emerging way of life' in the Kashmiri society, especially among the youth.

Social Deviance: With the introduction of violence and other effects of militancy after 1989, social deviance among the school-college youth is on rise which was observed never before. While it has disturbed the existing patriarchal authority and traditional pattern of parent-children relationship with the family institution, the conventional pattern of life and traditional moral ethos was exposed to new challenges, leading to the process of cultural erosion in some cases.

Juvenile Delinquency: In the situation in which illegal authority and social control became ineffective, there merged a tendency to consciously de-validate laws and rules, particularly among the youth. That is what has been happening in Kashmir in the recent years. A significant number of youth commit major and minor crimes [from theft to murder] and are neither punished for committing crime nor stopped to repeat the criminal acts. A minor study of Juvenile delinquency in Srinagar city revealed that there were many juvenile cases, only some of these have been booked by the police. In a small number of cases, the delinquents were arrested on charges of pick-pocketing, deceit, frauds, eve-teasing, stealing, and molestation. But, after they were produced in normal courts [as there are no Juvenile courts and juvenile homes in Kashmir], they could not be sent to 'juvenile homes'.

Crime: In comparison to the traditional Kashmiri society, about 50 years back, hardly any case of minor or major crime was committed or reported. But, the situation has changed radically to such an extent that every kind of crime is committed in Kashmir today. Not many criminals are caught and punished. The daily reports of police control room, radio-television, print media and official statements reveal a higher number of crimes including the major crimes. In reality, Kashmir experiences heinous crimes daily and has emerged as "one of the major spots of crime in the world". In other words, Kashmir joined the "global mainstream of crime". Some of these crimes are horrible and kill the human conscience.

Social Disorganization: The process of family disorganization has started as a result of the negation of patriarchal authority within and outside family, violations of moral ethos and ethical values, and not following desirable cultural traits. This process has also effected the 'marriage-market' wherein the phenomena of late marriage, no marriage, increasing demands of dowry, and demand for government jobs for girls has increased and intensified.

Gender Discrimination: The practices related to gender discrimination got expanded and strengthened during the conflict situation and there was not an organized movement to oppose it. In practice, thousands of women, young as well as old, were harassed and molested by security forces and other armed groups. The author's study revealed that this happened within their families, places of work, public transport vehicles and even at public places. Not only the security forces only were involved in these activities, distant relatives, neighbours and office colleagues were also found involved fully. Many cases of rape of local women by the security forces have also been established.

Permissive Sex Practices: In the situation of conflict, traditional values and norms could not be maintained in totality in Kashmiri society. As a result of this development, deviance from these ideal values and norms became an empirical reality. In this background, permissive sexual practices could hardly be stopped. Thus, the trends of pre-marital and extra-marital sex practices could not be avoided in urban areas. These illegal and immoral practices also contributed to the practices of prostitution and so on.

Legitimizing Corruption: At the national level, an unofficial survey about "corruption in India", the J&K state was graded as "No. 2 corrupt state" in the whole of India. This situation can be explained in terms of the abnormal social situation prevailing during the conflict period which corrupted state as well as society. In this situation, many illegal and amoral activities were carried systematically and in an organized way without any guilt, shame or feeling.

Mental Health Deterioration: One of the most important implications of conflict situation in Kashmir was identified as breakdown of the mental health whose prominent features were stress, anxiety, trauma, depression, PTSD, deprivation, emotional scars and suicides. The enormity and intensity of these psychological-psychiatric problems was that every family living in the valley had developed one or more such problems. In a brief study of suicides in the valley this author identified and analysed about 200 cases of suicides which were reported in the local press during the year 1999-2000

Unemployment: The problem of unemployment in Kashmir has surpassed the reasonable limits and huge number of unemployed accumulated partly due to increasing number or graduates and post-graduates in different fields of modern education from within and outside the state and partly due to blanket ban on recruitment imposed by the government during militancy. The situation has become so worse when about 1,00,000 jobs were lying vacant in different departments according to official information. As unemployment increases, so does the poverty and its other devastating effects. In this environment, frustration among the youth increases that leads to more violence and crime.

Social Pathology: In the social situation mentioned above, people in general and professionals-intellectuals in particular felt trapped in an inferno whose heat increases by time and intensifies the existing problems. This kind of social environment has created some degree of 'social apathy'. This has also given rise to the process of 'social pathology' in which most people hardly care for others living around them and think and act for selfish ends only.

Disabilities: The situation related to 'disability' which emerged as a direct effect of armed conflict in Kashmir stands grim. According to 2001 census, the JK state had a total population of persons with disabilities 3,03,670 who composed of visual disability 2.08,713, impaired hearing 14,157, speech disability 16,956, loco motor disability 37,965 and mental disability 24,879. Moreover, there were more than estimated 50,000 people of all age groups who were injured and became disabled partly or completely for whole of their life.

Widows and Orphans: Our research has revealed that conflict situation in Kashmir has effected women and children more than any other group or class. They, especially widows and orphans [whose number has been estimated 32,000 and 89,000 respectively], stood as 'ideal suferers' in this situation. While their life conditions have turned pathetic and miserable, they were not provided sufficient help by official or unofficial agencies and organizations. While most of these children have dropped from schools and have joined child labour force, their mothers were compelled to comeout of their homes and work to earn for their families.

Youth's Suffering: The conflict situation has effected in a big way the local youth. In actuality, the age group of 15 - 35 years was most active in the militancy related activities. Most of them got killed, injured and disappeared. Those who survived face the difficulties of life. This group also became the main target of the offences of security forces and state agencies.

Increasing Misery: The authors research [recorded in this and other publications] has clearly revealed that these suffering groups were not helped sufficiently and properly either by government agencies or by national-international NGOs. That has directly contributed to extremely miserable conditions among these groups. This in turn has given rise to certain serious and dangerous problems.

Keeping in view the increasing intensity of above-mentioned social problems in the Kashmir valley, this situation can easily be characterized as "alarming" social trends with dangerous consequences for all. In order to control this increasing 'social inferno', efforts should have been started long back. But, the crude reality stands that no such effort was carried out so far at the state or central level. Neither problems of pre-militancy period were responded properly nor problems of post-militancy were dealth realistically.

As a result, it is tragic to see thousands of local youth who died or were injured or developed any disability or suffered mentally and were not given proper and continued treatment on the part of the state. It was also bewildering to see thousands of widows, orphans and half-widows without any significant help and rehabilitation. It was again shocking to observe pathetic condition of mentally disturbed women and children without any medical or non-medical help. Thousands of suicides were committed and the state remained apathetic and unconcerned. Finally, the security forces and state police does everything which can easily be characterized as 'dehumanization'.

Despite having such alarming situation in J&K, the state had no specific declared social policy in this regard and so had not adopted any specific planing programme or scheme to tackle these problems.

Even the 'working group' constituted on the Prime Minister's initiative to recommend confidence-building measures related to Kashmir in the 'Round Table Conference' in Srinagar took cognizance of these problems and suggested various measures of relief and rehabilitation for these suffering groups. But, nothing has been done so far. In reality, the state has proved near-apathetic. It neither responded responsibly to this social crisis, nor attempted seriously to resolve these crucial problems. Taking a serious note of this type of behaviour in a relevant case, the State High Court observed that "all this only shows the casualness of government functionaries, not only in responding to the call of their duty but also in discharge of obligation cast on them in implementing the court order."

In the context of situation explained above what is needed immediately is to adopt a comprehensive social policy which will focus on crucial social problems in crucial sectors. In other words, a *comprehensive social policy* has to be formulated [by experts, professionals and bureaucrats], adopted [through various social agencies and organizations] in short-term and long-term planning perspective. But, at the same time, the society at large has also formally to initiate its efforts in an organized and systematic way mainly through credible NGOs and other self help groups. When both types of organizations will start their efforts seriously, a relevant and radical change may be observed in the near future in the state.

GLOSSARY

Naya Kashmir Programme	New Kashmir Programme
Maharaja	The Dogra/Hindu ruler in JK state till 1947.
Khilafat	The Islamic [Ottoman] caliphate.
Dogra	A Hindu ethnic group based in Jammu.
Tangawalla	
Atooth Ang	Inseparable part
Shah Rug	Life Line
Azaadi	Freedom
Hurriat	Freedom
Wazir-e-Aala	Chief Minister
Wazir-e-Azam	Prime Minister
Sadr-e-Riyasat	President of the State
Kashmiriat	The ideology of the people of Kashmir
Hanji	An occupational community living in Srinagar in houseboats.
Shikarawala	
Dral	Agent dealing with land transactions.
Mehr	An amount of money paid by Muslim groom to the bride at the time of marriage.
Sayyid	A descendant of the Prophet of Islam [PBUH]
Khan	*A descendant of a* dynasty.

Khane Damaad	A matri-local groom
Nikaah	The marriage agreement between two marriage partners
Phum	Pashmina wool
Shahtosh	A particular wool
Namdah	The wool-based thick sheet
Paper Machie	The Kashmiri Art
Mohalla Committee	A localty or colony committee
Masjid Committee	The mosque committee
Chinar	A heavy shadow tree
Shakhawat	Sympathy
Yateem	Orphan
Yateem Khana	House of orphans – orphanage
Koshish	Efforts
Muskaan	Smile
Chotey Tarey	Little stars
Shehjar	Deep shadows
Ikhwani	*Govt-sponsored Militant*
Mukhbir	An informer

BIBLIOGRAPHY

Ahuja, Ram, *Social Problems in India* [New Delhi, 1997, Rawat].

Ali, Aga Shahid, *A Country without Post office* [1994, U.S.].

Baba, Firdous, *The Poison of Waywardness, Greater Kashmir,* Srinagar, 13th March 2010.

Bamzai, P.N. *Modern History of Kashmir* [New Delhi, 1977].

Bazaz, P.N., *Daughters of Vetestha* [Srinagar, 1984, Gulshan].

Bazaz, Sajjad, "Governance and Conflict", *Greater Kashmir,* Srinagar, 9th May 2010.

Bonner, Arthur, *Democracy in India: A Hallow Institution* [Washington, 1994, A.U. Press].

Census of India, 1951-2011, Govt. of India, New Delhi.

Census of Jammu and Kashmir State, Govt. of J&K, Srinagar.

Cox, Peter, *Demography* [New Delhi, 1972, United Book Store].

Dabla, B.A., *Working Women in Kashmir* [Jaipur, 1982, Rawat].

...................., *Ideology, Polity and Societyin Modern Turkey* [Aligarh, 1988, A.M.U.].

...................., *A Sociological Study of Widows and Orphans in Kashmir* [Srinagar, 2010, JK Books].

...................., *Sociological Papers on Kashmir,* 2 Vols., Srinagar, 2010, JK Books.

...................., Report on *Impact of Conflict Situation on Women and Children in Kashmir; A Study of two Districts* [1994-Save the Children].

...................., Report on *Suicides in the Kashmir Valley,* [Srinagar, 2001, CSSCD].

...................., Report on *Tourism and Sex Practices in Kashmir*

[Srinagar, 2007]

......................, Report on *Emergence of Late Marriage in Kashmir* [Srinagar, 2008, DOSSW]

......................, Report on *Changing Marrriage Practices in Kashmir Valley* [Srinagar, 2010, DOSSW].

......................, *Domestic Violence against Women in Kashmir* [paper presented in national seminar]

......................, 'Domestic Violence in J&K' organized by Lawyers Fraternity, New Delhi In calloberation with I.M.P.A., J&K Government, Srinagar in October 2009.

......................., *Role of Region, Religion and Culture [RRC] in Economic Development:The Case of Kashmir* [paper presented in 35th annual conference on All India Sociological Conference at KU, Srinagar in October 2009.

......................., "Demographic Changes in Kashmir", *Radiance,* Delhi, 2nd January 1994; *News from In*dia [New Delhi], 21st March 1994; and *Kashmir Times,* Jammu, 2nd April, 1994.

......................., Demographic Changes in JK, *SRC Newsletter,* KU, Srinagar.

......................, "Violence Against Women in Kashmir", *Kashmir Life*, Srinagar, 11th July 2009.

......................, "Social Impact of Militarization", *Kashmir Life,* Srinagar, 19th September 2009.

....................., "Rising Graph of Suicides in Kashmir, *Honour,* Srinagar, September 2009.

....................., "Disability in JK", *Honour,* Srinagar, June 2010.

Drug Abuse in Anantnag District of Kashmir, [M. Phil. Dissertation submitted by Shahzad Wani in DOSSW IN 2009.

Durkhiem, Emile, *Suicide* [London, 18].

Eighth Report of NCPCR, New Delhi, 2009.

Fazili, Manzoor, *Socialist Ideas and Movements in Kashmir* [New Delhi, 1960, Euroka].

Geelani, Iftikhar, "Erased", *Kashmir Life, Srinagar,12th December 2009.*

Geelani, S. A., *Rodade Kafas,* Urdu, [New Delhi, 2007].

Gupta, C., *Mental Health Relations* [New Delhi, 1976].

Haq, Bashirul, *Unfortunate Muslims of Kashmir, Radiance*, Delhi, 8th April 1979.

Hardy, Justine, *Women of the Valley of Mist* [2009].

Inqilabi, M.A., *Navee-e-Subuh,* Urdu, [Srinagar, 2010].

Iyer, K. Gopal, *Agrarian Reforms and Rural Transformation in J&k* [Paper presented in 11th annual conference of NWISA at KU, Srinagar in September 2009].

Jagmohan, My *Icy Turbulance in Kashmir* [New Delhi, 1995].

Qureshi, Hashim, *Kashmir Ke Talakh Haqayik,* Urdu, Srinagar, 2010].

..........................., *The Undenieable Truths* [Srinagar, 2010].

Kazi, Seema, *Between Democracy and Nation: Gender and Militarization in JK* [New Delhi, 2009, Women Unlimited].

Khan, G. H., *History of Freedom Struggle in Kashmir* [New Delhi, 1984].

Lawerence, W. R., *The Valley of Kashmir* [London, 1895].

Majid, Z., "Released Militants seek Rehabilitation, *Greater Kashmir,* Srinagar, 20th November 2009.

Marshall, Gordan, ed., *Oxford Dictionary of Sociology* [New York, 1994, O.U. Press].

Mathews, Shasha, "Of Mental Health and Illness", *Greater Kashmir, Srinagar, 7th April 2010.*

Michel, Duncan, ed., *A Dictionary of Sociology* [London, 1987, R & K].

Mir, M., *Khidmat-e-Khaleq* [New Delhi, 2009].

National Conference, *Document on Autonomy to JK [Srinagar, 1984]*

Nayyar, Kuldip, *Distant Neighbours* [New Delhi, 1978,].

Nayeem, Hamida, "End this Culture of Impunity", *Greater Kashmir,* Srinagar, 18th April 2010.

Nazir, Mohd., "Hindu Rulers and Muslim Subjects", *Conveyor,* Srinagar, November 2009.

Patel, Vikram, *International Mental Health* [New Delhi,].

Peer, Basharat, *Curfewed Nights* [New Delhi, 2007, Rutledge].

Peoples Democratic Party, *Document on Self-Rule in JK* [Srinagar, 2008].

Puri, Balraj, "Azaadi, Autonomy and Self-Rule in Kashmir", *Human Rights Perspective,* Jammu, 9-10, 2009.

Rafiqi, Q. and Yasin, Madhvi, eds., *History of Freedom Struggle in Kashmir* [New Delhi, 1984]

Raja, Yasmeen, Qaidi Number 100 [Srinagar, 2009].

Sakamoto, Y., ed., *Asia: Militarization and Regional Conflict* [London, 1986, Zed Books]

Saraf, M. Y., *Kashmiris Fight For Freedom* [Lahore, 1977, Ferozsons].

Shariati, Shafi, *Qaudi Inqilab: Syed Ali Geelani,* Urdu, [New Delhi, 2009].

Sofi, G. M. D., *Kashir, 2 Vols.,* [*New Delhi, 1969*].

Throp, Robert, *Kashmir Misgovernment* [London, 1865].

Veijapuri, A. R., *Dimensions of Federal Nation-building* [New Delhi, 1992, Manek].

Voice of Kashmir, London, 1987.

Wani, Shamayil, [M. Phil. Dissertation on A Sociological Study of Juvenile Delinquency in Kashmir'submitted to DOSSW in 2010].

Wani, Khursheed, "Official Criminalization", *Kashmir Life, Srinagar, 7th June 2010.*

Daily Telegraph, London.

New York Times, New York.

The Times of India, New Delhi.

Telegraph, Calcutta.

Patriot, New Delhi.

Conveyor, Srinagar.

Kashmir Life, Srinagar.

Kashmir Times, Jammu.

Rising Kashmir, Srinagar.

Greater Kashmir, Srinagar.

Aftab, Srinagar.

Srinagar Times, Srinagar.

INDEX